European Encounters
with the New World

European Encounters with the New World

From Renaissance to Romanticism

Anthony Pagden

Yale University Press
New Haven & London · 1993

*For Chantal, and for our son Felix Alexander
on his second birthday*

Copyright © 1993 by Yale University

Reprinted 1993
First published in paperback 1994

Set in Baskerville by Best-set Typesetter Ltd., Hong Kong
Printed and bound in Great Britain by St Edmundsbury Press

Library of Congress Cataloging-in-Publication Data

Pagden, Anthony.
    European Encounters with the New World: from Renaissance to
Romanticism / Anthony Pagden.
        p.   cm.
    Includes bibliographical references and index.
    ISBN 0–300–05285–5 (hbk.)
    ISBN 0–300–05950–7 (pbk.)
    1. Europe—Intellectual life.   2. Europe—Relations—America.
3. America—Relations—Europe.   I. Title.
CB203.P3   1993   92–21947
303.48′2407—dc20   CIP

A catalogue record for this book is available from the British Library.

Contents

Acknowledgements

The idea for this book grew out of a series of conversations I have had with Bianca Fontana over a number of years. She may not recognize what she has helped to create, but it could not have been done without her. She also gave me my title. An earlier version of what has now become Chapter 5 was delivered as a paper to the Shelby Cullom Davis Center at Princeton University in September 1991. I would like to thank the members of that seminar for their observations, and in particular Natalie Zemon Davis both for having invited me, and for the characteristically perceptive critique she made of some of my claims. Anthony Grafton, as always, set me right on a number of issues and helped me to clarify the structure of the piece as a whole. Stephen Greenblatt read a version (subsequently published in *Representations*) of what has subsequently grown into Chapters 1 and 2 and their present form owes much to his comments. Peter Russell reminded me that America was not the only 'new' world Europeans encountered in the fifteenth century. To him I owe also a debt of gratitude for his encouragement and friendship over many many years. Donald Kelley instructed me in Roman Law. Joan Pau Rubiés i Mirabet taught me a great deal about European travel literature, and Fintan Ryan about science in seventeenth-century Britain. My understanding of Alexander von Humboldt owes much to a brilliant article by Michael Dettlebach, which mere citation cannot adequately capture. I am very grateful to him for having shared his researches with me. Girolamo Imbruglia set me right about Diderot, and instructed me in the textual complexities of the *Histoire de deux Indes*. My wife, Chantal Brotherton-Ratcliffe, read patiently through the whole text and did her best to unravel my syntax and to order my thoughts. Without her constant support I could barely have begun, and would certainly never have finished. Finally my gratitude, once again, to John Nicoll and Rosemary Amos at Yale, for being the very best and the most forgiving of editors.

London–Cambridge,
March, 1992

'O frati', dissi, 'che per cento milia
perigli siete giunti a l'occidente,
a questa tanto picciola viglia
de' nostri sensi che'è del rimanente
non vogliate negar l'esperienza,
dietro al sol, del mondo sanza gente.
Considerate la vostra semenza:
fatti non foste a viver come bruti,
ma per seguir virtute e canoscenza.'
Dante, *La Divina Commedia*, Inferno.
XXVI. 112–20

Introduction

Think onely what concernes thee and thy being,
Dream not of other worlds, what Creatures there
Live in what state condition or degree. . . .'
John Milton, *Paradise Lost*, Bk.viii. 174–6

i

From the deck of frigate *Pizarro*, early on the morning of July 16, 1799, Alexander von Humboldt saw for the first time the South American coastline. 'The quill-like leaves of the palms,' he recorded later,

> stood out against the blue of a sky whose purity was untroubled by any trace of vapour. The sun mounted rapidly towards its zenith. A dazzling light spread through the air, among the white hills dotted with cylindrical cactuses, and across the surface of an unmoving sea, whose shores were lined with brown pelicans [*alcatras*], herons and flamingoes, the splendour of the day, the vivid colours of the vegetation, the shapes of the plants, the varied plumage of the birds – everything was stamped with the great character of nature in the tropics.[1]

While sailing in the same waters some three hundred years earlier, Columbus had listened to the roar of the head-waters of the Orinoco as they met the sea, and stared at the massive vegetation which lined the banks of a river which he knew could only have risen somewhere deep within a continent. For the first and the only time in his life, he was struck by the possibility that what lay before him might not, in fact, be the 'Golden Chersonese', the southernmost promontory of 'Cathay', but instead a wholly unknown 'New World'.[2]

This book is an attempt to explore some of the implications for Europeans of their encounter, direct or indirect, with the 'New World' of America in the years which separated the unselfconsciously late-medieval discoverer from the self-consciously modern explorer. It offers an interpretation of a number of interrelated and overlapping attempts to make some sense of the process of interaction which resulted from

1

Columbus's landfall in October 12, 1492, on a still unidentified island once called 'Guanahani'. Each chapter is concerned with a single author or set of texts on a particular moment of encounter. Each may be read as an independent essay. But when read consecutively they constitute an inquiry into what soon became the most daunting of the many problems which the 'discovery' of America posed for Europe: the possibility, and for many the impossibility, of cultural commensurability.

Europeans have for long been preoccupied with the difficulties involved in encountering other worlds and their often fiercely 'other' inhabitants. Since antiquity European culture has been founded on the concept of the *oikos*, the *domus*, the household. The civilization which has shaped the normative behaviour of all Europeans has always been, by definition, a life lived in cities. Beyond the city, as Aristotle had said in the fourth century BC, there were only beasts and heroes. There were also, of course, the saints and the navigators. All had cast off the *civitas* and had gone out, whether for gain or in the expectation of sanctity, to the destabilizing worlds beyond. In all European cultures, before the aircraft effectively isolated the traveller from the consequences of travel, migration and nomadism were looked upon as either the 'barbaric' phase in the evolution of cultures, or as an integral part of the process whereby once civil peoples, who had been driven from their lands, became progressively decivilized. Such migrations had always been perceived as a menace by the inhabitants of the 'civilized' West. Modern Europe has never quite been able to forget that the great empires, first the Greek and then the Roman, which had brought some measure of cultural cohesion, and with it a political and moral life to the western world, had been destroyed by nomadic peoples whose capacity for movement had made them militarily superior to civilized man with his insistence on the civic benefits of immobility.

The image of the barbarian hordes massed on the crumbling Roman Empire's eastern and northern borders remains, for all Europeans, a nightmare out of a collective cultural past. But if movement was associated with disorder, it was also, in another sense, inescapable. For all men are in some part of their being *homines viatores*, as St Francis had described them, perennial movers. Just as even the fiercest of endogamous societies must, on occasions, allow its members to 'marry out' if they are to survive, so all cultures however concerned they might be with fixity have also to move if they are to progress. Like the stasis which Plato urged upon the inhabitants of his ideal *polis*, total immobility for most humans is simply not an option.

The traveller, however, has always remained a mediatory figure, and the journey has always served to divide one universe from another. The belief that travel involved not merely migration, but also an entering into 'other universes' is an old and enduring one. 'When I came among them [the Tartars],' wrote the Franciscan William of Rubruck in the thirteenth century, 'it seemed indeed to me as if I were stepping into a different universe,'[3] a sentiment echoed precisely some five hundred years later by the Spanish explorer Antonio de Ulloa. 'Distant lands, and in particular the Indies,' he wrote, 'strike the judgement of those who encounter them at a distance, as very strange. . . . From this it follows that when they recognize that what is in them is new, it is as if, in reality they had passed over into another world'. And, he concluded, it was for this reason that 'they have instantly given them [the Indies] the name "New World"'.[4] The spaces that separated the European from those 'others' he[5] was eventually to encounter were spaces of dissolution, menacing areas where civility could so easily dissolve into barbarism.

In the case of the Americas, this sense of detachment from all that was familiar was marked most starkly by the initial journey itself: the always terrifying and sometimes fatal ocean crossing. All those who travelled to America, Spaniards, Portuguese, English and French, saw the sea-journey as an ordeal, almost (as we shall see in Chapter 2) as a rite of passage which could convey either purity or a special kind of vision to those who suffered it and survived. For long periods of time the migrant was encased, to use Diderot's metaphor, by the walls of his floating world, 'contained and immobile'.[6] But what happened to him there was frequently unimaginable. 'Did he suffer much', is the first question A asks B in the dialogue which occupies much of Diderot's *Supplément au Voyage de Bougainville* (Supplement to the Voyage of Bougainville, 1773) on hearing of the French explorer Louis Antoine de Bougainville's circumnavigation of the globe.[7] In a sense the migrant passed through three separate existences. From Europe his living space was transferred to the floating castle which was to be his home, sometimes for months on end. Then, having stepped gratefully ashore, he immediately found himself in the new and wholly unfamiliar world on the other side. He was now, unless he was prepared to reverse the process, effectively isolated from everything that he had once known.

But the isolation could never be complete. The traveller would return home one day, changed perhaps, but still with some sense of where his *domus* was. For generations the settler looked to Europe as the source of legitimacy, and as a model on which to construct his Nueva España, New England, Nouvelle France. The difficulty, observes 'Barchilon', the main speaker in Pedro de Quiroga's *Libro intitulado coloquios de la verdad* (Colloquies of the Truth), which I discuss in Chapter 1, is how to

3

make your voice carry across these vast stretches of water. For to the traveller and the colonist, what was on one side of the ocean remained stubbornly insulated from everything that was on the other. The oceans divided entire social, cultural and political worlds in which it was possible, as was the case with Francisco Pizarro, to be an illegitimate, illiterate orphan on one side and a Marquis on the other. The process of transition could, however, destroy as easily as it could ennoble. The Pizarros and the Cortéses could not be what they had become in America anywhere but *in* America. The identities of all those who tried to carry back with them to the Old World what they had become in the New tended to wither like the tropical fruits which the early explorers had hoped to transplant in Europe. Take the case of the Wolof prince whom the Portuguese chronicler, Rui da Pina calls 'Bemoin'.

In 1488 Bemoin came to Portugal to ask for military assistance in a civil war in which he was then engaged. Bemoin was a king, and because the Portuguese accepted that *mutatis mutandis* all forms of government were identical throughout the world, John II, self-proclaimed 'Lord of Guinea', received him as he would any visiting prince once, that is, he had been provided with the proper clothing, silver plate for his table and a suitable number of servants. Bemoin, who had been a Muslim, attended mass, 'to see what it was like' and not surprisingly was so moved at the elevation of the Host that he immediately perceived the truth of Christianity. On November 3, 1488, together with six of the 'nobles of his retinue' he was baptized a Christian with the King and Queen acting as his godparents. Four days later he was dubbed a knight and provided with a coat of arms consisting of a gold cross on red ground, the borders edged with the *quinas* of Portugal. In Portugal, then, he had become a noble, a member of the royal household and a Christian vassal of the 'Lord of Guinea'. He had, that is, become a European in everything except the colour of his skin. Bemoin then returned to Senegal in a fleet of twenty caravels carrying men and military equipment to help him in the war. When the fleet had almost reached its destination, however, the Portuguese commander, Pero Vaz, killed him and then turned his ships around and set sail for home. The reason he gave was that he believed Bemoin to be plotting against him. Given Bemoin's dependence on the soldiers under Vaz's command, this was hardly credible, and Pina says that many believed that Vaz had simply grown weary and wanted to return to Portugal and had killed the Wolof king to make this possible. Whatever the reason, Vaz was in effect guilty of regicide, and, as Pina himself observed, even if Bemoin had been guilty of treason, the Portuguese commander's duty would have been to return him to Lisbon for trial. John II, although he was said to be very angry with Vaz, did nothing. This was surely, as Peter

Russell has argued, because 'his people would not tolerate the execution of a white Portuguese of noble rank for killing a black African, king or not'. But it was only partly that. For once poor Bemoin had slipped away from the mouth of the Tagus he had, for all those in Portugal, already lost his identity as the king's *afilhado*. He had become part of another world. In the African Atlantic, far from the reaches of the networks of kinship and culture which enlaced all men and made them what they were, Bemoin had become nothing but a 'black', a thing, like any other slave, who could be tossed overboard to shorten a tedious voyage. King John II's sense of paternity towards him, like all our sense of community, could not be expected to extend very far beyond the limits of his *domus*. The kingdoms of Portugal and Senegambia could only meet in the kind of legitimating rituals which had the power to raise to the level of the Kings' godson a man for whom, in any other circumstances, the Portuguese would have expressed only contempt. But those rituals had no validity, no power to compel the imagination, outside the limits of the culture which had created them. In any other place, and at any other time, the worlds inhabited by 'Bemoin' and Pero Vaz remained entirely incommensurable.[8]

Bemoin's tragedy was a complex case of the inevitable deracination with which all travellers have to contend. Movement of the kind to which Bemoin had subjected himself was always, and inevitably, traumatic. To protect themselves from the 'shock of the new', most Europeans carried about with them a cluster of notions, categories, suppositions about what it was that they would encounter out there. These, and the ways in which they affected the first European attempts to understand the peoples of America, I have tried to describe elsewhere.[9] This book is concerned with a different phenomenon. It is an attempt to explore some of the many ways in which the *newness* of America was recognized, confronted and explained, and the 'impact' that this was believed to have had on the history of Europe itself.

ii

For all Europeans, the events of October 1492 constituted a 'discovery'. Something of which they had had no prior knowledge had suddenly presented itself to their gaze.[10] A 'New World' had now to be incorporated into their cosmographical, geographical and, ultimately, anthropological understanding. The term 'discovery' – and its Romance analogues 'descubrimiento', 'scoperta', 'descobrimento', découverte' – all derive from a late ecclesiastical Latin word 'disco-operio', meaning to uncover, to reveal, to expose to the gaze. It carries an implicit sense that what has now been revealed had an existence prior to and independent of the viewer. Unlike the classical Latin term, 'inventio', it does not suggest that what has been found has also, in effect, been created or 'invented' by the discoverer, by the 'inventor'. There are some writers who refer to the 'inventing' of America. Martin Waldseemüller, the first to use the term 'America', is one of them.[11] But they are very few.

The load carried by words changes, however, over time. Europeans had always looked upon their own cultures as privileged, and upon all other cultures as to some degree inferior. There is nothing remarkable about this. Most peoples distinguish with equal clarity between themselves and all others. What is striking about the Graeco-Judaic, and subsequently Christian, view is that it is based, not merely upon an intuitive response to difference, but upon a claim about the way the world has been constructed. Nature – the argument runs – had been created in a state of potentiality, as an inert undriven mass whose *actuality* could only be realized through the purposeful action of men. All trees, as Aristotle said, were potentially, but not actually, chairs. It required man's art, his *techne*, to release from the tree its essential 'chairness'. *Techne*, or as we would say technology, and what in Latin, the other dominant language in our cognitive vocabulary, was called *scientia*, is man's capacity to transform the world according to his needs. 'Art itself,' the Scottish social theorist Adam Ferguson was later to observe, 'is natural to man . . . he is destined from the first age of his being to invent and to contrive'.[12] Europeans are also unusual in their belief that to transform nature in this way is a crucial part of what it is to be a man; for Nature had been given by God to man for his use. Men were thus encouraged to see in the natural world a design of which they were the final beneficiaries. Those who understood this, and hence could use science to control nature, were 'civil' or 'civilized', and those who did not were either 'savage' or 'barbarian'. Discovery in this sense had always been, and has remained, the prime objective of European science. And the discovery of America, in particular, came to be described, as we shall see in Chapter 3, and then mythologized as a supreme example of a particular kind of scientific achievement.

It is this supposition, the supposition that nature is a latent force which man is compelled to exploit, which is ultimately responsible for the technological mastery which the 'West' has achieved over much of the globe. And it is this which led to the implied assumption that the 'discovery' of Africa and America and, to a lesser degree, of India had, in some sense which was never specified, brought the peoples of these places into the world. Even Bartolomé de Las Casas, whose writings I discuss in Chapter 2, and who in the sixteenth century was both the most outspoken champion of the rights of the Native peoples of Central and South America and their most thorough historian, nevertheless regarded America as having been shrouded in darkness, ignored, unknown and, crucially, with no place in human history, until Columbus had stumbled across it. Las Casas's claim clearly established his gaze, the gaze of the European, as the only one which could confer existence upon the world. Once 'discovered', the Indians became Las Casas's enduring moral concern. 'Undiscovered' they had had no moral existence at all. Hence the role which Columbus plays in Las Casas's narrative. He is the bringer of light, the 'Christ-bearer', the discoverer and finally the – the pun is Las Casas's own – 'Colon-izer'. The gang of brigands who follow him, whose minds are fixed only on personal gain, are responsible for what Las Casas, in the title of his most famous work, termed the 'Destruction of the Indies'. Columbus, by contrast, is the agent of a pure act of creation. He had also, so Las Casas believed, been the inventor of a master plan for peaceful and co-operative colonization of the Indies of the kind which Las Casas himself had urged upon the Castilian crown time and again. This image of the Columbine voyages as a phase distinct from the murderous colonizing ventures that were to follow, survived well into the eighteenth century. It surfaces in the eulogy which the Abbé Raynal (whom we shall meet in Chapter 5) dedicated to the 'discoverer'[13] and in such works as Joseph Mandrillon's *Recherches philosophiques sur la découverté de l'Amérique* (Philosophical Researches On the Discovery of America, 1784) which describes Columbus as the creator of 'new routes across the ocean', whose real purpose had been to 'create links of fraternity between the two worlds'. The calamities which in fact followed were the consequence not of the discovery itself but of the 'imprudence and wickedness' of later centuries.[14]

In describing the Amerindians as having lived since the Flood behind the 'locked doors of the Ocean Sea', doors which Columbus had been the first to unlock,[15] Las Casas, however, was not alluding to their technical or political culture (which he believed to be as good as anything produced by ancient Greece or Rome), but was referring to the fact that, until Columbus's arrival, they had been in total ignorance of Christianity. They had been separated by the whole of the 'Ocean Sea' from the Word. And since for early-modern Christians the *communitas christianae* was the heir to the Greek *oikumene*, the community of man, exclusion from that community implied a species of non-existence. European moral geography offered the image of a carefully circum-scribed world. Beyond the limits of the known world there was only darkness. And to have remained so long in darkness suggested, at least to some, that there must be something unnatural about America. As the jurist Juan López de Palacios Rubios claimed in 1513, had the Native-

Americans been a more worthy race then surely God would have sent them missionaries before now, just as he had sent St Peter to Cornelius, St Paul to the Corinthians and St Augustine to the English, another race who lived out beyond the limits of the inhabitable world.[16] The fact that these Americans were also technologically inferior to their European conquerors seemed to support the lingering sense that these peoples and the lands they inhabited had been, in Las Casas's words, 'occluded' before 1492. The great debate over the supposed physical inferiority of America, its absolute geological newness in relation to the other three continents, which began in the eighteenth century and echoes of which can still be found in Marx, was the continuation of this supposition in another, more secular, idiom.[17]

Even Humboldt, whose cosmology attempted so hard to shrink distances, to encircle and contain the world, wished to preserve at least this distinction between the 'Old' continents and the 'New' one. America, he believed, was a more recent creation than Europe, and its peoples, for all their obvious achievements, were still at that stage where their arts – for Humboldt the supreme indicator of civility – could not be considered as anything other than of historic interest. By contrast, the peoples of Europe and even of Asia had evolved styles of representation which because of 'the harmony and beauty of their forms' had transcended time and space. 'Let us not be surprised,' he wrote,

by the grossness of style and the incorrectness of the contours of the art of the peoples of America. Separated, perhaps since the beginning from the rest of the human race, wandering within a country where man has had for long to fight against a savage nature which is forever in turmoil, these peoples, left to themselves, could only ever have developed slowly.[18]

Like Condorcet, who from his hiding place in 1793 had envisaged a future European empire which would bring to the peoples of America not servitude but 'Enlightenment', Humboldt looked forward to a future in which the European would be able to assist the Amerindian in his slow and painful struggle towards a 'civilization'. Such a civilization would, he argued, be characterized, as that of classical antiquity and its modern European heirs had been, by the capacity to create transcendent works of art, and to understand the cosmos through science.[19] On the frontispiece to his *Atlas géographique et physique du Nouveau Continent* (Geographical and Physical Atlas of the New World, 1814) he tried to capture this process. A fallen Aztec is being lifted up by the twin figures of Greece and Rome, represented by Minerva and Mercury. To this Humboldt has appended a caption from Book VIII of Pliny

1. Frontispiece to Alexander von Humboldt's *Atlas géographique et physique du Nouveau Continent* (Geographical and Physical Atlas of the New World, 1814).

the Younger's Letters: 'HUMANITAS. LITERAE. FRUGES, 'The Liberal Arts, Science, Agriculture'.[20] (See figure 1.) Humboldt could hope that one day the Americans might come to resemble the Europeans, Tibetans or Asians with whom he compares them. But in his own time, as in this illustration, his world and theirs were still wholly incommensurable. Intelligible now as part of a huge spatial and environmental scale, at one with the flora and the geology in which they had their being, the Native-American was, still fixedly, for the moment at least, 'other'.

iii

'Discovery' was, however, only the first moment of the European encounter with America. What followed was a slow and sometimes painful process of assimilation. The conquerors and colonizers of America did their best to transform this 'New' world, and its inhabitants, into a likeness of the Old. American flora and fauna were forced into classical botanical and biological categories, the Amerindians were located and re-located in a variety of temporal and spatial relationships to the European and the Asian. In all of these attempts to make the new continent to some degree commensurate with the old, the viewpoint was always unwaveringly European. As I have tried to demonstrate elsewhere, this was inevitable. It was far more than simple 'prejudice', or an unwillingness to encounter and to recognize the existence of the new. Most Europeans, and certainly all of those who travelled to America in the first three centuries after the discovery, belonged to intellectual cultures which were convinced that everything in the world conformed to a pre-ordained set of laws – the law of nature (the *ius naturae*) – and could be made explicable in terms of that law.

But most of those who actually went to America, the traders, the settlers and the missionaries, were all also ultimately compelled, to some degree, to meet those whom they encountered on their own cultural terms. They were, after all, literally on their own ground. Although they could only ever relate what they had seen back to a pattern of European conceptual expectations, those expectations were often very flexible. Most Europeans could recognize structures of power in almost any form. They could understand different marriage customs, alien principles of exchange, seemingly diabolical or infantile modes of worship.

Anything, however, which fell right through their conceptual 'grid' could only ever be relegated to the 'marvellous' or the 'wondrous'. Most of those who left Europe for 'other worlds', whatever their objectives, left with a repertoire of strange human and animal types which served to individuate what was otherwise an entirely amorphous category. Columbus believed that he had encountered cannibals and sighted the Earthly Paradise; an expedition was sent to find the Fountain of Eternal Youth; generations of Spanish explorers claimed to have uncovered evidence of the existence of giants; and even the otherwise sober Hernán Cortés very nearly found the kingdom of the Amazons. Such things existed out of real time and space. They could be accepted as true because the form in which they were expressed prevented the listener or reader from asking detailed questions of them. Once, however, the marvellous was given precise shape it had somehow to be fitted back into the grid, to be given a place in the scale of European normative expectations. So long as the wealth of the Great Kahn was described simply as 'fabulous' it was accepted as such. But when Marco Polo declared it to be '14,700,000 gold pieces' he was dubbed 'Il Millione' and urged by his friends on his deathbed to recant his lies.[21]

America, however, had always been a mixed world, a world where dog-headed men, or cannibals, might be encountered at the end of a city street, a world where, as one eighteenth-century Spanish traveller mockingly noted, the women urinated standing up and the men carried the children on their backs.[22] It was a world, as the eighteenth-century Italian missionary Filippo Salvatore Gilii complained, which was known not by its real qualities, which were similar to those of all other worlds, but 'distinguished only by its marvels'.[23] In this respect America had always been and would always remain disquietingly new. And like all things which were new it had a powerful capacity for absorption. As most European settlers discovered, no matter how much they might try to reconstruct for themselves self-sufficient European environments in the New World, they would, with time, slowly become something other than what they had intended, something inescapably 'American'. For this reason, if for no other, America seemed to offer to later generations of immigrants, who hoped precisely to leave behind them all trace of what they had once been, the promise of a truly 'new' life.

America was also different from all other 'other' worlds in that until Columbus's landfall its very existence had been unknown. If, as the Huguenot missionary Jean de Léry (whom I discuss in Chapter 1) had observed, America had been simply unfamiliar, then 'Asia and Africa could also be named new worlds with regard to us'. But it was far more than that. America was truly other, and some had suspected might even be part of some other and later act of creation. There had even been a number of thinkers in the seventeenth century, Andrea Cesalpino, Girolamo Cardano, and the heresiarch Giordano Bruno among them, who believed that the American Indians had been created by sponta- neous generation, or that they were the progeny of not one but many Adams, hypotheses which struck at the basis of that most cherished of Graeco-Christian notions: the integrity of the human race.[24] The sheer presence of America therefore became an inescapable component in the European understanding of the past. It provided a marker between two epochs, a convenient date with which to begin a distinctively modern period in European history, a period in which the vision of human time as the steady unfolding of a divine plan – St Augustine's *Ordo saeculorum* – was replaced by the image of a constant process of perfection, of the evolution of purely human objectives. The discovery of America also intersected with another powerful tradition in European thought. This was the dependence of all knowledge upon textual interpretation and exegesis. In this tradition all that could be known had to be made compatible with all that had once been said by a recognized canon of sacred and ancient authors. The discovery intersected with that tradition over a period when, as we shall see, it was also under threat from other, internal sources, from Baconian empiricism, Cartesian scepticism and, later, Galilean physics. As the royal confessor, Louis Genty, noted rather wistfully on the eve of the French Revolution, if men had paid proper attention to the full meaning of the discovery of America, had they allowed it to 'change the general impulse of the spirit and to turn it towards new objects more worthy of their researches', modernity might yet have been created without recourse to scepticism, and, as he saw it, the consequent collapse of the Christian faith.[25]

iv

Incorporating the discovery into a history of science as the history of man's self-perfection through the understanding of his world, however, did little to familiarize Europeans with what America actually was. China, Africa and India had been slowly, if also uncertainly, incorporated into the European imagination. All three had been known about and discussed since antiquity. The post-classical contact with these places had always, however, been tenuous. The Portuguese occupied islands – Goa, Macao, São Tomé – and built trading stations, San João da Mina, Arguim, Ormuz, in Africa and Asia. But only in America did the Europeans colonize on a massive scale before the nineteenth century. The Spaniards turned the native populations of their colonies into a subservient labouring class. In the process they drove what little remained of these people's cultures underground. Some features of the Amerindian world, such as the cultural apparatus which had sustained the 'Inka' and 'Aztec' 'Empires', vanished altogether. Others, the religious and social systems of the Yucatec Maya for instance,[26] managed to survive in a constantly changing relationship with Christianity and with the settler societies. The Portuguese, once they had discovered that the Circum-Caribbean tribes of Brazil made poor labourers, drove their indigenous peoples deeper and deeper into the tropical forests. The British, for their part, did their best to annihilate what one colonist called the 'beavers upon our streams'.[27] Only the French who, at least until the nineteenth century, operated always on the margins of Native-American society, developed in the famous *coureurs de bois* something approaching a mixed community so that in 1768 Peter Kalm was led to declare that 'the French in Canada in many respects follow the customs of the Indians'.[28] But this was only short-lived and even those, such as the picaresque Baron de Lahontan (whom we shall meet again in Chapter 4), while evidently sympathetic towards what he saw as the virtues of Amerindian life, was also prepared to participate in a war against the Iroquois whose ultimate purpose was to subdue or, if necessary, eradicate them in the commercial interests of the French Crown.

Colonization, and the dual experience of administration and acculturation which colonization involved, brought the hitherto semi-mythical, and often mythologized 'savage' far closer to the European world than he had been during antiquity and the Middle Ages. Hitherto the European traveller had only ever encountered him on his own territory. Men like Marco Polo or the Venetian Alvise da Ca'da Mosto, who has left us the most detailed account of the Congo of the fifteenth century, had been observers, privileged outsiders looking in. Their interest in the cultural practices of the peoples they encountered was considerable. As the American anthropologist James Boon has observed, it requires a considerable act of imagination on the part of a medieval merchant to ask of the Arab, with whom he is conversing through signs and a rudimentary *lingua franca*, whether that Arab marries, and if so if he marries his mother's brother's daughter.[29] This objectifying habit, in which so many European travellers seem to have shared, had clearly been imbedded in European culture from a very early date.

But it was colonization which brought that habit directly to bear upon the conflicts occasioned by the contact between different belief systems and different ways of life. For the merchant it was a matter of little immediate importance *whom* the Arab married. To the colonist and the missionary, however, it could be crucial. It was colonization which forced the 'savage' and the 'barbarian', and with them the problem of the intelligibility of other worlds, fully upon the European consciousness. In Europe the consequence of this was the gradual evolution of a powerful self-effacing myth which, in the early part of the eighteenth century, came to be known as the *bon sauvage* or 'noble savage'. The last two chapters of this book deal in different ways with different aspects of that myth.

The 'noble savage' was by no means a single or unambiguous image. Even those, Rousseau for instance and Diderot, who made the greatest use of him, offered a shifting range of attributes from Rousseau's feckless Carib to the wise *veillard* from Diderot's *Supplément au Voyage de Bougainville*. But whatever the character with which he is endowed, the 'savage' was always a representative of worlds we have lost. He spoke as we once spoke, and lived as we once lived. He came, therefore, to occupy a crucial position in a gradually evolving conjectural history of human origins. The term 'savage' itself, though it was used to describe human beings (originally it applied only to plants) in the seventeenth century, was first given its modern definition by Montesquieu in a brief but immensely influential passage in *De l'esprit des lois* (On the Spirit of the Laws, 1748). Here, speaking of the Tupinamba of Brazil, he characterized 'savages' as those who 'have not been able to unite' (*ne peuvent pas se réunir*). This distinguished them from the 'Barbarians' who, like the Tartar and Mongol pastoralists, were those who had been able to 'come together' in simple social groups.[30] To judge by the jottings in his *Fragments politiques*, Rousseau had hoped to write an entire 'History of Morals' on the basis of these distinctions.[31] The category of an wholly pre-social being, which Montesquieu had thus created, freed the early history of mankind from any contamination by the more obviously brutalizing stages on its painful progress towards civility, represented by the 'barbarian'. The savage stood at the beginning of human social time. He was a universal type, what all men had once been before they became, in Rousseau's term, 'domesticated', a specific sample of an enduring, and universal, 'human' nature.

Real 'savages', both in America and in the newly discovered islands of the Pacific, could now be used to provide the empirical details required for a number of conjectural histories of mankind, histories which were sometimes, as in the case of Rousseau's *Discours sur l'origine de l'inégalité parmi les hommes* (Discourse on Origins of Inequality Among Men, 1754), more or less explicitly intended to replace the Biblical account of the creation and diffusion of peoples. One of these histories, which I discuss here in Chapter 4, was that of language. The other is the history of sociability, and of mankind's progressive imaginative grasp on the world or worlds in which he lives. This I discuss in Chapter 5. Both such histories were the outcome of a series of encounters between Europe and its New World. To a large degree, both were meditations upon the consequences for Europe of the process of colonization. By the early nineteenth century, where this book ends, the legacy of empire had come to be a subject of intense criticism. For three centuries Europeans had been driven into close and prolonged contact with the American 'other'. But this had done little, or nothing, to bridge the cultural divide between the two worlds. Instead of 'Enlightenment', however understood, the Europeans had brought in the end only death and disease to the peoples they had conquered. And those travellers, explorers and settlers who had gone to America had carried back with them to Europe not a greater understanding of that allusive subject 'mankind', but only hordes of precious metals and a new breed of physical, imaginative and moral pollutants of their own.

CHAPTER ONE
The Principle of Attachment

Se aleja el Continente con bruma hacia más brumas,
Y es ya rincón y ruina, derrumbe repetido
Rumores de cadenas chirrirando entre lodos

America, mi savia: ¿nunca llegaré a ser?
Apresúrame, please, esta metamorfosis.

Jorge Guillén, *Maremágnum*

i

Gonzalo Fernández de Oviedo, author of one of the earliest histories of America, looked upon the native inhabitants of the Antilles with disgust. Despite their occasional outward beauty, they seemed to him to be bestial in their habits, over-interested in sex and lacking in any recognizable social order. They had, however, one curious redeeming feature. They were, or at least seemed to be, possessed of what he called a 'notable religiosity'. This devotion may have been misplaced, since what they venerated with such obvious enthusiasm was a god called 'Cemi' which, Oviedo assumed, was merely a local term for Lucifer. But for the observant Christian any form of devotion had its merit, whatever the intention of the devotee.

Columbus, so Oviedo tells us, had also noticed the Indians' devotion to their deity. The conclusion which Columbus drew from what he saw, however, must strike the modern reader as rather odd. 'The Admiral Don Christopher Columbus,' wrote Oviedo,

first discoverer of these parts, as a Catholic captain and a good Governor, after he had heard about the mines at Cibao, and saw that the Indians gathered gold in the waters of the streams and rivers, without having to dig for it, with the ceremony and the piety that has been mentioned, refused to allow the Christians to collect gold without first confessing and taking communion. The Indians, he said, spent the twenty days beforehand without touching their wives (nor any other woman) and fasting; and they said that if they touched a woman they would find no gold. Therefore, he said, if those bestial Indians observed such rituals, there was even more reason for the Christians to cease from sin and to confess their errors, and that, being in a state of Grace with God Our Saviour, He would give them more freely the temporal and spiritual goods they sought. 'This

17

sanctimoniousness,' commented Oviedo, did not, however, please everyone, for the men replied that, as for women, those who had their wives in Spain were more celibate than the Indians, and as for fasting, most of them were, in any case, on the point of dying of hunger.[1]

This anecdote is the earliest extended account we have of the encounter between the religious and social practices of a European culture and an Amerindian one. At first it may seem to be little more than the record of the incomprehension with which most Europeans of the late fifteenth century confronted cultural worlds other than their own. But even if we assume that all Columbus is doing here is replacing what he takes to be an act of 'bestial' piety by another of his own, then what he is doing is remarkable enough. A closer reading of his actions, unreflective though they clearly were, may carry us a long way, not only into the always opaque operations of Columbus's own mind, but also into the representational complexities faced by all the early settlers in America.

We may assume on the basis of what is known about other polytheistic groups with similar ritual habits that, for their part, the Taino of Hispaniola believed that substances in transition between the natural and the artificial were dangerous. They believed that what lies in water is neither above nor below the ground. They believed, too, that because of its potentially disruptive power, such material is always close to the numinous. As one of Columbus's companions, Ramón Pane, had observed, the Taino exercised similar ritual caution when 'making idols', for wood and clay were possessed, in their transitional state, by the same perilous instability.[2] Columbus, as a 'Christian Captain', however, knew nothing about the perils adhering to transitional substances. He was trying to make sense of an initially alien pattern of behaviour which was evidently capable of producing the instant results that he required, no matter how bestial it might appear. The Indians found gold, and they did so after performing a series of rituals which bore a striking resemblance to some of those practised by Christians. If Columbus wanted gold then it might seem not unreasonable that he, too, should perform the same kind of rites. However, to understand something more about what he was attempting to do by this apparent expropriation of an Indian practice, we have first to take a longer look at his much discussed attitudes towards gold.

Columbus was highly sensitive to the numinousness of gold. His journals and letters are filled with quasi-mystical references to the lure of precious metals. In a famous passage in the *Journal of the Fourth Voyage* composed in July 1503, he wrote:

> Genoese and Venetians, and all those peoples who have pearls, precious stones and other valuable things, carry them to the ends of the earth for trade and to convert them into gold. Gold is most excellent; with gold treasure is made, and he who possesses it, can do as he wishes in the world. It can even drive souls into Paradise.[3]

This is more than the banal claim that wealth is power, or that salvation can be achieved through the giving of alms. Gold was a symbol of divine wisdom. For Columbus – who assured Pope Alexander VI that on Hispaniola he had located the legendary mines of King Solomon – gold was a powerful independent agent, a food for the soul, as bread was the food of the body.[4] Every time Columbus was brought a sample of the metal, he retired into his oratory to give thanks to God.[5] In his mind, God and gold, mining and conversion, were not clear and distinct goals as the later missionaries to America were to make them. They were indissoluble. If, he wrote on his disastrous third voyage, the 'gold and other things' still eluded him, this might be, he thought, not because there was none to be had, but that because of the 'dissolute cupidity' of his men, God had hidden it from him.[6] On Christmas Day 1500 he recorded a vision he had had. 'When I was much afflicted,' he wrote to Doña Juana de la Torre, the nurse (*ama*) to the heir to the throne, Prince Don Juan,

> warring with bad Christians and the Indians, and on the point of abandoning everything and escaping, Our Lady miraculously consoled me and said to me, 'take courage, and do not faint nor fear, for I will provide in all things, for the seven years without gold are not yet passed, but in them and in all things I will give you remedy'.[7]

The Virgin's promises did not run to seven fat years of gold to follow the seven lean ones and, in the end, her consolations sound rather unhelpful. But the analogy with Joseph's dream is explicit. Christopher, the *Christum ferrens*, as he signed himself, the 'Christ-Bearer', would one day lead his people into a Promised Land of mineral abundance. There, too, they would settle as the Israelites had done, for if Columbus's baptismal name had marked him out as the Christ-Bearer, the name he had been born with – 'Colón' – meant, as his first historian Bartolomé de las Casas reminds us,

> someone who settles a land for the first time, the which surname was suited to him since through his industry and labours he was the

cause that, by discovering these peoples, an infinite number of their souls . . . was saved.[8]

From the day of his birth the infant Colón had been marked down as a future '*colon*-izer'. As Dr Johnson was later to observe, 'there is something in names one cannot help feeling'.[9]

All of Columbus's references to gold conjure with similar allusions to the language of biblical prophetics. They are also heavily indebted to the language of alchemy. The alchemist's quest was to transform base metal into gold, instantly and effortlessly. The Taino, it is true, did not quite do this. But they did, or so Columbus believed, successfully pan the gold *without having to dig for it*; something remarkable to a man who was accustomed to thinking of gold as a substance that had to be dug out of the earth. That they were able to do so, he could only attribute to their elaborate ritual preparations, preparations which shared one thing in common, at least, with some Christian rituals: sexual and dietary abstention. Since, for the Christian fundamentalist (and Columbus was nothing if not a fundamentalist), sexual abstention is perceived as a good no matter what the intention, it might be argued, as Oviedo seems to imply, that the ready availability of gold *was* a sign of divine favour. The Indians had understood this through natural reason; Columbus knew it through revelation.

Having thus noticed what he took to be the immediate effectiveness of the Taino rituals, Columbus was now poised to make what is a startling transition for any Christian from analogy and allusion to direct substitution. In asking his men to abstain from sex and food and to confess, so that they might be 'in a state of Grace with God Our Saviour', he was, in effect, laying Christian practices, whose objective was to acquire grace, over non-Christian practices, whose purpose, as Columbus perceived it, was to acquire gold.

In the long history of the European attempts to Christianize America, there are numerous cases of unorthodox substitutions. But all of them, including Hernán Cortés's seemingly unconcerned use of native 'priests' to tend his newly-created Christian shrines,[10] and the use of the names of Amerindian deities for Christian saints, sought to Christianize through the symbolic manipulation of pre-existent pagan customs. Only Columbus's blatant appropriation involved, if only implicitly, the substitution of a Christian for a pagan ritual in order to achieve the objective for which the pagan, not the Christian, ritual had been intended.

Columbus's behaviour was frequently bizarre. It seemed so to his companions, and on occasions it even seemed so to Bartolomé de las Casas, who did more than anyone to preserve his writings and safeguard his fame. Columbus frequently claimed to hear celestial voices; he insisted that the still imaginary wealth of the 'Indies' should be used to fund a crusade, and he regularly appeared at the court of the Catholic Monarchs in a Franciscan habit and once in chains.[11] But if we go still further into Oviedo's anecdote, it will become clear that the Christian Captain was doing something more than finding a characteristically eccentric means of acquiring gold, something which others, who shared none of his messianic veneration for precious metals, would replicate in different ways. He was also translating varieties of experience from an alien world into the practices of his own. He was doing this, however, not as so many others in America would do, by analogue or metaphor.[12] At this stage neither Oviedo nor Columbus allude to any similarities between Christian and pagan practices. European and Amerindian sacred rites are not said, as many later commentators would say of them, to be similar, the one either a diabolic inversion or a residual memory of the other. Indeed the supposed effectiveness of the rituals of the 'bestial Indians' excludes the possibility of any such claims. Instead, what is familiar, abstention and self-denial, is employed to 'attach' one unfamiliar action to another familiar one. The stark incommensurability of the two is, or seems to be, dissolved in the supposed common recognition of the danger of sex and of the cosmic worth of gold. I shall call this device, for we will come across it again, the 'principle of attachment'.

Here, then, the bestial Indian and the Christian are made to share a common, if only transitory, ritual terrain. In the process the 'otherness' of the Indians' world, although not eliminated (they still remain 'bestial', a mark by which Columbus's men can measure their own 'errors', has been made accountable. What follows from an act of attachment is an act of recognition. However reluctant Columbus may have been to see in the Indian – naked, polygynous and, to his ears, inarticulate – a fellow human, he was now equipped to recognize one aspect of Taino behaviour as compatible with his own. He had achieved this, however, only at the expense of *de*taching the original Amerindian practices from their contexts. By making the actions of the Taino recognizable in his terms, Columbus had re-located them in a context which would have made them unintelligible to their original actors. But recognition of this kind, however much it distorted what the Indians may actually have intended by acting as they did, offered at least an initial identification of humanity. Although it is clearly very far removed from what, ever since the early eighteenth century, has been regarded as acceptable ethnographical practice, it had the apparent effect of reducing, sometimes even of erasing, distance.

ii

Many of Columbus's other acts, and the language in which he described them, were similarly intended to shrink the distance between Europe and America, between himself and the geographical and cultural 'Other'. His initial cosmographical calculations, by reducing the real length of the degree, had shrunk the globe to two-thirds of its actual size. And all his life he insisted that what he had discovered was not a new world, but a new route to the old familiar world of Asia. Only once, when standing off the Gulf of Paria, and realizing that what flowed along the weed-encrusted hulls of his ships was fresh water, did he question this belief. If the Orinoco could set up 'such a great contest between the fresh water striving to reach the sea, and the salt water striving to enter the gulf. . . that both waters caused a great roar and thunder from east to west' then he knew that he must be near 'a very great continent which until today has been unknown'.[13]

But Columbus's faith in his mission, and in his own navigational skills, wavered only for a moment. If, he argued, this were a continent unknown to the Ancients, and if it lay to the south of the Malay Peninsula, as it must do if he were, as he knew himself to be, somewhere near Ptolemy's fabled Golden Chersonese, then this 'great continent' could only be the one, as yet undiscovered land mass: the Earthly Paradise, which Pierre d'Ailly's *Imago mundi* had led him to believe that he would find in a temperate zone beneath the equator. This claim, which struck even his contemporaries as absurd, was not, as the great nineteenth-century Prussian naturalist Alexander von Humboldt (whom we shall meet many times again) later claimed it to be, merely the conjurings of Columbus's 'poetic imagination' – a reminder, as Humboldt put it, that 'the creative fantasy and the poetic manifests itself in the discovery of a world no less than in every other form of human greatness'.[14] It was instead a desperate attempt on Columbus's part to 'save the phenomena' as he knew them, to preserve his own eccentric geographical vision which he had spent so many fruitless years peddling to the various monarchs of Europe. For he could see only too well that, 'if this river does not proceed from the Terrestrial Paradise, it comes from an infinite land to the South, of which no-one so far has had notice'. The vision of such a land, shattering the known, measured and mapped spaces of his imagination evidently terrified him. 'But I am very certain in my soul,' he immediately added, 'that this is, as I said, the Terrestrial Paradise, and I rest my case on the reasons and the authorities mentioned above'.[15] Having identified the source of what he could now assume to be the Ganges, and knowing that no mortal could set foot there, 'except by divine command', Columbus sailed on.

Columbus's 'constant endeavour', as Lord Acton later observed of him, 'was *not* to be mistaken for the man who had discovered the New World'.[16]

Columbus's contemporaries, however, were less persuaded either by his calculations or his explanations. The Milanese humanist at the court of the Catholic Monarchs, Peter Martyr, who wrote an eager, somewhat breathless account of the discoveries 'as they came in', laughed at Columbus's account of the Earthly Paradise. He laughed, too, at Columbus's laborious reasons for believing that the world was 'not round, in the shape they describe, but it is the shape of a pear' or, as he says later, 'like a woman's breast on top of a round ball'.[17] Martyr, who had only what he could pick up at court to go on, nevertheless knew what had happened. 'This Columbus,' he declared, 'is the discoverer of a New World'.[18] What Martyr meant by this, however, is uncertain. European navigators had for long suspected the existence of islands in the 'Ocean Sea' lying between them and India. These appear on maps and in the romances of chivalry, and the name of one of them, Brazil, in the end found its way to America. One thing, however, is certain. Martyr knew where Columbus was in relation to Europe, and he knew that this New World would bring with it problems of description and understanding which few, if any, previous discoveries had brought.

The subsequent settlement of the Caribbean, and the very rapid realization that this 'New World' was not a mere archipelago, but a vast land mass whose northern and southern extremities were unknown, brought with it the recognition that these were territories inhabited by a variety of strange peoples, not all of whom could easily be accommodated under some existing anthropological category. As more information became available it became increasingly difficult, even for Europeans with no direct experience of America, to ignore the sheer presence of its novelty.[19]

Columbus's immediate strategies for dealing with this novelty were in many ways unprecedented, and within a few years of his first voyage, they had become very largely unrepeatable. Columbus's act of ritual appropriation could never ultimately accommodate the range of alternatives with which America increasingly presented him. Even Amerigo Vespucci, to whose lurid sexual imagination America seemed, at first, to be the repository for a variety of classical exotica – the Earthly Paradise, the ceaselessly fertile, persistently ageless Amazons ('one hundred and fifty years old and sometimes more'), the Hyperboreans (whose bellies, even after many childbirths, 'were in no way different from those of virgins'), the cannibals and the giants – even Vespucci came finally to realize that when one got up close enough, 'nothing shows any conformity with the things of this part [of the world]'.[20] The divide which separated Amerindian cultural and religious practices from those of the Europeans was clearly too wide to allow for any direct assimilation of one to the other.

But the same principle of attachment which had underpinned Columbus's eccentric attempt to find gold, became an enduring feature of most European efforts to steady the initially vertiginous experience of being in a 'new' world. There was, however, an inherent danger in this, as in all unreflective action. The principle of attachment may give some degree of understanding, and it is doubtful that we could do very much without it when confronted, as Columbus and his immediate followers were, with the blatantly unknown. But it may (and indeed frequently does) lead us simply to assimilate the unknown to the known.

Oviedo, for instance, fell into this conceptual trap when he declared that since both the Thracians and the Taino practised polygyny, the Taino must also sacrifice all foreign visitors. As he freely admitted, he had no reason to suppose that the Taino in fact practised any form of human sacrifice, even if, on Columbus's evidence, they were cannibals. But Eusebius had said that this was what the Thracians did, and having 'attached' the Thracians to the Taino, he simply 'read off' onto them *all* their attributes.[21] Here recognition has been withheld. The distance which separated Oviedo the observer from the Indian whom he knew at first hand (and he was, as we shall see in the next Chapter, insistent on his status as 'eye-witness') had been increased by the distance, temporal as well as spatial, which separated Oviedo the reader from Eusebius's Thracians.

iii

The extent to which the principle of attachment endured, despite very large changes both in the range of objects of knowledge available to the traveller in America, and in scientific method, can be seen by moving forward some three hundred years. In July 1799, Alexander von Humboldt, accompanied by his friend and draughtsman the French botanist Aimée Bonpland, landed on the coast of what is now Venezuela. For the next five years, accompanied by a battery of scientific instruments, some of which Humboldt had designed himself – eudiometers, hygrometers, barometers, chronometers, inclinometers, sextants, quadrants, achromatic and reflecting telescopes, a cyanometer (this was used to gauge the blueness of the sky) and a Ramsden graphometer – the two men travelled throughout Venezuela, Colombia,

Ecuador, Mexico, Peru and Cuba.[22] It was the most extensive scientific exploration of America yet attempted. What Humboldt hoped to take home with him was America discovered, described, measured, mapped and sampled. He had, in his own image, captured an entire continent and laid it out before the critical gaze of those 'back home' who would now know it in no other way. Humboldt's account of this undertaking, the *Relation historique*, first published in French in 1814, made him famous. As Charles Darwin later acknowledged, 'my whole course of life is due to having read and re-read as a youth his *Personal Narratives*'.[23]

The shock with which Humboldt registered the unfamiliarity of America was to remain with him throughout his very long life. In all his writings, the same images occur and re-occur: images of contrast, of the new matched against the old, of the familiar set against the unfamiliar. Few naturalists have left such a detailed record of the aesthetics and the cognitive strategies on which they were engaged, nor struggled so long to get them into words.

He has also left us a vivid account of the scientist–traveller's sense of detachment on leaving Europe. 'It resembled,' he wrote, 'none of the impressions which we have received from our earliest youth. Separated from the objects of our most dear affections, entering, so to speak, into a new life, we are forced to rely upon ourselves, and we find ourselves in an isolation which we have never before experienced.'[24] Humboldt knew that to emerge from this isolation we have to find something to which we can attach ourselves. The sea offers nothing. It was, as he remembered it, only a massive undifferentiated waste. Even the night skies which might have provided the traveller with some point of orientation merely added to his sense of isolation, 'beaming', as it was, 'with stars other than those to which [the mariner's] eyes have been accustomed'.[25] And when in 1845 he came to write his most popular work, a great synoptic history of the universe magisterially entitled *Kosmos*, he recorded, in these terms, his own experience of what it was to come into contact again with a world which, though expectedly unfamiliar, offered some immediate possibility for attachment.

When far from our native country, after a long sea journey we tread for the first time the lands of the tropics we experience an impression of agreeable surprise in recognizing in cliffs and rocks, the same forms and substances, similarly inclined strata of schistous rocks, and the same columnar basalt which we had left in Europe.... But those schistous and those basalts are covered with vegetable forms of new and strange aspect. Amid the luxuriance of this exotic flora surrounded by colossal forms of unfamiliar grandeur and beauty we experience (thanks to the marvellous flexibility of our nature) how

25

easily the mind opens to the combination of impressions connected with each other by unperceived links of secret analogy . . . . The colonist loves to give the plants of his new home names borrowed from his native land, and these strong untaught impressions lead, however vaguely, to the same end as that laborious and extended comparison of facts by which the philosopher arrives at an intimate persuasion of our indissoluble chain of affinity binding together all nations.[26]

Here we are dealing with the natural world, not the world of human behaviour. The principle of attachment, however, operates in much the same way as it did for Columbus and for Oviedo. The observer recognizes immediately that the rocks of, in Humboldt's case, the Venezuelan coastline, are recognizably the same as those of his own 'mother country'. His eye steadied and assured by this perception he then attaches to the wholly unfamiliar vegetation familiar names. These, as most of the early botanists were soon to discover, were, in fact, singularly inappropriate to plants which are most striking precisely for their dissimilarity to everything which grows 'at home'. Yet this initial linguistic act, however misleading it might appear to be, 'points', Humboldt recorded elsewhere, 'as it were, instinctively to the truth'.[27] This is not simple catachresis, for the instinctive namer also arrives at the same condition *vis-à-vis* his perception of the relationship between rocks and plants, in the same manner as the philosopher arrives at his 'intimate persuasion' of the common identity of all mankind. The namer is able to do this, or so Humboldt suggests, because quite plausibly our eyes give an instinctive priority to what is familiar over what is unfamiliar. Our eyes and our scientific understanding move from the known to the unknown, not the other way. Having made the attachment, we name the unknown for the known. Having named we have recognized and, having recognized, we have also taken possession. What is, in effect, first-degree intuition is made to do the same work as second-degree reflection.

I shall return to Humboldt. His Goethian quest for natural unities, his belief in the capacity of the new to imprint itself immediately upon the mind and, perhaps more importantly in this context, his belief in a natural history of scientific understanding, are far removed from the concerns of Columbus and his contemporaries. Yet there is a continuity which links the two men which, as we shall see in Chapter 3, can in part be expressed in terms of the fascination which the one exercised over the other. Both were self-conscious discoverers; both knew, as Humboldt himself said of Columbus, how to 'seize the phenomena of the exterior world'.[28] Both were looking for homologies. Both saw the globe in terms of encirclement: Humboldt in terms of isolines, isotherms and the geography of plants, Columbus in parallels of precious metals – the 'gold line' which ran through Guinea and on round through the Malay Peninsula – and his 'line at which magnetic variation becomes nil' whose discovery Humboldt attributed to his 'almost instinctive lucidity of spirit'.[29] This, as Humboldt understood it, he had hoped to transform into a political demarcation, the natural meridian which 'divided the globe into two hemispheres with wholly dissimilar configurations and physical constitutions', whose marine frontiers were to be marked by the Sargasso Sea, a floating continent of weed, a world which had nothing *except* a location. When in 1494 the Treaty of Tordesillas divided the globe up between Spain and Portugal, the line of demarcation was established a long way from the divisions which Humboldt had attributed to Columbus. But it was certainly a reflection, as Humboldt recognized, of the same Columbine impulse to encircle, to divide, to contain and ultimately to possess.[30]

iv

Attachment led to possession. But most things possessed, if they are to be of any value to the possessor, have to be capable of mobility.[31] At one level mobility may be expressed in terms of exchange. This is why (as we shall see in Chapter 5) commerce came to be seen as the prime example of man's capacity for motion. For Columbus, gold was more prized than any other thing, because in his view it was the one commodity which no one would wish to exchange for any other. For him it seems to have been a thing in itself, to be exchanged only for such eternal and abstract benefits as the liberation of Jerusalem and a place in Paradise. Yet it was gold's transportability combined with its rarity and durability which had made its worth seem more than merely relative in the first place, precisely because it was these qualities which had made it so well suited to be a medium of exchange. Gold was a symbol, as paper money was to become in the eighteenth century, of the unique capacity of the human to carry with him what he is able to possess.

Like gold, names too were symbolic units which could, as both Columbus and Humboldt recognized, easily be transported about the globe. Just as maps could transform the un-possessable world into a series of lines and figures which could then be carried home to Barcelona or Lisbon, names had the power to reduce what still remained to be explored, possessed and settled into a single transportable set of phonemes. The first illustrated version of the famous *Carta a Santángel* depicted Columbus standing in his ship in the midst of what is, in fact, a contemporary map, and surrounded by the islands of the archipelago he had 'discovered' – although in the illustration he seems rather to have created them – each with the name he had given it (see figure 2). Like maps, names are also part of what the philosopher of science Bruno Latour has called 'immutable and combinable mobiles' – those 'charts, tables, trajectories . . . conveniently at hand and combinable at will, no matter whether they are twenty centuries old or a day old'[32] – which may be used to link the metropolis with the distant frontier. They make the unknown and the nearly unimaginable familiar enough for it to *become* imaginable to the awed explorer and the frequently indifferent people 'back home'.[33] In the end the history of science, as Latour says, comes to be the 'history of the many clever means to transform whatever people do, sell and buy into something that can be mobilized, gathered, archived, coded, recalculated and displayed'.[34]

Nothing terrifies so much as the unimaginable, incalculable, unmapable empty space which cannot be possessed or transported in this way. The classical and medieval geographers filled their uncharted, unexplored lands and seas with terrors, with dragons, man-eaters, vast whirlpools which could swallow entire ships, the 'Green Sea of Darkness' which the Arabs had located immediately to the south of Cape Bojador. These unknown lands were filled, too, with clusters of imaginary beings – the Amazons and the Anthropophagi, the Cephalapods – and with impossible places – the Mountains of the Moon, the Fountain of Eternal Youth, the Terrestrial Paradise itself – which were also at once both immutable and highly mobile. Columbus found Anthropophagi in the Antilles, Ponce de León sailed to Florida in search of the Fountain of Eternal Youth in Florida and Francisco de Orellana's description of the Amazons was so convincing that their name, not his, was given to the great river he was the first to navigate. In the early eighteenth century Joseph François Lafitau, Jesuit missionary and author of one of the earliest comparative ethnologies, even claimed that his Huron informants had caught sight of Cephalapods in what is now Canada proving, so he believed, that a land bridge had once existed between the Old World and the New.[35] At one level the entire sixteenth- and seventeenth-century debate over the origins of peoples, and over the origins of the American Indians in particular, can be interpreted in this way. To claim a Chinese, Scythian, Lycian or Spartan source for the human life in America made it possible to transport those new and troubling peoples back along the migratory lines which had first carried them away from the Old World. By making him mobile, the 'savage'

2. Illustration to the first edition of the *Carta a Santángel* (Barcelona, 1493), announcing Columbus's discovery.

could thus be domesticated in space, just as, through education and instruction, he could eventually be domesticated in time, his world moving ever closer up the evolutionary scale to our own.

The American 'savage', before ne had encountered the European with his passion for movement, had rarely shown any wish to move beyond the limits of his village, his community, his ancestral hunting ground. He was now to be forced out along the sea-routes with which Columbus and his like had patterned the world. Travelling, either along real or supposed migratory trails, or up (and sometimes down) putative evolutionary scales, or as migrant or semi-migrant labour in real space and time, as slaves or curiosities, the peoples of America would increasingly be compelled to follow the trajectories which the European scientific imagination had constructed for them. Never again would they be able to call either space or time their own.

The Europeans, for their part, may travel in their mind's eye in the other direction if, like Humboldt's 'imaginative scientist', they possess a 'sensibility towards works of art' and a 'cultivated spirit'. 'The European,' wrote Humboldt, 'isolated on his arid coastline can entertain in his thoughts the appearance of distant regions'. If he has the imaginative skills, and if he is sufficiently knowledgeable to raise himself up to what Humboldt called 'the grand conceptions of general physics', he may yet, from the depths of his solitude, 'appropriate all that the intrepid naturalists had discovered and travel the winds and oceans and penetrate into subterranean grottoes or raise himself up on ice-covered peaks'. It is the informed, 'sensible' resources of our imagination which bring us to the 'enlightenment and civilization [which] influences, for the most part, our well-being. It is this which allows us to live in both the present and the past, it is this which allows us to gather round ourselves at the same time all that nature has produced in different climates, and which puts us in contact with the different races of the earth'.[36]

The reflective, informed and 'sensible' being possesses the ability to be, in this way, literally in more places than one. And it is precisely this capacity for cognitive travel which constitutes his power of scientific understanding. For all scientific knowledge, and the power that that knowledge brings with it, demands just such movement. And all movement follows the same trajectory. It begins as a going out and ends as coming back. The Odyssey, as Auerbach noted long ago, is an image of all our mental worlds. The discoverer carries out with him his lexicon of names, his repertoire of classifications, his knowledge of the invisible isolines and parallels which link him to home. He returns with samples, exhibits, slaves. This itinerary, which is always invariable, is, as

Descartes may have been the first to recognize, the same 'journey' which every scientist must make.[37]

The process of going out and coming back which all this involved posed, however, serious technical and conceptual problems. Once the attachment had been made, the name given, the species seemingly identified, the resultant 'mobile' still had to be brought back to those, to borrow from Latour again, 'centres of calculation', the museums, laboratories, botanical gardens where they can be made intelligible for those who have never left Europe. The distances the traveller has to cover before he can reach home inevitably threatens to reverse the process I have been describing – to detach what has so recently become attached. For the one thing which cannot be preserved on the journey home is the context in which the initial attachment was made. In certain cases this presents no serious difficulty. Rocks, birds, plants, works of art can easily be 'made mobile' and shipped home. With his first letter from Mexico in 1519, Hernán Cortés sent Charles V just such a collection to which he added two native manuscripts to give his King some immediate idea of the 'the customs and riches of the people who inhabit [this land] and of the laws, beliefs, rites and ceremonies by which they live'.[38] Less transportable goods, tropical fruit for instance, could be replaced by drawings. In extreme cases, even humans could be sent home. In 1495 Columbus had sent some Taino back to Castile in part to demonstrate to Queen Isabella, whose own attempt to break the Portuguese monopoly on the Atlantic slave-trade had proved abortive, that these islands, if poor in the spices and the gold which should have been there, might still be rich in human merchandise. But he also brought them back as specimens, so that Their Majesties might see what people these Indies had in them.

Samples of minerals and plants, once relocated in their new 'centres of calculations', can be made intelligible by reference to other minerals and plants. Humans, however, rarely transport so well. They die or become meaningless in their new contexts.[39] What, in fact, happened to the savage as he disappeared into the thickets of European civilization? We have records of very few cases. Most vanished without trace. The Indians with which Columbus returned from his first voyage, the Tupinamba Montaigne met at Rouen, surface briefly as data used to embellish texts which have only transitory uses for them. Columbus loses interest when they are declared not to be slaves. Montaigne shifts his gaze back to the iniquities of his own countrymen. The Eskimo whom Martin Frobisher brought back from Baffin island – 'as a token from thence of his being there' – is put on display and then he, too, dies.[40] These creatures are only ever of interest as representatives of

31

their own worlds. Although they are here among us, they are so only because we cannot easily go to them. If, like poor Pocahontas, they leave the shelter of their own exoticism, they very soon perish. None of them has the option of discovering, like Voltaire's 'Huron' l'Ingénu, who turns out to be the son of a French army-officer – or like Tarzan – that they are Europeans after all.

Exposed to Europe, the 'savage' can only sustain his position of detachment for a short while. The critique of our ways which nearly all such visitors express, will lose its force the longer the critic remains absent from the culture which had made it possible at all. In Europe he runs the risk of becoming a mere ranter. What happens to him, as it must to all travellers, is a loss of identity. His journey has, like all journeys, resulted in a kind of knowledge, monstrous though it is in this case. François Delisle de la Drévetière's Canadian Indian, 'Arlequin sauvage', knows this. After his first day in France, he turns on the French sailor who brought him to Europe:

> May the Devil take you. Why then have you taken me from my country to show me that I am poor? Never in my whole life would I have know that without you. In my forests I knew nothing of riches or poverty. I was my own king, my master and my servant. And you have cruelly torn me from this happy state, to teach me that I am a miserable creature and a slave.[41]

Human specimens always have a similarly uncertain attachment to their attributes. And, once removed from their original environments, they may, like the 'spices' which Columbus, in his eagerness, brought home from his first voyage, turn out to have no useful properties at all. When Bougainville returned in 1769 from his circumnavigation of the world, he brought with him a Tahitian he calls 'Aotouru', the model for Diderot's Orou, whom we shall meet again in Chapter 5. Like most such exotic imports, Aotouru caused something of a sensation in the Paris salons. But Bougainville was a serious scientist who had hoped to use Aotouru to study a real savage society 'at home', and he noted sadly that the interests of most Parisians amounted to nothing more than

> a sterile curiosity which had resulted only in giving false impressions to men who . . . had never left the capital, who had never thought deeply about anything, and seized by errors of every kind, see things only in the light of their own prejudices.[42]

Spices that are not spices and men who turn out to be neither slaves nor adequate specimens, like the 'tanned skins of wild women' with

3. Greenstone mask now in the Museo degli Argenti, Florence. This may once have been part of the dowry of Vittoria della Rovere on her marriage to Ferdinand de'Medici in 1634. The mask is of Mexican origin, the frame and base of gilded and enamelled copper is European.

which Hanno returned from Africa and the foot, tusk and hair – 'fully a palm long' – of an elephant carried home by Ca'da Mosto from the Gambia, become, as did Aotouru and Frobisher's poor Eskimo, mere curios, tourist souvenirs. The same is true of the cultural artifacts which humans make. The sixteenth- and seventeenth-century cabinets of curios were, said the great eighteenth-century Spanish explorer Antonio de Ulloa, as close as the modern scientist could get to 'the archives of nature'.[43] But what most of them, in fact, contained, were the ultimate context-less objects. Such items as the greenstone Aztec mask, which one of the Medici had set with rubies and mounted in a gilded copper frame, is wholly incommensurate with its original purpose, function or value, as either cultural symbol or object of exchange.[44] (See figure 3.) Even those objects which were not modified in this way – the manuscripts, feather-work and obsidian statuettes the Medici also collected – served less to provide evidence of the identity of alien cultures than they did to illustrate what was believed to be a universal past of which Europe itself had once been part. Like so many of the exhibits in the modern museum, they had thus been absorbed into a particular European world and were as culturally insignificant as the mermen or unicorns' horns to be found in the same *Wunderkammern*.

v

The sequence attachment, recognition, naming constitutes the process of carrying back, the route by which the discoverer 'enters into' what he has discovered. It is also, like every process of discovery, one which ends with an act of possession. He who first 'sees' a new land, claims the right to possession over it. As André Thevet, cosmographer royal to Henri III of France, pointed out, 'of all the senses in nature the human gaze is the most active'.[45] And everyone, like Thevet, whose relentlessly active gaze had fallen on a 'new' land, instantly claimed rights of possession over it. These rights were then recorded and secured by the act of naming and by the appropriation, and frequently by the coinage, of titles. The Europeans, as they crossed and re-crossed the Oceans, became inveterate namers and possessors. The Portuguese kings assumed to themselves titles over lands which their captains had seen, but to which they could never hope to lay any effective territorial claim. Balboa named and took possession of an ocean by placing his foot in it. As Diderot's imaginary Tahitian sage protests in fury some three hundred years later: 'what is written on this metal blade: "This Land is Ours". This land is yours! Why because you have placed your foot on it!'[46]

Columbus was equally sensitive to the power which priority of sight bestowed upon the discoverer. He was highly conscious of his role *as* a discoverer, even if he resolutely refused to believe that he had, in fact, made the greatest discovery of them all. For Columbus, as Tzvetan Todorov drily noted, 'to discover' was an intransitive verb.[47] He was also aware that the titles to sovereignty – Admiral of the Ocean Sea, Viceroy of the Indies – with which the Catholic Monarchs had so generously (since they cost them nothing) festooned him, would remain empty until he had found something over which to exercise them. Having offered 10,000 *maravedis* to the first man to sight land, he took the money for himself, as he must always have intended to, because, Las Casas tells us, although 'a sailor called Rodrigo from Triana [the lookout on the *Pinta*] first saw land', it was Columbus who 'had first seen the light, which meant that it was he who had first sighted land'. Columbus had thus anticipated, after the event, his own role in the process of sighting. The contemporary belief that all land, even if uninhabited, emitted a light at night allowed him to pre-empt poor Rodrigo's claim to have been the first recorded European to have set eyes upon America. It was inconceivable (to him at least) that it should not have been he who first saw the lands to which he had for so long pressed such extravagant judicial and political claims. Little wonder that, as Las Casas tells us, he wore the 10,000 *maravedis* round his neck for the rest of his life.[48]

Having sighted and then landed on what he believed to be 'The Indies', Columbus then assumed his political authority over them by giving them names. In Las Casas's narrative of his voyages, it is at this moment that 'Cristobál Colón', Genoese mariner and geographer of genius, is transformed into 'The Admiral', an officer of the Castilian crown. For, as Las Casas pointed out, from 'here on it will be right to use the prerogative and illustrious dignity which the Monarchs had so graciously bestowed upon him'.[49]

Illustrious though he had thus become, Columbus always remained the servant of higher masters, God and the Catholic Monarchs. His own initial act of naming was therefore performed in accordance with a strict order of hierarchy. 'The first [island] that I found,' he tells us,

> I gave the name San Salvador, in honour of his Holy Majesty who has miraculously given all this. The Indians call it Guanahani. To the second I gave the name Santa Maria de la Concepción, to the third Fernandina, to the fourth Isabella, to the fifth the island of Juana [after Prince Don Juan, the heir to the throne, but islands had always to be feminine], and so on, each with a new name.[50]

'The Indians call it Guanahani.' With one clause the aboriginal identity of the place had been erased. Columbus, it is true, will name things, and even some places, with Indian terms, places of little significance, or things for which he can find no available European analogue. But only the divine and secular monarchs, and their immediate offspring, could provide worthy names for the first of the lands on which he had 'set his eyes' and then his feet, and over which, in *their* name, he was to exercise *his* power. To Columbus it would have seemed at least irreverent to have named any of these places 'Colombia'. His position, and his authority, depended upon his role as agent. When later he was accused in the late 1490s of plotting to alienate the discoveries from the Castilian Crown, his defence was that he could not hope to survive without a patron.[51] Whatever he did, the image of his royal masters stood behind him. In the most famous of his descriptions, the account of his landfall on 'San Salvador' on the morning of October 12, 1492, he is keen to stress the extent to which he is there on his illustrious patrons' behalf. 'I took possession,' he wrote, 'for Your Highnesses by proclamation and with the royal banner unfurled',[52] an echo of the passage in the *Journal of the First Voyage* in which he recorded

that, 'on the second day of the month of January, I saw the royal
banner of your Highnesses raised by force of arms, on the towers of the
Alhambra . . .'.[53] Here the two great defining events of Castilian history,
as Columbus saw it, had been brought together in a single symbolic act.
Columbus himself who had been a witness to the first had now become
the agent of the second.

It is perhaps only appropriate that America itself, which remained for
so long an uncertain space, with no northern or southern limits, no
precise geographical location or fixed relationship with either Europe or
Asia – as late as 1513 Cuba was still appearing on maps as 'a Part of
Asia' – should have acquired its name, not through an act by any of
its discoverers but because of the decision of a German mapmaker,
uncertain what to call the 'fourth part of the world'.[54]

vi

From Columbus to Humboldt the principle of attachment served to
make the incommensurable seem commensurable, if only for as long as
it took the observer's vision to adjust, in Humboldt's metaphor, from
the geology to the flora and fauna of the world he had come to inhabit.
Attachment allowed for the creation of an initial (if also sometimes
troubling) familiarity. It also allowed the discoverer to make some
measure of classification. Above all, it allowed him to name, and by
naming to take cognitive possession of what he had 'laid eyes on'. But it
did not get the observer very far inside what he had seen, in particular if
that was not an island, a promontory or even a plant, but instead a
complex social world, which offered very few outward signs as to what
the inside might ultimately contain.

The traveller, however, did not need to go very far nor to understand
very much. Even for the purposes of the collection and description of
the kind set out in the various travel manuals of the sixteenth century,
the 'ars apodemica' and 'prudentia perigrinandi', with their proliferat-
ing stemma of classification, simple attachment was sufficient. The
traveller went only to record what he had seen and by so doing to
understand himself better. Once the traveller had made his enquiries
(and the manuals which he carried with him frequently provided him
with model questionnaires to help him in this task)[55] and taken his
notes, he returned home carrying with him all that he required to re-
locate and, in the process, utterly to transform his experiences within
his own familiar world. His ship, his floating home, carries him out and
back and within his narrow space he can still take with him all that he
requires of the lands he has left behind.

For the migrant, on the other hand, a different register of understanding was both necessary and inevitable. After the initial and consoling familiarity of the basalt and schistous rocks, to return to Humboldt's metaphor, had worn off, and when persistent naming had diminished none of the stark novelty of the vegetation, the immigrant who, unlike the traveller, could not at that point simply return home, was faced with inescapable incommensurability. He had to remain and yet resist the lure of the native. For him recognition was a more complex business for which attachment was an inadequate strategy, since any prolonged exposure immediately raised the difficulty of context. Some of those difficulties are apparent in Humboldt's text. Attachment of the kind he envisaged (unlike the kind Columbus had practised which was entirely without context) sought to replace context with intuition. Humboldt's plant geography based, as it is, in a belief in the cultural force of vegetation – 'that empire exercised over all organized beings' – is an attempt to create stable global contexts for differing cultures. 'The man who is sensitive (*sensible*) to the beauties of nature,' Humboldt believed, 'will find there the explanation for the influence which the appearance of vegetation exercises upon the taste and the imagination of peoples'.[56] The moment we come into prolonged contact with a new and startling flora, as Humboldt had in Venezuela, once our eyes lose contact with the comforting geology of home, we begin also to lose the identities we once had. For the migrant always remains in an anomalous position. Born and reared, so to speak, in one botanical and geological environment, he has used his will to transport himself to another. It is this action, the journey itself, which will bring him finally into contact with *his* new world. And it is this contact which will make his vision particularly privileged. As Humboldt noted in the *Relation historique*,

the character of a wild or cultivated nature, lies either in the obstacles which oppose the traveller or in the sensations which he experiences of it. It is *he* whom one wishes to see ceaselessly in contact with the objects which surround him, and the more this local colour is suffused through his account of the countryside and its inhabitants, the more it will interest us.[57]

But in the process of overcoming all those unnamed obstacles, the traveller who has no immediate prospect of return will have made *himself* into a context-less being. His instinct for attachment may help him to orientate himself. But it cannot ever disguise the fact that somehow he has to become part of another context, one in which, in the terms of Humboldt's imagery, the Great Bear *and* the Southern Cross are simultaneously present.

In time, he will come to imagine for himself a new community. As we shall see later, eighteenth-century theorists attributed this process of acculturation to the climate or, more generally, to the environment. Herder mocked the sight of European houses and European clothing in non-European settings. These foolish attempts to export a world intact could never long survive what he referred to as Nature's revenge.[58] But adaptation was always a more complex process than Herder was willing to allow, and it demanded not so much a response to the natural conditions imposed by each environment, as the creation of a cultural *bricolage*, built up from habits, traditions, discourses and partially understood memories of a 'mother-country' which had now become remote in both space and time. To this the colonist added such fragments of the indigenous cultures as might serve his immediate purposes. Each component of this 'colonial-identity' had to be embedded in a new context if it was to have the imaginative force required to build a new cultural world. This process was a long and invariably painful one. The first step which every immigrant had to take was to overcome the disorientation of his initial encounter with the new.

vii

Here, then, is an example of another moment of encounter between a European traveller and the experience of first 'being in' America, although in this case it is a fictional one.

In 1555 a secular priest named Pedro de Quiroga, about whom we know nothing except that on his own account he had worked for several years in Peru, composed four dialogues. They were never printed during his lifetime and they remained buried and largely unknown in the library of the Escorial until 1922 when they were published in a limited, and now inaccessible, edition. Yet they provide one of the most striking series of images of the dislocating presence of America, images which play with a complex set of internal references to the illusions of time and place, of sleep and waking, which America inevitably forced upon the settler. Quiroga called his dialogues the *Coloquios de la verdad* (Colloquies of Truth). Their purpose was, he said, 'to provide a way to attract the Indians of the Kingdom of Peru to our Holy Catholic Faith, by indicating the inconveniences and the reasons which, until now, have prevented them'.[59] But they are much more than that. They provide a scathing and bitter picture of the conquest and evangelization of Peru seen through the eyes of a number of disenchanted, but highly articulate Indians, and through those of a Spaniard he calls 'Barchilon'. Barchilon is Quiroga's great creation. The name was given to a real person who subsequently became part of the mythology of the conquest of Peru, a wandering curmudgeon who, like Diogenes, had yet to discover an honest man among the living. But Quiroga also uses the name, which means 'Quack' or 'Nursemaid', ironically since in the *Coloquios* it is Barchilon's role to defend the true values of the Christian religion before those – the Indians – who can only see the actions of its declared adherents.

Barchilon is a long-time resident of Cuzco. Once he had been rich but now, the victim of unspecified misfortune, he wanders the land, a penitent despised and feared by his fellow Spaniards, 'because I have left the past of mundanity and favour the natives of this kingdom'. (As we shall see in the next Chapter, he bears a striking similarity to Las Casas in his act of rejection, if not in his choice of vagrancy.) He lives perpetually on the margins of the two societies which his words attempt perpetually to reconcile. Despised by his fellow Europeans, who yet cannot shut their ears entirely to what he has to say, he is never quite trusted by the Indians he has set himself to defend.

In the first colloquy, Barchilon discovers 'Justino', a former friend from Spain and soldier of fortune, who has just arrived in Peru. He is asleep under a tree. The journey has exhausted him. But for Barchilon, his sleep is only the prescience of death. 'Is there,' he asks the sleeping form, 'any image of death more lifelike, more vivid, than sleep? For what is it for a man to fall asleep than to be tired of living', and he shakes Justino awake. Justino, far from any intimations of death, has been happily dreaming that he is 'the most powerful and the richest man in the world'. 'That for certain,' retorts Barchilon, Freudian *avant la lettre*, 'will be the dream of the wealth of this land, and of this century, all of which is a dream and a mockery'. And Justino, who has undergone the agonies of a long sea voyage only to fall asleep, and on waking to discover that his dream is nothing but a dream, also discovers that his journey was not as he had imagined a voyage to a golden land of opportunity, but a descent into Hell. 'Do you know,' Barchilon continues to Justino's amazement, 'what madness you have done to go to such pains in order to come to Hell? You could have gone there straight from Castile and saved yourself the journey and the hardships of coming here'. 'Is it something unusual for men to come here,' replies Justino, who has apparently read all the best books on the subject, 'Did I by chance travel the wrong road? Why do you ask me these things, for I only came with a desire to see new lands and to improve myself (*valer más*).'[60] But Barchilon knows that America can enhance nothing, since nothing in it resembles anything beyond it. 'If you are to stay,' he warns Justino, 'you must forget everything you thought you knew at home'.

As the sea-journey was a kind of rite of passage, so the final rupture
with the comforting orientating images of home will be an initiation.
The would-be colonist must, as a later French observer phrased it,
'abandon your country, your dear-ones, your friends, and all the objects
with which habit has drawn a protecting wall around you which cannot
be broken without suffering'.[61] Huge distances separate the Old World
from the New, and nothing ever arrives on the other side in the same
condition as it departed. Complaints – and Barchilon clearly believed
that there were many causes for complaint – made in America could
barely reach all the way to Europe, and if they did, 'they arrive cold
and the tears and blood with which they were first made have all
dried'.[62] No outward sign remains of the experience which generated
them, or of the suffering which prompted the complainer to write in the
first place.

And just as these long-distance messages reach back to Europe
stripped of their contexts, if they arrive at all, so, reciprocally, the
migrant from Europe travelling the other way, if he is to survive in the
New World, must learn to shed his context – the conceptual isotherms
with which he has always ordered his own social and cognitive worlds.
'Just open your eyes,' Barchilon tells Justino, and he will see that here
'everything is the reverse of what it is in Castile.' Nothing can be
trusted to be quite what is seems. What appear to be correspondences
often turn out, in fact, to be inversions. Indeed, it is the apparent
similarities between Europe and America, between Indian and Christian
devotional customs, that for Columbus had seemed to offer the possibility of immediate and direct translation, to which Barchilon now
points as evidence of their utter incommensurability.

'Here,' insists Barchilon, 'there can be no exchange, no direct
substitution'. 'Certainly,' Justino admits in reply, 'this land weakens
the judgment, disturbs the spirit, harms and corrupts good customs,
engenders unfamiliar conditions, and creates in men effects contrary to
those which they previously had'.[63]

But even such powerful forces as these can, surely, be countered by
prayer and a meticulous attention to duty. 'No,' replies Barchilon,
'Have nothing to do with the things of this land until you understand
them, because they are different matters, and another language'.[64]
Here, then, the neophyte has to learn to speak again. Literally nothing
that 'he imagines in Castile' will be of any service to him. But he first
has to learn something of the spaces which lie between his understanding and the realities of the American world. For Barchilon, the land,
like its inhabitants, speaks in muttered garbled sounds which can only
confuse and baffle the newcomer. 'Do not learn,' Barchilon warns him,
'the language of this land. Nor even listen to it, for I tell you that if you

do, one of two ends will befall you, for it will either drive you mad or you will wander restlessly for the rest of your life'.[65]

For Barchilon it is incommensurability itself which is, ultimately, the *only* certainty, the only possible context in which America can be made at all intelligible. In a world where no translation is possible, silence is the necessary condition of speech. For it is only out of silence that a new American language, and with it a new American identity, can be created. If Justino is to survive, and to escape Barchilon's own fate as a wanderer in the interstices of two cultures, he has to begin again. His dream, which was one of possession, must become one of disinheritance, but also, possibly, of re-birth.

Yet Barchilon is also aware that if Justino, metaphorically and literally, has to learn the language of America and, more literally, the languages of the American Indians, he has to do so only in order to tell them things in them, the catechism, the Trinity, transubstantiation and the calendar of saints, which he himself has placed there, which are as far removed from their world (and their languages) as they are from his (and from *his* language). We shall come back to the question of language. For the moment, however, these strange garbled Indian tongues – harder to learn, says Barchilon, than the difference between a pineapple and the prickly-pear – may stand, as they stood for him, as a metaphor for the cognitive distances the immigrant had to cross. At the end of the dialogue, the newly-arrived Justino has come to understand that the sea voyage, for all its horrors, and despite the fact that to many it seemed to be a rite of passage, a pilgrimage that might somehow ensure future success, had merely placed him on another shore. His real journey is only now beginning.

viii

The traveller, the discoverer, the settler, the immigrant, the missionary and the colonist: all such people came to America with battered ambitions, different expectations and different objectives. But if they were at all sensitive, they all in time came to see that, culturally at least, incommensurability was inescapable. In the real world beyond the high wooden walls of Bougainville's ship, the stark differences between worlds could not be reconciled by the simple transportation of samples, the identification of geological forms, the naming of the unfamiliar for the familiar. Justino, the adventurer, was one kind of immigrant who had been compelled to confront this incommensurability. There were also others. Those, for instance, who came to convert, to transform unfamiliar cultures of which they had no prior understanding, into something recogizably like their own. Most of these, the missionaries, failed at any but the most elemental level. Amerindian cultures were transformed certainly, but they remained, and remain, stubbornly Amerindian. The struggle of the missionaries to understand, not the cultures themselves, but the process which constituted an understanding of alien worlds, was altogether more successful. Most of the great Spanish missionary narratives of America – those of Bernardino de Sahagún, Toríbio de Motolinía, Diego Durán – are records not, as they have so often and so obstinately been read, of their author's vision of otherness. They are instead the, often fragmentary, histories of an attempt to register just what incommensurability *is*. Sahagún, for instance, begins his great *Historia general de las cosas de la Nueva España* (General History of the Things of New Spain, 1547–77) with the observation (some of the implications of which we will explore in the next chapter) that: All writers attempt to authorize their writings as best they can, some with reliable witnesses, some with the writings of those who have written about the same subject before them.

'But,' he continued, since he was confronting a very different kind of reality, 'none of these foundations would serve to authorize the twelve books that I have written.' He is, therefore, compelled to refer not to a text but to a method. 'I have not,' he concludes, 'found any other foundation for authorizing [my book] than to set out here the diligence with which I have attempted to discover the truth of all that is written in these books'.[66] The novelty of his approach, which was based on the interrogation of carefully selected witnesses and the patient collation of what they had told him, was the only strategy for measuring the distance which lay between him and his subject, a distance which, good Christian that he was, he hoped one day to be able to eradicate as – the metaphor is his – a doctor might cure a pernicious disease.

ix

The best example of this process, however, partly at least because it comes from what might initially seem to be such an unlikely source, is that of the Huguenot, Jean de Léry. Léry's *Histoire d'un voyage fait en la terre du Bresil* (History of a Voyage made to the Land of Brazil) has, perhaps more than any other missionary narrative, been treated as a triumph of early-modern anthropological science, 'the breviary of the anthropologist', as Lévi-Strauss once called it. Léry had been a member of the first, and only Protestant mission to Brazil which lasted for only two years between 1556 and 1558, although he did not begin work on the *Histoire* until 1563, long after he had returned to France, and it was not published until 1578.[67]

Léry was a European and he was a Calvinist. For him the line between 'us' and 'them' was not only cultural, it was also eschatalogical. The Tupinamba of Brazil, descendants of Ham, father of Canaan, had been cursed. They had no capacity for Christianity and there was, therefore, never any possibility that they might come to form part of the Elect and thus achieve salvation.[68] Léry was a missionary who could never have any belief in his mission, and perhaps because of this, he had no need to search for those similarities between Indian and European cultures, which all attempts at conversion require if they are to be at all intelligible. Unlike his Catholic counterparts Léry had no need to persuade the Indians that they had misunderstood God's purpose for the world, nor to demonstrate to them that their cultural and religious practices were the corruption of the innate ideas provided by the law of nature, or that their mental and social worlds were the outcome of the Devil's busy handiwork. For Léry, the Tupinamba had been since the Flood, and would remain until the end of time, utterly 'other'. Because of this, his relationship to them was not, as Lévi-Strauss had perhaps understood, so very far from that of the modern ethnologist. He was therefore able to offer his readers a comprehensive ethnology of the Tupinamba, a detailed account of the appearance, dress and customs and 'what might be called' their religion which has been much praised (and justly so), both for its detachment, probable accuracy, and for its apparent sympathy for Tupi social practices. Yet what is truly striking about Léry's account is the degree to which he is conscious of his own presence, of his own gaze, as a significant part of what it is he is trying to describe. Unlike Sahagún, the dispassionate doctor attempting to cure the disease that was Aztec culture, through an objective and detached description of tis symptoms, Léry is concerned with what it is to describe those symptoms. His narrative is not the detached account of the curious practices of some savages in a remote corner of the world. It is a history – in the precise sixteenth-century use of that term – of what it means, even if only in the imagination, to attempt to make fully commensurable what is necessarily incommensurable. And it is, albeit unselfconsciously so, the record of the impossibility of any such project.

Léry begins his account of the Tupinamba, however, in an appropriately detached mode, with a detailed description of the 'exterior of the bodies of the Americans'. He then asks his readers to 'represent to yourself a savage'. This, he says, is to be done by means of six separate and progressive 'contemplations'. 'Imagine in your understanding (*entendement*),' he wrote,

A nude man, well-formed and with well-proportioned limbs, all of whose hair has been shaved off him in the manner I described. The

43

lips and cheeks slit, with pointed bones or green stones set in them. His ears are pierced with pendants in the holes. His body is painted, his legs and thighs being blackened with a dye from the fruit called *genipap* which I have mentioned. And he wears necklaces made from many little pieces of a large sea-shell which they call *vignol*.

For 'the second contemplation' the reader is asked to 'remove all the flourishes described above, and after rubbing him with glutinous gum, cover his whole torso arms and legs with little feathers finely shredded like red-dyed down . . .'. The third and fourth contemplations follow in a similar manner. The 'nude man' is stripped and then dressed again, 'before our eyes'. At the final contemplation, however, this imaginatively reconstructed savage is forced into European costume, 'the breeches and jackets of our coloured cloth, with one of the sleeves green and the other yellow'. Having thus been compelled, if only in the imagination, to cross over into the reader's own world, the once noble, if garish, Tupinamba is reduced to little more than a jester. 'You will judge,' concludes Léry, 'that he no longer needs anything but a fool's bauble'.[69]

What Léry is doing here is to show us what may happen when we try to make the 'other' as much like a possible 'us' as we are able. If we can, in the end, only carry our imagined Indian across the line as a figure of mockery, as carnivalesque as the Indians whom Montaigne had met at Rouen, that is because, as Léry suggests elsewhere, such crossings always involve a loss of humanity. Those who make them, voluntarily or involuntarily, become re-contextualized, and re-born as other (and inevitably lower) kinds of being. Indians decked out in European clothes and made to ape European habits become nothing more than figures from a European carnival. But those Europeans who themselves travel in the opposite direction, as Léry had seen, may suffer an even worse fate.

In order to get his Indian from 'a nude man, well-formed and with well-proportioned limbs' to the Jester, Léry has invited his reader to perform a traditional Aristotelian act of *phantasia*. Like Aristotle, however, he makes no clear distinction between mental images and the reception of sensory perception,[70] and because of this, the final picture of the Brazilian 'savage' will be not unlike that of some tangible object in the natural world. So he has depicted him, he says, together with his other natural attributes: his woman, 'who in their customary way is holding her child in a cotton scarf', his fishing arrows, and 'the figure of the fruit they call Ananas'.[71] In the engraving which Léry commissioned for his book, the last of these appears many times life-size, as if to emphasize the point. (See figure 4.)

4. A Tupinamba warrior and his family from Jean de Léry, *Histoire d'un voyage fait en la terre du Brésil autrement dite Amerique* (Geneva, 1580).

Léry's account of the Tupinamba is one of the most sensitive and detailed we have. He had, he tells us, spent so much time 'in observing all of them, great and small, that even now it seems that I have them before my eyes, and I will forever have the idea and image of them in my mind'. He even includes an imaginary conversation (in both French and Tupi) with his 'savages', which assumes a level of familiarity quite unlike anything the more traditional missionary would wish to aspire to. In the end, however, Léry came to recognize that the use of representation to make cultures mutually intelligible, however imaginative, however 'fantastic' in the original sense of the term, will never amount to much more than drawing pictures of arrows, hammocks and pineapples. 'So that without any epilogue here, let the reader, by this narration, contemplate them as he will'.[72] Commensurability, however, demanded more than this surrender to the reader's will. It demanded that the observer and the observed occupy some common cultural ground. And that seemed to demand direct experience. 'Their gestures and countenances,' Léry at last felt compelled to admit, 'are so very different from ours that I confess my difficulty in representing them in words, or even in pictures. So that, to enjoy the real pleasure of them, you will have to go and visit them in their own country'.[73] But visiting them in their own country meant leaving one's own.

'Have you come?' enquires the Tupinamba in Léry's imaginary colloquy.

'Yes, I have come,' replies the Frenchman.

'Have you left your country to come and live here?' insists the Tupinamba.

'Yes,' replies the Frenchman.

'Then,' says the Indian, 'come to the place where you will stay'.[74]

Stay, and once there never return.

Léry fully understood the dangers that would face his imaginary Frenchman once he had crossed the invisible line which divided one culture from another. Like most of those who stayed in America for any length of time, he had witnessed at first hand the fate of those who had 'gone Indian'; who had, in their bid for survival in an alien environment, shed the humanity with which in Léry's view, for all his obvious sympathy for the Indian, only a culture that was European and Christian could possibly clothe them. The nakedness of the Tupinamba, on which Léry constantly harps, was more than a mere metaphor for their difference from him. It stood as a mark of what we, too, might all become. So, also, of course, did the 'crime against nature' for which the Tupinamba had already become famous when he wrote the *Histoire*: cannibalism. The Tupinamba were habitually, aggressively naked. (In particular the women: 'although we several times tried to give them dresses and shifts,' Léry observed, 'it has never been in our power to make them wear clothes'.)[75] They were also inveterate cannibals. And just as too great a familiarity might lead the European to un-clothe himself, so it might drive him to consume human flesh. Léry had seen for himself that it could happen. 'To my great regret,' he wrote,

> I have to admit that certain interpreters from Normandy, who had lived for eight or nine years in that country, accommodated themselves to the savages and lived the lives of atheists. They not only polluted themselves with all manner of lascivious and base behaviour among the women and girls by whom one of them had a boy (who was about three years old when I was there) but some of them, surpassing the savages in inhumanity, even boasted in my hearing of having killed and eaten prisoners.[76]

Living among 'them' requires constant vigilance, however sympathetic the observer, since a full understanding cannot stop this side of transformation. Léry's journey, as Michel de Certeau observed, had been precisely a journey 'from the self to the self, through the mediation of the other'.[77] But anyone who actually became the 'other' as the Norman translators did the moment they had tasted human flesh, could never come through, and hence back, to his own self as himself. Like Gulliver, who had also crossed over – although, in his case to a special kind of civility – such a person could never hope to mix again with his fellow creatures.[78]

God had created the cultural barriers between his creatures, just as he had created barriers between those he had chosen and those he had not. Léry's *Histoire* is a natural history, the record of an encounter with new and baffling flora and fauna and with a distinct human species. Beneath Léry's gaze the Tupinamba are still men, but in a sense, they are so only in a universe where the genus *homo sapiens* contains more than one species. As we shall see, this was an image of incommensurability which was to be taken up again at the end of the eighteenth century, principally by another of Calvin's heirs, Johann Gottfried Herder, although with different objectives in mind and with very different intellectual consequences.

x

In their different ways, Columbus, Barchilon, Léry and Humboldt had all tried to confront the problem of incommensurability with which their own discoveries of America had presented them. Each had done so by some variation of the principle of attachment. Because they had come to America with different objectives (and at different historical periods) they had come to very different conclusions. But each of them had come to the recognition, as would countless other less articulate, less motivated travellers, that being in the 'New World' demanded complex strategies if it was to be made not merely intelligible, but commensurable in any degree with the only world which they knew.

They were all also writers. They had, at one level or another, attempted to transform their experiences into some kind of narrative. Columbus's diaries and letters, Pedro de Quiroga's *Coloquios*, Léry's *Histoire*, Humboldt's many and varied scientific writings, all sought to record and replicate what their authors claimed to be unique personal experiences. The traveller's narrative is, at once, the most complex and the least stable thing which he can bring back with him. Taken from their contexts, words, too, lose their certainty just as objects do. A 'King' among the Wolof is not a 'King' in Lisbon and, as we have seen, at sea, between two worlds, a Wolof King, even if he is also the King of Portugal's godson, may be merely a 'Black' of no more worth than the ship's ballast. Humboldt, who had always had difficulty finding between words, charts, instruments and figures, the appropriate language for his cosmic vision, knew this well. 'This,' he tells us,

> is why I left Europe with the firm intention of not writing what it is usual to call the historical account of a voyage, but to publish the fruits of my researches, in works which would be purely descriptive. I have arranged the facts, not successively in the order in which they have presented themselves, but according to the relations which they have between themselves.[79]

Finding and mapping, measuring the context and pinning it to a graph was Humboldt's prime concern. Most botanists had been wholly concerned with finding and describing new species, an activity which, he said, was useful and necessary for the advancement of those sciences 'which treat of the medicinal properties of plants or their cultivation or their application to the arts'. But this had little to do with understanding the plants in themselves, too many of which 'do not yet exist except as names'. Science was the plotting of relationships, of a set of universal contexts, of a 'general physics' to which everything, ultimately even man, belongs.[80] In place of an unreliable and personal record, Humboldt would send back charts and floral catalogues, and the records of isotherms, isodynamics, isogonics and isolines. For the discoverer, unlike the modern 'physicien' (as Humboldt consistently described himself), and for all who were interested in those things which could only be incompletely reduced to Humboldt's 'physics of the earth', the narrative was the only certain thing with which they *could* return.[81]

Narratives set out 'the facts . . . successively in the order in which they have presented themselves'. But the things, which in Humboldt's reluctant, but also very long, *Relation historique*, stand so uncertainly besides the charts and graphs, the measurements and the diagrams, cannot be retrieved so easily as Humboldt supposed. Making the narrative authoritative, giving voice the same certainty as the mute but certain chart, became, as we shall now see, the prime objective of all those who tried to convey their special vision of America to Europe.

CHAPTER TWO
The Autoptic Imagination

> The person who speaks with understanding
> must insist upon what is shared by all,
> as a city insists upon its law.
> Heraclitus, DK, 114.

THE FIRST MOMENT

i

In the end Jean de Léry had capitulated before the presence of the new. His plea to his readers that they should visit the Tupinamba 'in their own country' was, as he knew, a vain one. They were in France (as, of course, was he), and in no danger of de-contextualization, of falling prey to either nudity or cannibalism. An act of *phantasia* was the only thing which could transport them to Brazil. And since *phantasia*, as Léry also knew, is an attempt to translate initial sensory perceptions into mental images via language, it is a process which inevitably lays great stress upon the authority of the translator. It is the traveller's narrative, his power to conjure up the required mental images in all their intricate details (in Léry's own words 'to leave nothing out, if that is possible')[1] which alone allows the reader to 'see' the Indian. Hence the repetition in so many of these narratives of first-person 'utterance markings', to use Michel de Certeau's term, 'I saw', 'I heard', 'I was there'. 'My intention,' as Léry claimed of his *Histoire*, 'has been to set down only what I did, saw, heard and observed'.[2] 'Only the appeal to the senses', as de Certeau has said of Montaigne's use of such phrases, 'and a link to the body...seem capable of bringing closer and guaranteeing, in a single but indisputable fashion, the real that is lost in language'.[3]

Léry's claim belongs to a category in ancient rhetoric called 'autopsy'. It is the appeal to the authority of the eye witness, to the privileged understanding which those present at an event have over all those who have only read or been told about it. The use of phrases like 'I saw', 'I found', 'this happened to me', as Léry told his readers, was not a device to 'show myself off'. It was evidence that 'these things are within my understanding, that is from the experience and sight I had of them', and because 'I will speak of things that it is very probable that no-one before has ever seen, much less written about'.[4] In America this was to dominate the long and bitter struggle over the nature,

51

representation and status of the New World and of its inhabitants. The ability to 'bear witness' in this way was, for obvious reasons, to mark off those who had 'been there' from those who had not. Inevitably, it was also to sharpen the boundary which divided the Old World from the New, and the 'them' from the 'us'.

The role which autopsy played in the construction of this early history can only be fully understood, however, in the context of a theory of knowledge by which the cognitive practices of all the early historians of America were bound. This relied very largely upon exegesis and hermeneutics, and claimed that the external world and all human life was legible, *secundum scriptura*. Understanding the world, that is, was dependent upon the interpretation of a determined canon of texts: the Bible, the Church Fathers, and a regularly contested although in practice restricted corpus of ancient writers. There was an obvious difference in status between these texts. There was an equally obvious difference in genre, between a narrative (the Bible) in which, in Paul Ricoeur's phrase, God is 'the agent of a history of deliverance';[5] a theology (that of the Church Fathers and their successors, both essentialists and nominalists alike) in which there can be no agency (other than the uncertainty of Grace); and a Graeco-Roman natural and moral science in which nature and man himself may both be agents. These differences inevitably created not only occasions for conflict – the traditional *disputatio*, which was based upon competing interpretations of different texts – it also allowed for some often far-reaching manipulations of the canon. When required, the Bible and the Fathers could be called upon to discredit the authority of the Ancients. Thus, Bartolomé de las Casas, to whom I shall return, could, without any sense of contradiction, defer to the authority of Aristotle on the necessary conditions for civility but, when it came to describing the condition of the *psyche* of 'barbarians', dismiss him as 'a pagan burning in Hell'.

Some objects of description might also appear, as they sometimes did to 'Barchilon', to fall so far outside the range of the structure which this canon provided as to seem to be merely inversions of some recognizable component within it. But nothing could be made intelligible in terms of an alternative non-scriptural authority. Whenever an alternative structure did present itself it was likely, at least at first, to be dismissed as false simply because it *was* an alternative. All that could be seen or demonstrated by experiment had ultimately to be made intelligible in terms of one or another component of the canon. As the Spanish Carmelite Domingo de Santa Teresa stated in the late eighteenth century, although Descartes's epistemological scepticism *seemed* to be intelligible, it had already been refuted *a priori* by 'the authority of Aristotle and St Thomas and Scotus, and all the other doctors and theologians who thought the contrary'.[6] For such people – and they are largely representative of the intellectual world to which nearly all Europeans before the mid-seventeenth century belonged – there was no possibility for immediate and authoritative knowledge outside the 'structure of norms' provided by the canon.[7] The world of the American Indians, and of all those other 'others' whose behaviour seemed initially unaccountable, could never therefore be explained, as later ethnographers such as the French Jesuit Joseph François Lafitau were to demand, 'in their terms' since, for these early writers, 'their terms' could never be detached from 'ours'.[8]

I am not suggesting, as Hobbes claimed for his own rhetorical purposes, that before the seventeenth century *all* philosophers had become so dependent upon what others had written that 'their teachings no longer deserve to be called philosophy, but merely "Aristotelity"'.[9] In practice, scientific understanding was built up by a process of continuing negotiation. When it became possible to see a marked discrepancy between the object under observation and the text, it was ultimately the text which had to give. The Jesuit historian José de Acosta, for instance, tells us that on finding himself cold at midday yet with the tropical sun directly overhead – an impossible situation according to ancient meteorology – he 'laughed and made fun of Aristotle and his philosophy'. The difficulty, however, was always *seeing* the discrepancy between the observation and the text, particularly since no observation or experiment was ever conducted *with the purpose* of verifying (much less falsifying) the statements made *in* the text. When experience directly contradicted the text, it was the experience, which was unstable because of its very novelty, which was likely to be denied or at least obscured. The simple experience of the heat, which Acosta should have felt but did not, and the cold which he should not have felt but did, would have been difficult for him to overlook no matter how much he might have had invested in the absolute accuracy of Aristotle's *Meterologica*. But more complex matters – the nature of belief, kinship relations, the vocabulary of emotions, even the properties of plants and the appearance of animals – could be ignored with far greater ease in the interests of preserving the status of a powerful textual authority. Acosta may have laughed at Aristotle's meteorology, but he accepted all of his psychology, and most of the sociology and the anthropology to be found in the *Politics* and the *Ethics*.[10] It was also obviously the case that not only did the canon determine what could be said with any degree of conviction within any given community, it also established what the objects of inquiry might be in the first instance. It determined, that is, what *could* be seen. Columbus's own voyages were paradigmatic of this process. Having found evidence (or so he believed) in the ancient geographers, St Augustine and the Bible, that the world was far smaller than it in fact is, he set off confident that 'Cathay' lay more or less where America does lie. Having discovered what every shred of external evidence should have told him was a 'New World', he then referred back to the canon to demonstrate what only he, because of the authorities which had dictated his original hypothesis, could not accept.

ii

The tensions which were created by the very different responses to the presence of the 'new' of America derived, at one level, from the problem of how to create a text where none had existed before. This led to the invention of new genres or, at least, to new versions of old genres. Few of the early writers on America, however, make any direct reference to the problem of genre. What Las Casas described in traditional Aristotelian manner as the 'formal, material and efficient causes' of his *Historia de las Indias* (History of the Indies) referred only to its author's intentions.[11] Under the general heading of the term *Historia* he was content to combine a number of different genres: chronicle, autobiographical narrative, natural history, legal deposition. The first writer to recognize not only that the presence of America demanded a new kind of writing, but also to theorize about what form that should take was Acosta, whose *Historia natural y moral de las Indias* (Natural and Moral History of the Indies) of 1590 was, as he claimed, the first 'philosophical history', the first moral history – as history that is of *mores*, 'customs' – of the New World.[12]

At another and far more complex level, however, the question in a culture whose scientific procedures were so bound by the appeal to *auctoritates*, was how to endow any text, once created, with authority. One answer might be to follow an ancient model. This was the solution suggested, for instance, by Oviedo and, with differing degrees of emphasis, by many others. But this did not really achieve very much. Copying an authoritative model was another form of attachment, and in a world of experience for which there existed no obvious genre or recognizable representational types, such imitation might offer some degree of cognitive security. But the ancient or patristic text had not acquired *its* authority because of its form. It had acquired it precisely through its membership of a canon to which no mere imitation could belong. Commentary which was directly parasitic upon a canonical text could hope to acquire some of the *auctoritas* of the original, which is why so much early-modern theology and medicine took this form. But obviously no natural historian of America could write his work *as* a commentary. Even the move by Philip II's physician, Francisco Hernández, to smuggle American botanical species into his Castilian translation of Pliny's *Natural History* does not work, any more than do the various attempts to find a place for tobacco in the Dioscoridean system of classification.[13]

Oviedo, therefore, could not appeal to Pliny except as a guide. Nor could he appeal to the internal coherence of his narrative, nor to the logic of argument, since before the radical epistemological changes which Descartes and the sceptics introduced in the seventeenth century, neither consistency nor tautology could be made to stand as evidence for the truth of any given statement. Under such conditions, authority could only be guaranteed (if at all) by an appeal to the authorial voice. It is the 'I' who has seen what no other being has seen, who alone is capable of giving credibility to the text. If the reader chooses to believe what he reads, he does so because he is willing to privilege that writer's claims to authority over all others and not, in this case, because what he reads might seem to him to be inherently plausible or internally consistent. Indeed, as José de Acosta pointed out, it was only the authorial voice, the inherent credibility of the 'I' who has 'been there', which made the distinction between reading about America and reading the romances of chivalry.[14] An analogous claim holds true for the texts within the authoritative canon itself. We – the members, that is, of this particular discursive culture – believe what Aristotle, Aquinas or St Jerome have to say not, at least in the first instance, because of any particular properties of their texts themselves, but because they are the works of Aristotle, Aquinas and St Jerome. Michel Foucault made much the same point when he observed that 'it [the author's name] has other than indicative functions: more than an indication or a gesture, a finger pointed at someone, it is the equivalent of a description'.[15] And, one might add, a legitimation.

The obvious difficulty was, of course, that the authority of the 'I' that was Aristotle, Aquinas or Jerome, derived not, as did that of the American observer, from privileged access to information and experience. As Hobbes had noted, it derived precisely from a cultural standing which was believed to confer authority. Aquinas and Jerome had been favoured by God, Aristotle by membership of a past society which was believed, more contentiously, to have had a unique understanding of the natural world, and whose works had been sanctioned by Aquinas. The observers of the American world, whose authority rested solely on their status *as* observers, had,[16] therefore, to raise themselves as authors (and with them the texts that they had written) to a level which, if it was not directly comparable with that occupied by either the Church Fathers or the Bible, was, nevertheless, as distinctive and authoritative as the scientific works of antiquity.

iii

Until the second half of the seventeenth century, all attempts to represent America and its peoples constitute, at some level, an attempt to resolve this tension between an appeal to authorial experience and the demands of the canon. The lineages of this struggle can best be seen in the works of two men, rivals and opponents, both of whom were engaged in conceptually similar types of project, however unalike the final outcomes might have been – and each of whom despised and excoriated the other. The first we have already met. Gonzalo Fernández de Oviedo y Valdes was the author of the earliest, and certainly the bulkiest history of the flora, fauna and human inhabitants of the Americas, the *Historia general y natural de las Indias* (General and Natural History of the Indies). Oviedo, who came originally from a well-placed Castilian family (as he constantly reminds his readers), spent many years in America first as overseer (*veedor*) of the mines at Darien and later as the governor of the castle of Santo Domingo. Although his *Historia general* had, he claimed, been written in order to make known 'to all the states of the world' the uncontested greatness of 'these states which God has granted to Your Royal Crown of Castile',[17] he held much the same low opinion of its inhabitants as other, less articulate, Spanish colonists in America. The complete text of his work remained unpublished until the nineteenth century, but a version of the first part appeared in Seville in 1535.[18] This proved to be enormously popular and won its author recognition as, as Humboldt said of him later, the 'Pliny of the New World', an epithet which Oviedo had himself worked hard to acquire.

The second of these rivals is the famous 'Apostle to the Indians', Bartolomé de Las Casas. Las Casas wrote a large number of quasi-legal tracts in defence of the rights of the Amerindian peoples. But he is, perhaps, best known today for his descriptive works: the *Historia de las Indias* composed between 1527 and 1559, the *Apologética historia sumaria* (Apologetic history of the Indies) written sometime after 1551, and the *Brevíssima relación de la destrucción de las Indias* (Short Account of the destruction of the Indies) published in 1552, the only one to appear during his own lifetime. All of these, together with a number of his other works, were composed in awareness of Oviedo's *Historia general* and sometimes in explicit opposition to it. For Las Casas, Oviedo was always that 'utterly vain trifler' (*vanissimus hic nugator*), that unashamed fabricator of 'monstrous lies . . . from which he stupidly promises himself immortality'[19] whose writings, because of their undoubted popularity, had done more, in Las Casas's view, to harm the peoples of America than any other.

Both Oviedo and Las Casas, however, were in agreement on one point: that only those who had 'been there' could possibly have any significant understanding of America and its inhabitants. Las Casas's most serious intellectual threat came from the humanist Juan Ginés de Sepúlveda with whom he had a now famous 'debate' in Valladolid between 1550 and 1551. But he always knew that it was ultimately Oviedo's claims as witness – the claims on which Sepúlveda had rested his own theoretical assertion that the Indians were 'slaves by nature' – which he had finally to refute.

For his part, Oviedo carried away from his experience of the Indians the picture of a creature of sub-human status. He said that their heads were not as the heads of

> other men. They were not, in fact, heads at all, but rather hard and thick helmets, so that the most important piece of advice the Christians gave when fighting in hand to hand combat with them was not to strike them on the head, because that broke the swords. And just as their heads were hard, so their understanding was bestial and evilly inclined.[20]

Las Casas, by contrast, claimed that what his vision of America had revealed to him – and, as we shall see, the ocular metaphor was central to his argument – was that the Indians, though technologically primitive and frequently mistaken in their interpretation of the natural law, were, in all crucial respects, 'men like us'.[21] With time, instruction in the Christian faith and prolonged exposure to the more uplifting aspects of European culture, they would cease entirely to be 'other'.

Both Oviedo and Las Casas had to persuade their readers of the accuracy and authority of *their* vision; both, by implication had to demonstrate the falsity of the other's claims. Oviedo, it is true, seems to have been barely aware of Las Casas's presence. But he makes frequent references to

> some person who from Spain (about whose name it is better that I am silent and do not mention) speaks uncertainly about those things

he cannot know nor understand without either being there (*sin su presencia*) or being informed by those who know.[22]

which seems to be a description of Las Casas who did, indeed, spend much of his long life in Spain.

Both men were aware of how frail all claims to authority could be when made by a single voice. Like Léry they, too, had heard 'what is commonly said, that since neither the old nor travellers to distant parts cannot be contradicted, they give themselves a license to lie'.[23] For this reason, both were insistent upon the amount of time they had spent in America. Las Casas had, as he proudly tells us at the beginning of the *Historia de las Indias*, arrived in Hispaniola in 1502 on the largest of the fleets ever to have sailed to the New World, and that by the time he came to write his *Historia* he was 'one of the oldest to have passed over into these Indies'.[24] Oviedo claimed that he had spent 'thirty-four years in these parts', and that during this time he had crossed the Atlantic – which, like so many others, he came to regard as an initiation into knowledge through fear – eight times. For all the clumsiness of his prose style, this extended exposure to the realities of the world of America had conferred upon him the power to write 'a true history, so unlike those fables which others have presumed to write on these matters without moving a foot from Spain'.[25] Neither man was above claiming that the majesty of the person to whom his work was addressed (Charles V in the case of the *Historia general*, Philip II in that of the *Brevíssima relación*) was a pledge of their accuracy. Who, asked Oviedo, would lie to Caesar?[26]

But Oviedo was far less polemical in his objectives then Las Casas, if also more insistent upon his role *as* an author, and far less certain of his standing with God. Unlike Las Casas, whose entire project was to minimalize the differences between Europe and America, Oviedo was constantly aware of the very 'newness' of the 'New World'. He was also more sensitive than his opponent to the enormity of the descriptive task which faced him. At times, indeed, it seems almost to have overawed him. 'I know well,' he admitted to his readers at the very beginning of his *Historia general*,

> that I am at the very end of my life, and yet I perceive that I am only just at the beginning [of my understanding of] the marrow of these great and innumerable secrets, which remain to be discovered in this second hemisphere and in these parts which were unknown to the ancients.[27]

The sheer distance which separated him from his potential readers seemed to daunt him as much as it had 'Barchilon'. In an attempt to pre-empt all possible criticism, he warned that those who 'have to hear me from so far away should not judge me unless they have seen this land about which I write'.[28] Like Pliny, whose *Natural History* had been his inspiration from the beginning, he marvelled both at the existence of the sea routes which linked such distant parts of the world, and at the (as he saw it) design of nature, which had made such routes possible. He wondered, he said, echoing Pliny, at the fact that a simple plant, the flax from which linen sails were woven, had made of 'Egypt the neighbour of Italy'; that 'from a tiny seed something is born which can cross the world from one side to another'.[29]

Oviedo's *Historia general* is also unlike any of Las Casas's texts in the consciousness it displays of the sheer diversity of America. Whereas Las Casas, in his bid to make the Indian familiar to his European reader, tries to erase difference and create a suitable natural and human environment for Cicero's 'republic of all the world', Oviedo moves in the opposite direction. No matter how prescient the eye of the observer, claimed Oviedo, nor how diligent the historian, not only would much of what he *could* see lie beyond the range of his vision, but even those things with which he did come into immediate contact might still elude both his understanding and his representational skills.

America seemed sometimes to overwhelm all Oviedo's self-confessedly meagre capacity for description. The flora and the fauna could be described or depicted with reasonable accuracy. But to get close to the human inhabitants required skills which he admitted were very often beyond him. 'What ingenious mortal,' he asked, 'could understand such a huge diversity of languages, of habits and of customs as those practiced by these Indians?'[30]

Since he could not master all the knowledge nor be in so many different places at the same time, he recognized that his history had, if it were to be 'true', to incorporate not one but many voices.[31] Yet he also knew that reliance upon a source which was at even one remove from the narrator could cast doubt on the authenticity of the narrative. Careful inquiry of enough of 'those who know' might produce a reliable alternative to the autoptic vision itself. But he was never prepared to vouch for it. 'I wrote these things down in my notes (*borradores*),' he tells us of the interviews he conducted among 'those who know'. 'But,' he goes on, 'I never wrote it out in full until I had seen these things for myself, if it was possible to see them, or until I had found contexts which satisfied me'.[32] Oviedo was aware that, no matter how plausible his informants' tales might be, they could only have meaning when placed beside other narratives for whose truth-value he could personally vouch. Once again the narrator had to find a context, a context which, with no classificatory guidance to help him, could only be located within the same discourse as the thing to be contextualized. The context which would 'satisfy' Oviedo could only do so because of the privileged position in which Oviedo, not his readers, now found himself. Once the immediate attachments which, in the first instance, had bound the old to the new had been loosened, there simply was nothing *but* America.

For this reason America in Oviedo's narrative, as in the narratives of so many other of the early historians (although not in Las Casas's), appears so frequently as the exotic, the 'other'. In the late eighteenth century, an Ialian missionary resident in what is now Venezuela, Filippo Salvatore Gilii, set out as Oviedo had done to compose a natural history of America in imitation of Pliny. No one, he complained, not even Oviedo, had been able to write about the place 'in a just and simple light'. Every other part of the world, he continued, was distinguished by precise features by 'the number of men, by their worth, and their intelligence'. America, in contrast, was 'distinguished only by its marvels'. Yet in America,

> as in every other part of the world there is good and there is bad, rich provinces and poor, healthy countries and sick ones, beautiful skies and ugly ones, fertile land and infertile ones, plains and mountains, just as there are with us.

But Gilii's eyes had had nearly three hundred years to adjust.[33] Oviedo had been able to see very few of these points of engagement with the lands he had left behind. What he could see, and set out to record, was precisely a world which was 'new', vast, largely unexplored, and filled with things for which there was no adequate classification, no known terms; and with sights like his famous tree, which, flaunting a brief knowledge of Italian painting, he claims could only be depicted by someone with the skill of Leonardo or Mantegna, 'or better still seen rather than being either drawn or written about'.[34]

Like Pliny he knew how difficult it was, in Pliny's words, to 'give authority to what is new, brilliance to what is commonplace, light to the obscure, attraction to the stale, credibility to the doubtful'. Like Pliny, too, he may have found some consolation in the fact that any true work of creation was a process which could never be complete, which is why only the foolish and the vain declared their works to be 'made by so and so'. The truly great, said Pliny, simply inscribed their creations with such words as, 'worked on by Apelles or Polyclitus'.[35]

But incomplete though Oviedo's *Historia general* inevitably was, it too, like the *Natural History*, was, as he repeated time and again, the work of one whose authority derived from his personal vision. 'I,' he says at the very beginning of the work, 'do not write with the authority of any historian or poet, but as an eye witness'.[36] He had gone out to 'discover', as Columbus had done, and, like Columbus, had returned with the material for a narrative. The certainty of that material could be guaranteed before the incredulous reader by the suffering which he personally had undergone in order to acquire it. Those, he says in a taut and anguished passage, who attempt to 're-create the narratives' of the natural world in this way and who 'go searching for the natural things which are unknown to those who have not seen them [*no communicados a los ausentes*]', are driven to endure

> indifferent food supplies, the unhealthy and unpropitious waters and the winds which blow through the plains and through the uplands, the wild animals, the tigers, lions, serpents, and other noxious beings, and other innumerable difficulties which I could not express in a few brief lines.

At one point he went so far as to suggest a comparison between his own determination to discover the truth about America – to 'continue with', as he puts it, 'and to conclude, these matters which are here treated' – and the determination of Job to withstand the plagues that his God has heaped on him, and still to offer witness to His goodness.[37]

And if finding out the truth required these harrowing experiences, the construction of some kind of narrative could be equally arduous. Forcing what was so remarkably new into a compelling and intelligible literary form demanded skills which he, like Las Casas and like nearly all the early historians of America, claimed that no modern author possessed. 'To give substance (*encarnecer*) to the greatness of the Indies,' wrote Las Casas, 'one would need all the eloquence of Demosthenes and the hand of Cicero'.[38] The only alternative to Demosthenian and Ciceronian eloquence, was the simple unadorned prose style. Indeed Oviedo hoped that his lack of eloquence and his very inability to cultivate the 'art and beautiful form in which to narrate these things'[39] would nevertheless generate immediacy precisely because 'these things' can be truly represented only as the viewer finds them in nature. It would certainly, he believed, dispel any doubts as to the authenticity of the experience which the words sought to capture. Ironically it is on these occasions, when he is trying to capture the experience of writing about America in America, that his prose is most carefully worked. By contrast, the long descriptive passages which made his *Historia general* famous are indeed, as he claims, plain, repetitious and discursive.

Once he had overcome the problem of style, however, Oviedo, like Las Casas and later Acosta, was immediately faced with one of genre. Here the difficulty was how to distance his account of a new and seemingly bizarre world from those described in the romances of chivalry. Readers in Spain, he tells us, frequently confused what they had read about America, with what they had read about in 'Amadís of Gaul and Palmerín of England [two of the books which would turn up later in Don Quixote's library] and those that derive from them'.[40] Oviedo's fear that his true history of America might be identified too closely with the evidently untrue histories offered by such works was not unfounded. Indeed, as one latter critic of European colonialism pointed out, the *conquistadores* had been driven by 'the remnants of the spirit of chivalry ... to seek for riches in distant climes, which presented to their eyes an opulence they could not hope to find at home'.[41] Unsurprisingly, the romances were very popular reading in America and many of the *conquistadores* fell back upon the descriptive terms which they offered when they made any attempt to construct a narrative of their actions. As they marched across the causeway into Mexico City in 1520, Bernal Díaz del Castillo remembered years later, the soldiers in Cortés's army turned to each other and 'said that it seemed like one of the enchanted things which are told about in the book of Amadís'.[42] The chivalric romances' explicit and implicit claim to be 'true histories' also seem sometimes to have been taken literally, to judge from remarks made by both Hernán Cortés and Bernal Díaz.

This was not so surprising in a world of only partial literacy, and one which had no great familiarity with the rhetorical claims to the literal certainty of the text which was traditionally employed by every descriptive genre. Every romance began with precisely the same kind of explanatory text as did most histories. Furthermore, by insisting on their status as 'true histories', most attempted to locate themselves within an authoritative tradition of ancient historical writing, which was precisely the tradition with which every 'true' historian also wished to associate his work. The prologue to the most famous of them, *Amadís de Gaula*, for instance, draws implicit comparison between its author, or authors, and the *names* of both Sallust and Livy. To enforce the point, it also condemns the Greek poets for writing 'feigned histories in which wonderful things out of the order of nature are to be found',[43] thus implying that the 'wonderful deeds' of Amadís are neither feigned nor, despite their inherent improbability, 'out of the order of nature'. As Oviedo said on another occasion, his potential readers in Spain had 'never known anyone but their neighbours', and thus had no exterior measure by which to judge the accuracy of his report. He was well aware that 'ancient history' had itself, through too frequent association, become a genre which, in the vulgar mind, was now virtually indistinguishable from romance. The true 'true' historians (such as

Oviedo and Las Casas claimed to be) had therefore to perform a double task. They had to separate out the ancient historiography from romance, and they had to secure acceptance for the claim that *their* texts were indeed what the romances purported to be – namely true; although their subject matter was quite as fantastic as anything to be found in *Amadís de Gaula* or *Palmerí de Inglaterra*.

For Oviedo, the problem was particularly immediate because, in 1515, during a brief spell in Spain, he had himself written just such a romance, the *Libro del muy esforçado y invencible Cavallero dela fortuna propriamente llamado don claribalte* (The Book of the Very Valiant and Invincible Knight Errant Properly Called Claribalte).[44] It is worth a moment's consideration, not because of its plot (the story of a young nobleman's rise from 'Knight-Errant' to become 'Emperor of Constantinople'), nor because of its laboured prose, but because of what Oviedo himself says about it. Like all romances it too claims to be a 'true history', and, also like all other romances, it claims to be a text without an author. In the preface, Oviedo tells us that he 'travelled across much of the world and in so doing found the kingdom of Phirolt which is very remote from the region [i.e. Europe] and language of the present treatise'. He then polished it up 'from that barbarous and inaccessible language in which I found it by means of a Tartar interpreter, for the aforementioned kingdom of Phirolt is in the region of Tartary', and subsequently 'rendered it into Castilian'.[45] He did, he admits, write out the whole story again once he had returned to Hispaniola, 'so that it is not now so brief as it once was'. But his editorial modifications were, he assured the reader, done without in any way deviating from the 'substance and the historical accuracy' of the original. What the dedicatee, Fernando de Aragona, Duke of Calabria (then in prison in the Castle of Jativa) had before him was, therefore, not so much a work by Oviedo as a palimpsest. Successive layers of text, and two, possibly three, languages (the exact role of the Tartar interpreter is left vague) are piled one upon another. A fragment found in 'Phirolt' written in 'Tartar' and then re-written in Castilian by someone living in the Indies, tells a story which begins in somewhere named 'the Kingdom of Epirus which was once called Serpenta and is now called Albania' and finishes in Constantinople.

Amadís and Palmerín start in similar though less confusing ways. The claim which all their authors make, to have found something not their own and which they have merely edited, translated, and made accessible to the world which their readers inhabit, is intended, as Jean Starobinski has said of Montesquieu's (entirely more imaginative) use of the device in the *Persian Letters* (*Lettres persanes*), to make a plea for the authority of real life. It is to give to the work . . . the prestige of an origin which is entirely independent of any literary tradition; it is to deny [to the text] . . . every imaginary provenance.[46]

The readers of Amadís or Palmerín or Claribalte, like Usbek and Ricart, Montesquieu's Persians in Europe, find themselves 'in another universe'. The purpose of all this is precisely to convince the reader that no matter how seemingly remote this universe might be, the account that has been given of it is factually accurate. For – the argument runs – this is the truest possible kind of history, the kind of history from which the presence of the historian himself has been entirely effaced. This is a narrative which has been not made but found. And since the only kind of authorial voice with which the reader is confronted is one which immediately seeks to erase itself, he is not called upon to question its authority, nor does the author need to demonstrate the force of his claim to absolute veracity. The text alone is thus made sufficient unto itself.

This, of course, is the very reverse of the kind of history which Oviedo himself was offering his readers in the *Historia general*. There the text depended at every stage upon the presence of its author, and he prefaced nearly every book with a 'proemio' which was intended to keep Gonzalo Fernández de Oviedo firmly before the reader's gaze. In the *Historia general* he makes no mention of *Claribalte*, but he makes occasional contemptuous references to the habitual readers of the romances as 'a generation so stuffed with fables, that I am ashamed to hear that in Spain, they continue to write such frivolities that they have forgotten the Greeks'.[47] Elsewhere he called such works 'vain treatises, fables filled with lies, founded in errors, luxury and gibberish'.[48] And it is not difficult to read in these comments a heightened concern that his readers should not confuse the absent, self-effaced novelist with the autoptic recorder, the disengaged 'I'.

Establishing a proper distance between true history and romance was, however, only part of the historian's problem. There still remained the difficulty of actually *writing* about America *in* America. For here, too, confusion with fiction was a constant danger. The romances of chivalry were often set in a series of remote outlandish places – England, the distant East or the far North – places as far from Europe and whose geographical identity was as uncertain as was America itself. These fantasy worlds were places which could be swiftly translated or erased from the memory, or peopled at will with Cephalopods, Amazons or Giants. Distinguishing, or failing to distinguish, between these imaginary spaces of the world and the real, but barely credible ones like America, became part of the rhetoric of the romance. The constant mobility of the imaginary geography of medieval Europe also allowed for its repeated erasure and re-creation. Forgetting, for instance, became a means of deliberate dislocation. When Thomas More came to write it down, he was able to recall in every detail what Hythlodaeus had told him about the island of Utopia's civic and political structures; but he could not remember exactly where Hythlodaeus had told him it was, except that it was somewhere near the Americas. (Since it was, of course, also 'Nowhere' there is a double geographical joke intended.) Cervantes begins his great anti-romance with a similar act of wilful forgetting: 'In a place in La Mancha, whose name I do not wish to recall . . .'.

Claribalte, whose adventures begin in a place which has changed its name three times, also inhabits a geographically uncertain world accessible only to the imagination through successive layers of language. By contrast, the America which Oviedo the historian is writing about has to have a precise and fixed geographical location. Hence the long digression in Book 16[49] on the location of the New World in relation to Asia. Hence, too, the long final section of the *Historia general* on the horrors of the sea-voyage, entitled 'Misfortunes and Shipwrecks'.[50] This was meant to provide a further contrast with the romances, *Claribalte* among them, whose heroes, unlike the navigators in the real world Oviedo was describing, were able to travel immense distances, by hippogriff or magic ship, in an instant, and in complete ease.

Because in *Claribalte* Oviedo the author had been replaced by Oviedo the collector, polisher and continuer of other peoples' texts, the struggle to make the imaginary seem real was hidden from the reader's gaze. For Oviedo the historian, however, that difficulty is manifestly on display as an integral part of the task of gathering the 'truth and the secrets of nature'. Incomplete and untidy though the *Historia general* is, it was, so Oviedo hoped, a book. It was, furthermore, a book which had had to be created *ab initio* out of the raw material of the human and natural world, not through the embellishment or 'beautifying' of someone else's discarded fragments. Like Pliny, Oviedo too could say that 'there is not one person among us who has made the same venture'. And such a venture, he warned his readers, would be new, if not in style or format then at least in content and in language. 'Alien and barbarous terms', he warned, were a necessary part of any attempt to represent 'novelty'. This, too, is an echo of Pliny:

> My subject is a sterile one – the world of Nature, that is to say, Life; it thus employs either rustic or foreign, that is to say, barbarous terms.[51]

But unlike Pliny, who tells us that he wrote his *History* in his garden and in his leisure hours, Oviedo knew the difficulty not merely of incorporating such terms into a recognizable discourse, but also of doing so while still confronted by the enormity of this material. In America there was no possibility of retreat from the immediate presence of what he had set himself to describe; there was, as he put it, 'no Grecian garden' of the kind in which some authors may find the opportunity 'to note with tranquility what they have written'.[52] Here, he complained, he had to live among savages whose very presence seemed to deny the possibility of existence to those 'rules and opportunities which other authors who write in lands populated by civil and prudent people' have at their disposal.[53] Such conditions of authorship demanded from his readers not merely the traditional benevolence towards his clumsy prose, but something more: the recognition that his work constituted a new kind of writing. Pliny, who claimed that he was the first to have 'treated every branch of the subject',[54] provided the only known antecedent for the project on which he had embarked. But whereas Pliny was still moving across familiar terrain, and doing so by reading books, Oviedo's writing had been dragged out of the treacherous nature of the land itself. In Oviedo's text, complaints about the conditions of composition rapidly slide into complaints about the conditions of life. Once again the narrator fashions himself as a sufferer. The chronicler of 'these things over here', he moans, lives

> with much thirst and hunger, with exhaustion, in warfare with his enemies, and in both war and peace, he struggles with hostile elements and great needs and dangers. Here he is wounded without a surgeon, sick without a doctor or medicines, hungry without food, thirsty without water, tired without being able to sleep, needy with nothing in which to dress himself, and with no shoes for his feet. He who should ride on horseback walks on foot, and he who cannot swim has to cross many great rivers.

Suffering is the inevitable fate of the author in the New World, but it is also that suffering which authenticates and ennobles the text he will finally be able to write. These men, said Oviedo, speaking partly of himself, partly of those he had gathered together to be his informants, who have been driven into exile among savages, were 'more trustworthy' precisely because of their displacement, than those who have never left home and who have 'never known anyone but their neighbours'.[55]

Like the 'simple and rough man' who had told Montaigne of the habits of the Tupinamba of Brazil, and who was thus, in Montaigne's view, 'of the proper condition to bear accurate witness',[56] Oviedo, though neither simple nor rough, had also in Michel de Certeau's terms been 'put to the test of travel'.[57] For this reason he claimed, to Las Casas's lasting disgust,

> I know that my writings will not vanish, for they have passed through the doorway of truth, which is so difficult and heavy that it will sustain and prolong my vigils.[58]

The language is, and is intentionally so, that of Christian martyrdom. Christianity is, of course, a religion of observance. It affords those who believe in it an image, a vision of the divinity. Those, like Paul, who are converted to it by divine intervention, are first blinded that they might see better. They are in the most literal sense of the term enlightened. The heroes of Christianity, other than Christ Himself, are those 'Martyrs' – a word whose original Greek root means simply 'witness' – who having 'seen' but failed to persuade others of the unique authenticity of their vision, would rather die in any number of imaginative ways than deny the truth of what their eyes had revealed to them. 'When the soul is composed, ordered,' said St Augustine of the experience, 'made harmonious and beautiful, then it will see God'.[59]

All the early historians of America, faced with phenomena for which their often rudimentary intellectual training had given them very little preparation, fell back upon these discourses of privileged vision. Only Oviedo and Las Casas, however, because only they had attempted projects of such magnitude, needed to press for the uniqueness of what they had seen and recorded against that of all possible others, and crucially against each other. Oviedo, hard though he claims his life in Hispaniola to have been, did not suffer actual martyrdom. But like Las Casas (as we shall see) he edged himself as close as he dared to a secularized, scientific analogue of that state.

Oviedo also knew that physical hardship was only part of what the historian of anything so startling as America would have to endure. For once he had collected his data, verified his findings, checked it against the testimony of 'innumerable eye witnesses', and transformed it into a book, he then had to face his readers. This, too, was a kind of martyrdom. Who, Oviedo asked bitterly, will protect the historian, after all that he has endured in the interests of truth,

> who will protect him from the mutterers, those who speak about things they do not understand and scorn those things they could not achieve and do not know how to do, and who degrade the historian for having given them information about things of which they were

ignorant, they who cannot refrain from biting those who most deserve their gratitude.[60]

Oviedo's confidence in his capacity to 'bear witness' is unusual. His initial rejection of *all* textual authority hides, perhaps, an unease about the way in which any text which is itself so empty of scriptural references, secular or sacred, will be received at the hands of 'the mutterers'. Oviedo's 'General History' is certainly rambling and sometimes indiscriminately inclusive. In this, as its author might have pointed out, it is not unlike Pliny's own. But it offers very little that would have been immediately familiar to the contemporary reader, skilled as he was in moving from citation to citation in reading a narrative in terms of the references it provided him, and of the network of inferences that those references suggested in their turn. Oviedo, by contrast, is, as he so often says, only seeking to describe what he has seen and known. In place of all those other texts, therefore, he offered only a stream of claims to autoptic authenticity. Ptolemy, he pointed out, had 'rightly described geography as a mode of painting'.[61] 'I wish only,' he then added, 'to give what many and diverse witnesses [including his own] have provided of the painting or place that is this New Land of the Indians'. Instead of the authoritative word, the reader of the *Historia general* is offered the accurate image. In Oviedo's texts, geography and history, description and depiction are made interchangeable.

This is as far as Oviedo goes in confronting the problem of how to assimilate his text to all those others which for him, no less than for Las Casas, constituted the authoritative canon, and with which he hoped (again to Las Casas's disgust) that his own would one day belong. There is very little by way of analysis in his book and what there is is often hastily brushed aside by the arrival of new data. Neither is there any consideration in the numerous claims he makes to have evaluated all the stories which those 'many witnesses' he had questioned had told him, of what establishing the truth value of *their* statements would consist of. But then it is unlikely that he would have seen the need for any. The method, if it can be so called, which he employs in the *Historia general* consists in the simple forensic appeal to the multiplicity of 'eye-witnesses'. Like any competent jurist, he demands to know details about how and where his informants saw or heard what they have told him. But that is all. Since he is merely describing, merely painting with words, he does not even spend much time in vilifying the customs of the Indian whom he so obviously despised. All he need do to damn them forever in our eyes, so he tells us, is to recount them.

THE SECOND MOMENT

i

Like Oviedo, Las Casas was also caught by the need to authenticate his own voice in terms of *his* experience. Neither he nor Oviedo were impartial, neutral observers, nor did they wish to be. They made no claim – as their often disingenuous eighteenth-century successors were to do – to be above the fray, to act as dispassionate recording angels. It is very likely that they would not even have understood such an objective. Their histories belonged to clearly defined political and moral projects. For Oviedo, as we have seen, this was precisely to refute those, like Las Casas, whom he rightly saw as the enemies of the Spanish imperial mission and, at the same time, to reveal to an envious world the full range and greatness of that mission. Las Casas's *Historia de las Indias*, by contrast, was, said its author, 'a book of the greatest and ultimate necessity', and it had been written to demonstrate that there was no people on earth, no matter how seemingly 'barbarous' their condition, who could be denied membership of the 'Christian family'. His motive for writing all his works was 'the very great and final need to make known to all Spain the true account and truthful understanding of what I have seen take place in this Indian Ocean'. He had been compelled, he said, to utter, to write book after book, only by the enormity of the vision of 'so much harm, so many calamities, so much destruction, so many kingdoms devastated'. He was, he claimed in the *Brevíssima relación*, the only reliable witness to what had taken place in the Americas, 'wherever Christians have set foot', for only he had been willing to break the 'conspiracy of silence about what has really been happening'. 'It has become the custom,' he complained, 'to falsify the reports sent back to Spain about the damaging nature of Spanish actions in the New World'. Those few who, like himself, were prepared to risk official disapproval and more dangerous still the fury of the settlers, found that their 'reliable eye-witness accounts' were 'totally discounted' by indifferent royal auditors who returned statements which were at best 'hazy and unspecific', and who were always more concerned with any financial loss to the Crown than they were with the ceaseless haemorrhage of human life.

The testimony of Las Casas's is the only one that is true, he is claiming, not simply because it does not fudge the facts, but because it alone deals with the one feature of the Spanish settlement of America which matters: 'the massacres of innocent people'. This was, he argued, of such magnitude that not only did it 'silence all talk of other wonders of the world', it also threatened to destroy the existing world-order, 'to bring a collapse of civilization and to presage the end of the world'. Little wonder, then, that when Las Casas told his story to those he met in Spain, they 'listened open-mouthed to his every word'.[62]

But dramatic though his story-telling was, story-telling of itself was not sufficient. His project was more ambitious than merely to shock his readers, and ultimately the ministers of the Crown themselves, with the vividness – not to mention the repetitiousness – of what he, and only he, had seen. It was to prove that the American Indians possessed the same political civil rights as their conquerors, and to do this by demonstrating the complexity and sophistication of Amerindian culture. To achieve this end he was, as we shall now see, driven to use his voice as a means to interpret the authoritative canon in what he believed to be not so much a new as the *only* true manner.

ii

Las Casas's project was to establish the unique status of his voice. Most of his writings are, therefore, implicitly or explicitly, autobiographical. His *Historia de las Indias* has rightly been called an *apologia pro vita sua*.[63] Certainly no historian of America is so tirelessly self-referential. It is not surprising, then, that he should have chosen an account of a personal experience, the most significant of his entire life, to provide what is, in effect, a representation of the necessary relation between the cognitive status of text and experience. This was his now famous conversion. And this, or so he tells us, is how it came about.

Although he was to become the most outspoken defender of Indian rights, Las Casas spent much of his early life as a lay priest and a colonist in Cuba. He was, on his own account, better, more gentle perhaps, than other colonists, but he was also, like them, the master (*encomendero*) of Indians whose labour he, like they, unquestioningly exploited. On the Sunday before Christmas 1511, however, Las Casas, together with the other members of the tiny colony of Hispaniola, received a rude shock, which marked the beginning of his brief and dramatic journey from colonizing priest into Indian apostle.

That morning a recent arrival on the island, the Dominican Antonio Montesinos, delivered a sermon in the main Church of Santo Domingo. Taking his text from St John, he drew an analogy between the natural desert in which the Evangelist had chosen to spend his life and the human desert which the Spaniards had made of the once fruitful, 'paradisiacal' island of Hispaniola. He then turned upon the colonists. 'With what right,' he demanded of them, and with what justice do you keep these poor Indians in such cruel and horrible servitude? By what authority have you made such detestable wars against these people who lived peacefully and gently on their own lands?

'Are these not men?' he concluded. 'Do they not have rational souls? Are you not obliged to love them as yourselves?' The last three questions were to become the referents of every subsequent struggle to defend the rights of the indigenous peoples of the Americas. For Las Casas, in particular, the third – 'are you not obliged to love them as yourselves?' – was to guide his actions for the rest of his life.[64]

Las Casas's immediate response to Montesinos's sermon, however, was unremarkable. He did not share the indignation of the rest of the colony which demanded Montesinos's recantation and immediate repatriation to Spain. But neither does he seem immediately to have grasped that the full implication of what Montesinos had said was, as he finally came to recognize, that 'one could not in conscience possess Indians' and still claim to be a Christian. Later that same year he accompanied Diego Velázquez to Cuba where he witnessed, seemingly for the first time, the massacres which he was to describe so vividly in the *Brevíssima relación*. We must assume that he took no part in them. But although Las Casas is careful to point out how much better his behaviour was towards the Indians than that of any of his fellow conquerors, how they came to him because of 'the great pain and pity' with which their plight filled him; and although, so he tells us, he remonstrated furiously against the atrocities committed by Panfilo de Narváez in Caonao, he nevertheless served Velázquez well enough to be granted a large *encomienda* in Canarreo, near the port of Xagua.[65] How such a troublesome, lay priest came to be so well rewarded he never explains.

Three years later Las Casas experienced his 'conversion', which he describes in the *Historia de las Indias* in terms intended to convey a discrete but inescapable analogy with the conversion of St Paul. This was to result in his transformation from Indian-owning cleric into the 'Apostle to the Indians', and ultimately from lay priest into Dominican friar. Las Casas's moment of illumination, however, – conceived precisely as the bestowal of a power to understand through experience – was not the consequence of an encounter with a divine revelation of the kind which had struck Paul from his horse on the way to Damascus; nor did it come to him as the result of his observation of the misery of the Indians, although, as he says, he had seen much of that. As with Augustine, whose own conversion was triggered by the famous *tolle lege*, the child's voice saying 'pick up and read', so Las Casas's, too, was the consequence of an encounter with a text, Ecclesiasticus 34: 21–2, which he 'began to consider' in preparation for his Easter sermon:

The bread of the needy is their life. He that defraudeth him thereof is a man of blood. He that taketh away his neighbour's living slayeth him, and he that defraudeth the labourer of his hire is a bloodletter.

For Las Casas it was this text that led directly back, and gave meaning to, the sufferings of the Indians of which he had been a hitherto unreflective witness. 'From that very first hour,' he recalled, 'in which the darkness of that ignorance which had enveloped him' (Las Casas always spoke of himself in his pre-conversion state in the third person to emphasize the nature of the transition from 'other' to 'self') he understood 'the misery and the servitude in which these people had suffered'.[66] It was God's word which, in characteristically Augustinian terms, had restored through Grace the eye's capacity to see. 'We might say,' Charles Taylor has written,

that where for Plato the eye already has the capacity to see, for Augustine it has *lost* this capacity. This must be restored by Grace. And what Grace does is to open the inward man to God, which makes us able to see that the eye's vaunted power is really God's.[67]

Las Casas was always in this way 'God's eye', 'God's witness' in America, and it was his unique experience which had given him this role. When in 1515 the Dominican Pedro de Córdoba asked him to return with him to Spain in order to harass the Crown on behalf of the Indians, Las Casas says that although he was troubled by the prospect,

he was not dismayed, for it seemed that God had given, and gave him, the desire and the zeal which was needed to secure the safety of those wretched souls, and with it God gave him great perseverance.[68]

This was the closest he could come to revelation. Las Casas could not, of course, make claim to the status of a true visionary any more than could Oviedo. He could never pretend that God had spoken to him directly, and this, as we shall see, was to prove a serious inconvenience. But his conversion stands at the centre of his hermeneutical struggle with the 'cruel and implacable enemies of the Indians'. He had, if only with his 'inward eye', seen. The same could not be said of Oviedo. He might have suffered discomforts for the sake of his history. But these could have none of the heuristic force of Las Casas's conversion.

Indeed, for Las Casas, Oviedo is only a bearer of false witness. Before the 'conversion', both men were in some sense comparable. But whereas God had granted Las Casas illumination, he had taken from Oviedo what little natural vision he had once possessed. 'God for his crimes had blinded him,' declared Las Casas, 'so that he was unable to see the good disposition of the Indians'.[69] This must seem, at best, a curious argument, but Las Casas's intention here is to recall Paul's condemnation of all those who would not hear *his* message:

the God of the world hath blinded the minds of them which believe not, lest the light of the glorious Gospel of Christ who is the image of God, should shine upon them. (2 Corinthians 4: 4.)

The vision which Las Casas's conversion had granted him could not, however, stand alone. For, since he was neither a 'Martyr' nor even a real apostle, this vision too had to be linked directly to the canon if it were to acquire any meaning beyond its place in his personal biography. It was, he tells us, further texts yet which had verified precisely what it was that the moment of illumination had revealed to him. It was, as he was later to claim, 'every book' he had read 'in either Latin or the vernacular which in forty-four years were infinite'.[70] Here the text made sense of what he had seen, but what his blinded eyes had not allowed him to 'witness' for years, and what he had thus experienced led back round the hermeneutical circle to yet more texts.

The project to which Las Casas subsequently dedicated the remainder of his long life – the establishment of the Indians' claims to full humanity, and hence full legal equality with the Spaniards – depended upon the reconciliation of the competing claims to authority of text and experience which his 'conversion' had allowed him to achieve. Only an interpretation of the canonical texts, primarily of those texts which had been used against them, could secure the human status of the Indians before a community for whom exegesis was the only access to knowledge. His own knowledge of the canon was, he insisted, equal to that of any professional jurist or theologian, and to prove it he loaded his writings with more citations than any contemporary jurist or theologian would have thought necessary. As the great Dominican natural-law theorist, Domingo de Soto, said wearily of one of his depositions, and could have said of them all, 'it was as copious and diffuse as have been the years of this affair'.[71]

Learning on this scale was, Las Casas insisted, the result of an intense and prolonged intellectual labour, itself a kind of mental pilgrimage. 'For forty-eight years,' he told his colleagues in Chiapas and Guatemala, with pardonable exaggeration,

I have worked to inquire and to study and to set down clearly the law [on these matters]. And I think that, unless I deceive myself, I have delved so deep into the waters of these matters that I have reached their source.[72]

But it was also the case that the primacy of his *interpretation* of 'the Law' depended not so much upon the range of his knowledge, as it did upon the depth of his direct unmediated contact with what he called 'the fact'. As in the court of law, before which he so frequently imagined himself, it was the facts of the case which provided the basis for an authoritative reading of the text. For, he wrote – alluding to the famous adage of the fourteenth-century jurist Petrus Baldus de Ubaldis 'ex facto oritur ius' – 'it is, the jurists say, from the true account (*relación*) of the fact, that the Law is born'.[73] The Law, as Baldus had said, was based not on theory but on 'the experience of things'.[74] In order, however, to ensure the authority of *his* account over that of all possible others, Las Casas had to present his experience of the facts as uniquely privileged. His voice, particularly since he was forever conscious of Oviedo's voice making the same claim to autoptic authority but to very different ends, had to triumph over all others. 'God has given no man,' he claimed,

> neither living nor dead (and that only through His goodness and through no worth of my own) so much experience (*noticias*) and understanding (*sciencia*) of the facts and the Law natural, divine and human, as I have of the things of these Indians.[75]

'Facts and the Law', 'hecho y Derecho', 'ius et factum'[76] the coupling – which occurs again and again in all his writings – determined the crucial relationship between the canonical text and a direct experience of the external world as the only certain instrument of interpretation.

The terms *ius* and *factum* belong to a foundational distinction in Roman law, and in particular to the law concerning possession (*possessio*). The best-known instance of this distinction is that between things which belong to someone *de facto* and those which belong to him, or to her, only *de iure*. True possession, the jurists argued, had to reconcile both *ius* and *factum*. Las Casas had shifted the location of the term *factum* from the legal or civil to the natural. His 'facts', that is, are not legal facts. They are facts about the world. Here Las Casas seems to have taken up a powerful debate among the post-glossators and the commentators over the extent to which juridical experience should be made to conform with experiential reality.[77] His argument seems to be that as all acts of interpretation are also acts of possession, the correct interpretation will be the one which reconciles *factum* and *ius*. Where no such reconciliation is apparently possible then it is the law, which must have its source in fact, which must change. This seemingly unremarkable claim, at least from the juridical point of view, was Las Casas's most original theoretical contribution to the debate over the status of the American Indians. The men whom Las Casas had always identified as the enemies of the Indians – Juan Ginés de Sepúlveda in particular – had always maintained that it was the law which had to be upheld – for the law of course belonged to the canon – and that any data which could not be fully accommodated by the law should be disregarded. Sepúlveda, for instance, never denied that some Amerindians possessed notable technical and social skills. He merely denied, when faced with what he believed to incontrovertible proof of cannibalism and human sacrifice, that these skills were at all relevant to their case. Las Casas, in contrast, maintained, as had the Roman glossators, that any legal description had to begin with the facts, and it had to include *all* the facts. The *Digest*, the great repository of Roman law, after all, had in origin been only a collection of data, and jurisprudence itself was not so much a body of moral precepts as a method of interpretation.[78]

And if this were true for any act of legal understanding, it was particularly so for the understanding of anything to do with America. For everything about America, in the words of the opening sentence of the *Brevíssima relación*, was 'so extraordinary that the whole story remains quite incredible to anyone who has not experienced it at first hand'.[79] And only Las Casas had fully understood what that involved. In 1535, he wrote

> I can swear before God that, until I went to this royal court, even in the time when the Catholic King Don Ferdinand was still alive, no-one knew what thing the Indies were, nor of their greatness, their opulence, their prosperity . . .

nor, he added, 'of the destruction which had been wrought in them'.[80] In the prologue to the *Historia de las Indias*, a long and somewhat disjointed essay on the identity and purpose of the historian's task, he said it had been his objective 'to give clarity and certainty for readers of ancient things, to the principles which have been discovered about the machine of this world'.[81]

In order to achieve this end, he had become a recorder, an historian in the proper, ancient sense of the Greek term, 'historia', 'which', he said, quoting Isidore of Seville, means 'see' or 'know'; for no-one among the ancients dared place himself in any position other than among those where he had been present, and had seen with his own eyes that which he had determined to describe.[82]

Only a history of this kind could provide the data necessary for the correct interpretation of the authoritative canon, as it applied to America. And, to borrow Clifford Geertz's pun, only the '"I" witness' could be relied upon to compose such a history.

iii

Throughout all of Las Casas's writings there is the same insistence on the primacy of *his* eye, and consequently, of the uniqueness of *his* text. He knew that seeing, like interpretation, constituted a form of possession, analogous to that by which (and this was a claim Las Casas never denied) the Castilian crown 'possessed'[83] the New World. The claim to prior possession through sight also assured the uniqueness and authority of the text composed by the seer. 'I am,' Las Casas told Charles V's minister, the Seigneur de Chievres,

> the oldest of those who went over to the Indies, and in the many years that I have been there and in which I have seen with my eyes, I have not read [other] histories which could be lies, but instead I have experienced.[84]

Only I, he told the Council of the Indies, who have been 'an eye-witness for all the years since the Americas were discovered' who have 'wandered through these Indies since very nearly the year 1500',[85] 'only I can be trusted to know what I write'.[86] By contrast, Oviedo had only 'fabricated his history – or better his trifles – from stories', stories, so Las Casas claimed, which had been told to him by 'one of those pilots, called Hernán Pérez, who never leave their ships either then or later'. And he had turned for corroboration for these fictions, not to the evidence which lay before him, precisely because he had lost all power to 'see' these things, but to 'histories that are nothing but sheer fables and shameless nonsense'.[87] All such men, wrote Las Casas in a remarkable, if also characteristically obscure passage,

> who have written not what they *saw*, but what they did not hear so well . . . , and wrote with great detriment to the truth, have been occupied only in dry sterility and with the fruitlessness of the surface, without penetrating into the reason of men.

And, he continued,

Because they failed to till the field of this dangerous material (*peligrosa materia*) with the rake of Christian discretion and prudence, they sowed an arid seed, wild and unfruitful of any human or worldly sentiment, and as a result a mortal discord has greatly grown, produced, burst forth, in many, in very many, scandalous and erroneous sciences, and perverse consciences, so that, as a consequence, the very Catholic faith and Christian customs, and the greater part of the human race has suffered irreparable harm.[88]

Here the agricultural metaphor holds together the notions of experience, ocular testimony – that 'dangerous material' – and the skilful manipulation of hermeneutic knowledge – 'Christian discretion and prudence'. From the cultivation of the one by the other comes the true science which has eluded all previous commentators. Experience, as Las Casas's own 'conversion' had shown, was not an alternative to hermeneutics; it alone made true prudential interpretation possible.

The true witness, the historian, is then the only reliable guide to those 'ancient things' which constitute our knowledge of 'the machine of this world'. The historian, however, provided more than the accurate grounding for the interpretation of an old text in a new context. From Diodorus Siculus, whom he declared to be 'more like a holy theologian than a damned pagan philosopher', Las Casas had learnt that 'through such a presentation of events', the historian may also provide his readers with what Diodorus called 'a most excellent kind of experience'. For just as providence had

brought together the orderly arrangement of the visible stars and the natures of men into one common relationship, so history, in recording the common affairs of the inhabited world as though they were those of a single state have made of their treatises a single reckoning of past events and a common clearing-house of knowledge concerning them.[89]

But the process of transmuting personal experience into a text which would itself then provide 'a most excellent kind of experience' was not unproblematical. Las Casas knew that, for the most part, historians wrote, as he did himself, with a purpose. Most had done so for the glory of their patrons, or because they 'have felt within them a great number of polished and limpid words, the sweetness and beauty of gentle speech'; or, like the 'Greek chroniclers', who were 'very partial to their own worth and particular honour', they had written 'not what they had seen and experienced, but that which formed the subject matter of their personal opinion'.[90] Oviedo, he suggested on more than one occasion, belonged in this camp.

Las Casas's own motives, however, were like those of Josephus, the historian of another race – the Jews – who had been destroyed by a rapacious imperial power, and to whom his own theoretical remarks are heavily indebted. Like Josephus, he too had written 'to bear witness for the benefit of many' to 'great and noteworthy deeds' which the official record would prefer to have silently forgotten or presented as something other than what they were.

The result of this strict adherence to the immediate fact had been a text which was, as was Oviedo's, inescapably 'uncured'. 'The eyewitness,' Stephen Greenblatt has observed, 'possesses the truth and can simply present it: he who has not seen for himself must persuade'.[91] The very 'poverty of vocabulary, humanity of the style and lack of eloquence' of the *Historia de las Indias* will, therefore, Las Casas claimed, 'be good witnesses' both to its accuracy and to its author's sincerity.[92] Las Casas's writings are strewn with similar observations on style – his own and others. Columbus's prose, for instance, is also praised for its directness, since Columbus, too, indubitably had had the kind of direct access to experience to which Las Casas wished to lay claim.[93] This device, known in the language of Ciceronian rhetoric as *captatio benevolentiae*, was a familiar one.[94] For Augustine, who frequently provided Las Casas with his formal rhetorical models, the plain style of the Bible – the very feature which had provoked his contempt when he was a young academician teaching rhetoric – was construed as a formal and outward sign of its truth-telling power. As we have already seen, Oviedo, too, had insisted upon the unpolished nature of his texts, and that *only* a direct unadorned, unselfconscious prose could hope to unlock 'the truth and the secrets of nature'.[95] In Las Casas's case, however, the claim was intended to do more than appeal to a native simplicity, to establish a boundary between true history and romance, or even to ward off potential criticism from his remarkably unwieldy prose. It was a declaration of faith in the essential innocence of his eye.

For in order to secure the authority of the 'I', he had to give back to the language of description not merely its directness – its lack of formal rhetorical elegance – but also its transparency. He had, quite literally, to re-write the history of the discovery and conquest of America, since there was, or so he believed, a sense in which those who stood most to gain by misdescribing the Spanish enterprise in America had created for themselves a new and wholly mendacious vocabulary. The *conquistadores*, he bitterly recorded, frequently compared their activities to those of the Christian heroes of the Reconquest of Spain from the

Arabs. New arrivals in the Americas often had masses said on landing for the soul of that legendary hero of the Reconquest, El Cid.[96] By such acts of self-representation, these men were explicitly and self-consciously acting out in another place what had come to be thought of as the defining event of the Spanish past. And because the Indians, unlike the Arabs, were not 'worthy enemies',[97] their 'conquerors' had been compelled to re-describe their military capabilities and their political and technological expertise. America, Las Casas insisted, had not been 'conquered'. It had been overrun, invaded. 'This term "conquest",' he wrote in a memorandum of 1542, 'is tyrannical, Mahommedan, abusive, improper and infernal'. A conquest, he argued, can be conducted only against 'Moors from Africa, Turks and heretics who seize our lands, persecute Christians and work for the destruction of our faith'.[98] You can only speak to the woefully under-informed of 'conquering' peoples so gentle that they would flee rather than fight, whose wars were 'no more deadly than our jousting, or than many European children's games',[99] and whose arms – even those of the Inka – were 'a joke'.[100] 'Conquest' belonged with those other terms by which the *conquistadores* had transformed their shabby deeds into events from the romances of chivalry and the Spanish border – ballads – with 'Victories',[101] which designated only massacres, 'uprisings', which described the Indians' terrified attempts to escape their persecutors, 'rebellions', which characterized legitimate resistance to 'the forces of plague and carnage',[102] 'pacification', which meant 'killing God's rational creatures with the cruelty worthy of the Turk'.[103] For Las Casas, the ballads and the romances of chivalry, where his fellow countrymen had found a lexicon with which to fashion for themselves a comforting image of their 'pestiferous deeds', served as a model only because they offered a compelling image of a world gone mad. 'All that I have seen,' he wrote to his fellow Dominicans in 1563,

> and your reverences have heard, will seem perhaps like the fables and lying tales of Amadis of Gaul, for all that has been done in these Indies is by natural, divine and human law, null, inane and invalid, and as if it had been done by the Devil.[104]

Las Casas's claims for the transparency of his own vocabulary, as with the crucial coupling of 'Law and Fact', are heavily indebted to forensic rhetoric. It is precisely to those features which in any other circumstances would have reduced its value in its readers' eyes, that the 'true' historian can appeal as evidence that the translation from lived experience into language has been direct.

Similar analogies with recognized legal practices determined not only Las Casas's methodological claims; they also informed the formal structures of much of his narratives. The rapid transition within single chapters from recorded action and recorded speech to lengthy quotations from authoritative texts; the use, in the *Historia de las Indias*, of different temporal registers for the events of his own life, for those of Columbus's voyages, for the discovery and conquest of the Canary Islands, and for the subsequent conquests in America, all have identifiable legal analogues. So, too, does the frequent and circumscribed use of secondary evidence. Las Casas had not been present at all the events he describes. He had witnessed the conquest of Cuba, had spent some time in Venezuela and in parts of Mexico. But he had never set foot in the areas of the largest, most devastating conquests, central Mexico and Peru. When dealing with these areas he substitutes another's eyes for his own. 'I was told', 'I heard it from one who was there', 'he told me so', and similar 'utterance markings', are employed to retain as far as possible the illusion of the immediate personal contact with 'the real'. Sometimes, too, he incorporates entire documents into the texts. The Franciscan Marco de Niza's account of the killing of the Inka Atahualpa, for instance, reproduced in the *Brevíssima relación*, is a deposition, a sworn testimony, countersigned by the bishop of Mexico, and written by one who had had 'first-hand experience of these people' and was thus able to bear 'true witness'.[105] Much of the text of the *Historia de las Indias* and of the *Brevíssima relación*, despite the former's claim to be organized according to the traditional causal divisions of Aristotelian logic, reads less like a 'History' than a series of overlapping depositions.

iv

The *Historia de las Indias*, like all of Las Casas's writings, was meant, just as Josephus's history of Vespasian's war had been, to set the record right; the record that only he as the true witness could hope to provide. That record, however, was not only one of the deeds of the Europeans in America. It was also, crucially, a record of the conquered peoples. Here, too, Las Casas's project exactly resembled that of Oviedo. But whereas for Oviedo the Indians were little more than brutes, for Las Casas they were simple, outwardly pious 'primitives' (although he himself never used the term) who merely stood lower on the scale of cultural evolution than their European conquerors – and, as he tells us on many occasions, they were none the worse for that.

Part of the *Historia de las Indias*, and all of the *Apologética historia*, are studies in comparative ethnography. But Las Casas was not an ethnographer in any modern sense of the term. He observed, and he collected such data as came his way. But he had never intended to 'get himself into a culture'.[106] His project had been to collect the material necessary to establish a new reading of the law and, by so doing, to establish the Amerindians as peoples who could then be made fully intelligible to the European eye. If not yet entirely civil, he argued, they were nonetheless no more 'barbarous' than had been some of the remote cultural ancestors of the modern Europeans. To prove this point the *Apologética historia* provided the reader with series of detailed analogies between the practices of those cultures and the practices of the Indians. For Las Casas the new did not indicate, as it did for Léry, a stark unfamiliarity.[107] It indicated a precise cultural relationship in which distances in space could be expressed as distances in time. America was new in the sense of being initially unaccountable; it was new, too, in the sense that its peoples were still culturally unformed; just as, centuries before, the Greeks, the Celts, the Egyptians and the Romans had been. Given time, and now also the instruction that the Christian missionaries could provide, Indian cultures would in all important respects come to resemble European ones. However difficult it might be to make the act of imagination required to find the analogies between the ancient Mediterranean and modern American worlds, those analogies once again made the seemingly incommensurable, commensurable. Once he had passed through the theoretical grid of Las Casas's comparative method, the 'other' came out looking, after all, very much like 'us', albeit a now remote, barely imaginable 'us'. In Diodorus Siculus's striking phrase, Las Casas had, indeed, succeeded 'in recording the common affairs of the inhabited world as though they were those of a single state' and had thus made his 'treatises a single reckoning of past events and a common clearing-house of knowledge concerning them'.[108]

v

Columbus on Hispaniola, Barchilon in Peru and Léry in Brazil had all attempted to counter incommensurability by appealing ultimately to unmediated experience. When, by contrast, Las Casas turned instead to authorial experience, he seemed to offer a means of mediating between an authority-dependent hermeneutic culture and the presence of the 'facts'. All his works led, as Las Casas's own conversion had done, round the hermeneutic circle from the text to the experience and back again, in an attempt to find a place for America within the authoritative canon, to use 'the Fact' to interpret the 'Law' and the 'Law' to situate the 'Fact'.

But the strategies employed by both Oviedo and Las Casas and, indeed, by all other 'eye-witnesses', also placed upon the author just that weight of asseveration which, in their different ways, Columbus, Barchilon and Léry had attempted to avoid by making direct appeals to the senses. Las Casas was not, either by formal training or institutional affiliation, even a member of a recognized interpretative cadre. He may, indeed, have had a profound knowledge of both theology and the law, but he was neither a professional theologian nor a jurist – something of which his enemies frequently reminded him. He had, therefore, to mediate between the extreme solipsism of his claims to authority, and the equally extreme limitations imposed by the interpretive community to which he belonged. Las Casas's story of his conversion was intended to hint at the presence of a semi-divine source for his experience. God, he implied on more than one occasion, had sent him to America to act as a witness, the sole witness who, if any would listen to him, could prevent God's anger ultimately from destroying Spain, 'as divine punishment for the sins [committed] against the honour of God and the true faith'.[109] But since he could make no more claim to prophetic than he could to apostolic status, he could only hint and suggest. In the end, his ability to interpret the authoritative canon relied solely upon his own, purely human, vision.[110] It was, indeed, central to his claim for the rationality and humanity of the Indians, that all men, even the hated *conquistadores*, would be able to see as he did if only they were not so 'anaesthetized to human suffering by their own greed and ambition'.[111]

But although the authority of the 'I' may save 'true history' from confusion with romance, it cannot silence criticism of the author himself. As one of Las Casas's fiercest critics, Bernardo de Vargas Machuca, pointed out when he discovered an obvious error in Las Casas's population figures, 'if one proposition can be shown to be false in part, it may be presumed that the rest is false too'.[112] As Clifford Geertz has noted of the modern ethnographer's not dissimilar dilemma, 'to be a convincing "I" witness one must . . . first become a convincing "I"'.[113] The problem with Las Casas is that he was never a wholly convincing 'I', partly, as Vargas Machuca had seen, because his polemical objectives were always too stridently in evidence. His voice could never escape precisely those criticisms which Las Casas himself had levelled against the infamous 'Greek chroniclers'.[114] Nor could it escape from the noise which surrounded it, the noise produced by all those other reports, histories and relations – Oviedo's among them – which suggested the very opposite of what Las Casas was arguing. Re-writing the narrative of an event like the conquest of America required more than the repeated claim – however powerfully made – that this text, and this text alone was the only one which could be considered *the* 'true history'.

The uncertainty of Las Casas's, or of Oviedo's claim to autopsy, however, derived less from the proven unreliability of any particular 'I' than it did from the fact that before the emergence of the idea of the autonomous self in the seventeenth century, reliance on 'I' as a source of *authority* could only ever be tenuous.[115] For the Cartesian sceptic, the appeal to individual witness made perfect sense. To an Augustinian like Léry, or to a Thomist of Las Casas's stamp, both of whom belonged to cultures whose scientific procedures were bound by the appeal to *auctoritates*, it could only ever be highly problematical. For all those whose intellectual habits had been formed by the canon, the self had little existence beyond the plurality of the texts.

It was not until much later that a critical historiography would emerge that was capable of making some interpretative sense of the conflicting claims of these early historians. As Humboldt was to observe in the early nineteenth century, it was not until the publication in 1780 of Francisco Javier Clavigero's *Storia antica del Messico* (History of Ancient Mexico) that anyone would be in a position to pay much heed to 'the facts attested to by a crowd of eye-witnesses, all of whom were enemies of each other'. Before Clavigero had (or so Humboldt believed) sorted through the mass of conflicting information offered not merely by Las Casas and Oviedo, but also by such later chroniclers as Acosta, Torquemada, Garcilaso and Herrera, scepticism had been mandatory in the interests of truth. 'It seemed to be the *duty* of a philosopher,' said Humboldt, 'to deny what had been observed by the missionaries'.[116]

vi

Oviedo and Las Casas were also confronted by a further difficulty. Not only was there no obvious place in the culture to which he belonged for the detached and authoritative self. It was also the case that, although both men had aimed at providing *true* accounts, neither had aimed at providing a disengaged one. Both, as we have seen, were committed to particular and declared anthropological and political objectives. In their texts the observer's voice and those of the natural scientist or comparative ethnologist are fused. They could both offer compelling arguments for the primacy of their vision. But they could never, nor did they claim to, offer any proof of their *objectivity*. Yet they were addressing scientific cultures which had already begun to think in terms of objectivity and detachment and, as a consequence, to demand a disjunction between theory and observed fact. This move towards objectivity and empiricism was the outcome of the slow development of an objective – it cannot yet be described as a project – which is most closely connected with the work of Francis Bacon, to create a true 'natural' history of mankind.

Such a history would offer not, as Las Casas had hoped for his texts, a means of accurately interpreting the canon; it would instead be a substitute for all that had previously been written. And it was this objective which underpinned the great collections of travel narratives – from the *Navigazioni e viaggi* (1534) of Giovanni Battista Ramusio (whom Oviedo claims to have known well[117]) to the *Histoire générale des voyages* (1746) of the Abbé Prévost – whose declared purpose was *only* to provide the raw material with which the new natural historian would work.

The first part of the *Navigazioni e viaggi* is dedicated to the physician poet Girolamo Fracastoro, the author of *Syphilis sive morbus gallicus* (1521) the first extended treatment of that most famous of American imports. Ramusio tells his readers that he has chosen Fracastoro as the beneficiary for what might at first seem to be a work far removed from any interests of Fracastoro's own precisely because he is one of those 'who does not – as so many do – merely imitate, or go from one book to another, modifying, transcribing and declaring other men's things'. He is instead a true discoverer who, 'with a subtlety of mind', has 'travelled the world collecting many new things never before heard of, nor even imagined by others'. Ramusio's collections were similarly intended to extend the range of these hitherto unimaginable things. Their purpose was to provide a body of material which would replace the statements of the Ancients which Fracastoro had so wisely avoided. They would offer to the new empirical sciences the kind of data which all previous studies of the behaviour of man had lacked, truly *objective* information based upon first-hand, eye-witness accounts. And the guarantee of objectivity would be the detachment and scientific probity of the *collector*, not the status of the observer. These narratives, claimed Ramusio, with an implicit reference to Bacon, would lead to the greater understanding of mankind in the same way as

> the most subtle argument for homeocentricity, and in philosophy the secret method which have created in us the intelligence and the [hitherto] unknown route to those miraculous causes which have been hidden to past centuries.[118]

Ramusio's project, however, could only be achieved by detaching the raw material to be found in the texts which he had collected from the statements made by those whom the seventeenth-century English compiler Samuel Purchas, following self-consciously in Ramusio's foot-steps, called the 'Universal Speculators'. The texts that Purchas had collected in his *Hakluytus Posthumus or Purchas his pilgrimes* of 1625 (which included, among the works of several other Spanish authors, Las Casas's *Brevíssima relación*) constituted, he claimed, everything which 'a world of travellers have by their own eyes observed'. But this miscellaneous information had been collated, he emphasized, *not*

> by one professing Methodically to deliver the History of Nature according to rule and Art, nor Philosophically to discuss and dispute; but as in a way of Discourse by each Traveller relating what is the kind that he hath seene.

The observer's record of 'the kind that he hath seene', he believed, should provide only the data which the natural historian required, 'as *David*', he continued,

> provided material for Solomon's Temple or (if that be too arrogant) as Alexander furnished *Aristotle* with Huntsmen and Observers of Creatures to acquaint him with these diversified kinds and natures; or (if that also seems too ambitious) as Sense by industry of particular yeeldeth the Premises to reason's Syllogistical arguing . . . so here *Purchas* and his Pilgrimes minister individual and sensible materials (as it were with Stones, Birches and Mortars) to the universal Speculators for their theoretical structures.[119]

It was in this way, by detaching the 'speculator' from the 'observer', that America, and more significantly the Americans, were finally incorporated into something resembling the original Baconian project. When, in 1746, the Abbé Prévost (remembered today as the best-selling author of the sentimental romance, *Manon Lescaut*) composed his massive *Histoire générale des voyages*, he, too, made a clear distinction between the kind of texts whose parallel histories he was writing. Prévost, who knew that travellers' accounts rarely fell unaided into the neat distinctions offered by Purchas, set out to create a set of new texts by dismembering the works of his chosen authors. Thus, he said, he had created one category composed of *Extraits* which would

> contain the Journal of each voyage, the adventures of the traveller, and the other events which he recounts, together with the descriptions of places exactly as he has given them, so long as he has not been contradicted by another traveller,

and a second category entitled *Reductions* which would

contain the remarks made by the travellers on each country, on their inhabitants and on their natural produce, from which will be produced a body [of writings] which will form an orderly description.[120]

The final stage in the development of this project was to raise the level of philosophical speculation, so as to incorporate all this disparate material into a truly philosophical account, what Dugald Stewart – speaking of Adam Smith's *Considerations concerning the first formation of languages* (1761) – called a '*Theoretical* or *Conjectural* history'.[121]

The authors of such histories stayed at home. Only the security of their own environment would provide them with the detachment they required. 'I have interrogated the living and the dead,' wrote the Abbé Raynal, author and compiler of the *Histoire philosophique et politique des deux Indes* (Philosophical and Political History of the Two Indies) over a century later, 'I have weighed their authority. I have contrasted their testimonies. I have clarified their facts'. From text to text he had travelled the whole world, from the pole to the equator, in search of the precise, the wholly truthful witness with 'the august image of the truth' always before him as his guide. And if his work should find any future readers this will be because he, as author, has been entirely 'disengaged from all passions and prejudices'. With characteristic disingenuousness he predicted that such readers would be unable to tell by reading his book under what government he had lived, what employment he had or which religion he had professed. And, as Diderot (who, as we shall see in Chapter 5, was the author of a great part of the *Histoire*) added, only the historian of this kind, 'raised above all human concerns', so that he could 'glide above the atmosphere, [so that] one can see the whole globe beneath one',[122] would be able to make sense of the vast and conflicting body of data which the human race offered him. This was truly an history *de haut en bas*.

The self-conscious heir to this aspect of the Baconian project was, however, Humboldt. From the perspective of the early nineteenth century Humboldt was able to look back, with perhaps unwarranted confidence, over the long history of the attempts to describe America, and through description to make sense of her. The age of autopsy had clearly passed. And with it had gone the need for the scepticism which had cast doubt on all the narratives the travellers and the missionaries had attempted to bring home. Now, Humboldt believed 'a happy revelation has come about in the manner in which we envisage the civilization of peoples and the causes which have favoured or arrested their progress'. He, at least, had devised a new method of studying places and peoples, 'far from the style of which the Greeks left inimitable models' – those same Greeks who had so impressed Las Casas.[123] For, as he set off into the rain-forests of the Orinoco, Humboldt was confident that his narrative would be assured of its absolute truthfulness, not only because of the battery of instruments he carried with him to substantiate what he claimed to have measured, not even because of what Hans Blumenberg has called his 'total lack of mistrust of language',[124] but because he could be certain of the authority of his 'I' – the eye of the 'man of science'. But between Las Casas and Humboldt the status, role and image of the observer had been transformed. So, too, had the place of America in the European consciousness.

CHAPTER THREE
The Receding Horizon

Ich möchte nicht gern in einem andern Jahrhundert leben, und für
ein andres gearbeitet haben. Man ist eben so gut Zeitbürger, als
man Staatsbürger ist.

Friedrich Schiller, *Über die ästhetische Erziehung des Menschen*

i

Las Casas's attempt to preserve the claims of the 'law' in the face of
an ever-increasing awareness of the challenge which the discovery of
America presented to traditional modes of explanation, could only be
of limited success. No matter how it might come to be regarded, the
discovery was proof that the authority of the canon could be a perilously
fragile one. As the Italian historian Francesco Guicciardini noted in the
1540s, the mere existence of a 'New World' had, at least, thrown a
number of hitherto seemingly unquestionable assumptions into serious
doubt. It had even required a new reading of Psalm 18.5 – 'Their sound
has been spread throughout the world and the Word had reached to the
ends of the earth' – which had always been interpreted to mean that
the Gospel had been preached in every part of the globe.[1]

In America, it seemed, Europe had not only discovered an unknown
geographical space. It had also discovered something about its own
past: that the accumulated wisdom of the Ancients might be, if not
entirely false, at least seriously flawed. If the knowledge of the Ancients
had been so limited in this geographical respect who could know, asked
Erasmus as early as 1517, in what other as yet undiscovered ways it
might also turn out to have been in error?[2]

Erasmus's observation was meant only as a warning. He was himself,
after all, much committed to the sacredness of the text, and to the
peculiar authority of the writings of the Ancients. For many, however,
and in particular for those who had come to see science as the expression of ordinary experience, as a domain which, in theory, was
accessible to any willing observer, the discovery could be interpreted as
a liberation from the limits of knowledge imposed by the accumulated
statements of the past, a proof of the power of lived experience over
any theoretical claim based upon exegesis. For unlike so many of the
other 'discoveries' in early modern science, America was demonstrably

a reality. Even William Temple, the most ardent champion of the Ancients, could not deny that it had been unknown to Europe before 1492, although he did claim that had the Ancients been aware of the 'customs and manners of so many original nations, which we call barbarous', they would have done a lot more with the knowledge than the 'Moderns' have done.[3] The discovery of America, wrote a triumphant André Thevet, had finally trumped 'these toadstools of philosophers', and their preposterous claims to be able to 'argue with sophistry against what ordinary experience teaches and upholds'.[4] '1000 Demosthenes and 1000 Aristotles,' Galileo would say later, 'may be routed by an average man who brings Nature in'. Like Galileo's 'average man', Thevet's Columbus seemed finally to have freed the artisans of 'ordinary experience' from the bonds imposed upon them by the voices of the dead.

Thevet's views were also expressed, in a more reflective, if no less triumphant mood, by the Italian humanist Pietro Pomponazzi, professor of natural philosophy at the University of Padua, the author of a contentious treatise on the immortality of the soul and a rebarbative champion of reason, experience and the *principia naturalia* as the sole criteria for truth. On March 18, 1523, Pomponazzi was lecturing to his students on Book I of Aristotle's *Meteorologica*. Having explained what Aristotle had said about the impossibility of finding human life below the Antipodes, and what Aristotle's twelfth-century Arab commentator, Averroes, believed Aristotle to have meant by saying it, Pomponazzi turned to his students. 'That gentlemen,' he said, in the mixture of the vernacular and Latin which the contemporary professorate used when their enthusiasm overcame them,

> that is what Aristotle and Averroës think. But what should we today think? I am of the belief that where experience and reason [by which he meant the reason derived from the study of the canonical authorities on which he had been lecturing] are in conflict, that we should hold to experience and abandon reason. Averroës had himself said this, but then had failed to do so, for his reasoning is truly sophistical.

'And,' he continued,

> you should know that I have received a letter sent to me by a Venetian friend [probably Antonio Pigafetta] who accompanied the Papal nuncio to the King of Spain, and who, finding himself there,

went on an expedition sent by that King to the southern hemisphere and he travelled for twenty-five degrees after having crossed the Torrid Zone. Now he writes to me that having passed through the Pillars of Hercules, they have sailed in the southern hemisphere for three months and came across more than three hundred islands each separate from the next, which were not only inhabitable, but which were also inhabited. These arguments which the commentator calls 'demonstrations', how are they demonstrations? For one cannot make demonstrations contrary to truth. Because . . . if we are ignorant about things on earth which we can see, how will we know about the heavens?[5]

Pomponazzi's denunciation of Aristotelian meteorology should not, however, be taken as a condemnation of Aristotelianism. Pomponazzi had no quarrel with either Aristotelian metaphysics or Aristotelian moral philosophy. Indeed, as his final attack on 'the commentator' makes plain, his whole project had been to return philosophy to a purified form of Aristotelianism stripped of the corrupting accretions laid upon the text by such later interpreters as Averroës. Nor was Pomponazzi's rejection of 'reason' in favour of experience actually *caused*, as he suggests, by Pigafetta's letter.

But it still remained the case that if Aristotle had been wrong here, he might be wrong elsewhere. However suggestive his philosophy might still be, his claim to authoritative status had collapsed. And furthermore, it had collapsed in the face of a single piece of empirical data. The rhetoric of Pomponazzi's address was nicely and carefully turned to this effect. To his listening students, the force of the implied claim that it *was* indeed a single letter, a single experience – if itself one already transformed into a text – that had driven Pomponazzi suddenly to 'abandon reason', widened immeasurably the potential distance which lay between experiential knowledge and rational conjecture. A letter, Pomponazzi was saying, the written testimony of an ocular experience, can change the shape of the world, and can radically undermine hypotheses upon which an entire geography and possibly a cosmography had been erected. 'How great a difference there is,' as Kepler told Galileo nearly a century later, 'between theoretical speculation and visual experience, between Ptolemy's discussion of the Antipodes and Columbus's discovery of the New World'.[6]

None of this implied, however, that the painstakingly collected, carefully collated, great texts together with the massive intellectual systems which had been erected upon them, had lost their credibility entirely. Even Tycho Brahe's mathematics and Galileo's observations had not achieved that. It was clearly possible to save parts of the ancient corpus while discarding others, just as it was possible, until late in the seventeenth century, to modify the Ptolemaic picture of the universe to accommodate some of Copernicus's conclusions, while withholding recognition of the heliocentric theory itself. But both Copernicanism and the discovery of America – with which it was so often linked in the scientific discourses of the seventeenth century – cast a long and menacing shadow over the authority of the whole of the ancient corpus. And although in both cases it might seem that it was only a single authority – Ptolemy – or at most a single category of authorities – ancient cosmography – which had been discredited, most Europeans spoke of the Ancients as if they constituted a single if varied text, speaking with a single if modulated voice. The discovery of America, like the demonstration that the earth revolved around the sun, was clearly a triumphantly modern achievement. As the poet Alessandro Tassoni remarked in 1636, however willing modern cosmographers might have been merely to repeat the follies of Ptolemy and Strabo, they had

> discovered the sources of the Nile [this was not, in fact, true], had travelled to the farthest limits of Ethiopia . . . and crossing the immense Ocean had found in the Antipodes a New World of which the Ancients had not even dreamed.[7]

This discovery became, then, not a simple proof of the superiority of one scientific procedure over another. It was also evidence of the superiority of one historical period over another, the one already closed, the other still in a state of becoming. It thus rapidly became part of a prolonged debate on the merits of the modern world over the ancient.

The so-called 'quarrel between the Ancients and the Moderns', which broke out in the late seventeenth century, was in part a dispute over the interpretation of development: had the 'Moderns' actually done anything which the 'Ancients' had not done better?[8] It began as a struggle over literary excellence. But it was hard to maintain the claim that the modern world was something other than the mere re-molding of ancient types, and harder still to claim that modernity was in some respects quite unlike Antiquity, without very quickly being drawn into a dispute over competing world views.[9] And, at the base of any dispute over world views would inevitably be found a dispute between the omniscience of the (Ancient) text, and the uncertainty of (modern) empirical knowledge. In the context of that debate, 'Antiquity' came to be seen not as the collective achievement of a group of historical persons, but as a distinctive body of knowledge capable of extensive manipulation. This is what Socrates, in Bernard de Fontenelle's *Nouveaux*

Dialogues des Morts (New Dialogues of the Dead, 1683) means when he cautions Montaigne,

Be warned of one thing, Antiquity is an object, of a particular kind. Praise can enlarge it. When something commonplace happens which has been predicted in Antiquity, or when anyone has some quarrel with his own century, Antiquity profits by it.[10]

Seemingly infinite in extension, 'Antiquity' thus became a single category, divided from the world of the 'Moderns' not by the passage of time but by its claim to authoritative status. The 'Moderns' for their part belonged to a world which, because it had discarded the belief that truth was a function of origins and therefore to be found in texts, had discarded also the notion of permanence.

Unlike the theoretical speculations of either Aristotle or Ptolemy, however, and unlike any statement to be found in an ancient text, discoveries in the world were clearly *events*. The authoritative text was authoritative precisely because it was believed to be entirely timeless. What Aristotle had said in the fourth century BC was just as true in the sixteenth century AD. Events, however, belonged to history. And because the discovery of America had so unsettled the customary intellectual practices of an entire world, those who came to write the history of that discovery could only conceive of it as a moment of decisive change, a point at which one epoch had ended and another begun. 'The greatest event since the creation of the world,' declared the Spanish historian López de Gómara in 1552, 'excluding', he added cautiously, 'the Incarnation and death of He who created it'.[11] And Voltaire, for whom the Incarnation had no place in world history, was by no means the first to observe that the act of discovery itself constituted 'a species of new creation', and one which because it was owed solely to human agency, had made 'all that has seemed grand until then . . . vanish before it'.[12]

With the discovery of America, the historical process itself, concerned not with the operations of God's purpose in time – the *operatio Dei* in Augustine's phrase – but with the record of purely human acts, now became a mode of authority. In this new history, what drove men forward was not the divine *telos*, the ineluctable movement from the Fall to the Redemption. It was instead human curiosity. Since with the discovery, 'the self-confirmation of human curiosity', as Hans Blumenberg has written, 'had become the form of its legitimation', a new *telos* become possible, one expressed in terms of progress; of the constant, if unsteady, process of the fulfilment of purely human objective. 'History', to quote Blumenberg again, 'had become an authority to which to appeal against metaphysics'.[13] As Kepler argued, Seneca's supposed prophecy in the *Medea* (lines 375–9)

> There will come an age in distant years when the Ocean shall unloose the bonds of things (*vincula rerum*), when the whole broad earth shall be revealed, when Tehys shall disclose new worlds and Thule shall no longer be the limits of the land –

had once been taken to be little more than a literary conceit. Now it had to be regarded as a scientific hypothesis, reached by intuition alone, but demonstrated to be true centuries later by experiment.

Even in sciences so self-evidently text-bound as early modern medicine, even in theology, whose sole objective was exegesis, what Columbus's discovery suggested – at least to the 'Moderns' among their practitioners – was that the wish to venture beyond the established limits of the canon could be self-confirming. The sixteenth-century mathematician and physician, Girolamo Cardano, called for the discovery of new worlds in medicine to match those made in geography and cosmology; and as early as 1519, the Scottish logician and theologian, John Major, then resident in Paris, had argued in defence of his use of Greek moral philosophy in a predominantly theological discourse, that it was only when all the sources of human knowledge, human and divine, had been brought together – as they were in his works – that theology would be able to make discoveries of the kind which had been made in America. Nearly a century later the Italian magus, neo-Platonist and prophet of universal empire, Tomasso Campanella, made a similar observation. The empiricists' argument that theology had made no advances since the New Testament (and, indeed, given the kind of text-dependent science it was, *could* make no advances) was, he protested, the methodological equivalent to denying the reality of the discovery of America and the new knowledge of the heavens.[14]

Traditional theology, however, like traditional medicine, remained bound to interpretation, and through interpretation to a stable and controllable past. However, in all other areas of learning the discovery of America, by showing that the past could be radically incomplete, seemed also to have thrown the future suddenly and alarmingly into disarray. When in the 1512 Preface to his edition of Pomponius Mela's *Cosmographia*, the Nuremberg humanist Joannes Cochlaeus (resurrected for us by John Elliott), declared that 'whether [the discovery] is true or a lie has nothing to do with cosmography or the study of history' he was voicing exactly this disquiet. For the study of history belonged to that enterprise of textual scrutiny to which the humanists were as dedicated, if dedicated in different ways, as the scholastics. Now that, *pace* Cochlaeus, the whole of Ptolemaic geography and Aristotelian meteorology had been discarded, and with it the foundations on which the claims of the Ancients to authority had rested, literally anything had become possible.

An image of a future filled with new Americas arose before the Moderns. As Bernard de Fontenelle says to the Marquise de G . . . (in fact, the Marquise de la Mesangire of Rouen) in his *Entretiens sur la pluralité des mondes* (Dialogue on the Plurality of Worlds), who can ever be certain that we will not one day walk upon the moon? 'Recollect,' he says,

> the situation of America before it was discovered by Christopher Columbus. The minds of its inhabitants were in the state of the most profound ignorance. They had no idea that men might be carried by animals; they believed the ocean to be an immense space impassable by man and bounded only by the sky to which it is joined. You might suppose that they would not have easily believed anyone who told them that a navigation was carried on which was infinitely superior to theirs, that by its means every part of the ocean might be reached. . . . After thinking of that I will not say that no connection can be established between the earth and the moon.[15]

'You are mad,' replied the Marquise.

But the point that Fontenelle – permanent secretary to the *Académie des sciences* in Paris, and a man who believed as firmly in the possibility of life on other planets as he did that the Southern Hemisphere was inhabited – was making, was the point that since we all stand in our own time we cannot conjecture in safety about the condition of the future. If we study the past with the same scientific rigour which Leibnitz had brought to it, we may, he insisted elsewhere, be able to use it as a basis for making predictions about the future.[16] But we can only do so in the certain knowledge that, in the end, we are all in the same state with respect to our possible futures as the poor American Indians. Literally anything, including moon-flights, may one day be possible. Columbus had shown us that. We stand in our own time, but that is only one stage on a road whose end is unknown. The ancient physician Epistratos in the *Nouveaux Dialogues des Morts*, brought forward in time by Fontenelle to argue with Harvey, is like the ignorant Americans. ('You tell me such wondrous things,' he is made to exclaim. 'What! The blood circulates though the body!)[17]

There can be no difference in kind between 'Ancients' and 'Moderns'. All men are equal as regards their abilities and aptitudes. It is only historical time which separates them. All the speakers in Fontenelle's

Dialogues can understand each other. Epistratos may be astounded at Harvey's discovery, but he has no difficulty in understanding it. 'This is how it seems to me', Fontenelle wrote elsewhere, 'the great question of the Ancients and the Moderns [is] empty. The centuries impose no natural differences whatsoever between men'. Nor, he added, did climates. In matters of time and space, 'we are all perfectly equal, Ancients and Moderns, Greeks, Latins and French'.[18]

Equal, in that when confronted by the natural world, we are all equally capable of understanding it. Our achievements, however, are not all alike nor, of course, equally valid. If the centuries that lie between Harvey and Epistratos have created no natural distinction between these two men, it is nevertheless still the case that the worlds which they inhabit are strikingly different. The difference was to become the subject of a new history, a history of progress, of the final triumph of modernity and, ultimately, of 'Enlightenment'. In this history, all human time is divided into epochs. Although the historical process itself might be teleological, even deterministic, it was also discontinuous. It would also be a history quite unlike those dismal chronicles which Locke had already characterized as nothing more than the records of the deeds of the 'Great Butchers of Mankind'.[19] Instead, it would be a record and a celebration of the achievements of the great from Galileo to Newton. As Jean d'Alembert – mathematician and, together with Diderot, architect of that map of modernity, the *Encyclopédie*, phrased it – such a history would be one 'of the uses which men have made of the production of nature, in order to satisfy either their curiosity or their needs'.[20]

Such histories demanded clearly visible and effective figures to mark the boundary between one epoch and the next.[21] And although, to use another of Bruno Latour's images, Columbus may no more have discovered America than Tolstoy's General Zutozov won the battle of Taratino, an authoritative narrative account of the triumph of human agency clearly had to be provided with similarly powerful human agents.[22] The agent of the now richly symbolic 'Discovery of America' was, of course, Columbus himself. But the historical Columbus as he emerges from his own writings – the man who insisted that he had discovered Asia, that his principal aim had been to bring Christianity to the heathen, that he had found his inspiration in the Book of Isaiah, who once wrote that gold could buy a man's way into heaven and who was buried wearing a Franciscan habit – that man was clearly ill-equipped to play the role of epoch marker. A more suitable character was thus created to take his place.

Within a few years of Columbus's death, the image of the discoverer had already begun, perceptibly, to change. For Las Casas, as we have seen in Chapter 1, Columbus was primarily the agent of a divine plan. He was the 'Christian Admiral', the bearer of the Gospel to the inhabitants of the New World, the *Christum ferrens*. He was God's instrument who, as Las Casas phrased it, had gone overseas not in pursuit of the wealth of Cathay but 'to open wide doors so that the divine doctrine and the Gospel of Christ might enter therein'.[23] But it was crucial for this account that God should have chosen not merely a visionary, but also a rational and intellectually inspired one. Las Casas, therefore, dedicated six long and ponderous chapters of his account of the voyages in the *Historia de las Indias*, to describing and defending Columbus's geographical and navigational theories.[24] In these he is portrayed as someone who, by skilful manipulation of the textual evidence, had persuaded himself ('very reasonably', in Las Casas's view) that the 'Torrid Zone' was habitable, and that there must be more lands in the Atlantic 'to discover'.

Oviedo's Columbus is similarly gifted. He was, Oviedo believed, a 'learned and well-read man in the science of cosmography' who in his reading of the Ancients had 'discovered' a world which, although it had been familiar enough in Antiquity, had subsequently 'been forgotten'.[25] Columbus, according to Oviedo, was also the first to know how to navigate 'by the sun and by the North Star' (a patent absurdity) 'since this is a science which cannot be executed entirely, so as to know the use and experiment of it, if it is not practised in large gulfs and at a great distance from land'. Columbus was, therefore, doubly gifted. Not only was he the first man 'who had learnt the secret and the art of navigation', he also knew precisely where this knowledge would lead him.[26]

Although Las Casas's and Oviedo's accounts have clearly gone some distance towards creating a more rationally compelling portrait than the one which emerges from Columbus's own writings (despite the fact that many of those bear the mark of Las Casas's editorial hand) they still describe a recognizable historical person. During the late sixteenth and early seventeenth centuries, however, as the fact of the discovery slowly began to be felt in increasingly wider and more varied cultural circles, Columbus the Christian visionary, even Columbus the colonizer, the creator of new worlds, is steadily replaced by a more obviously modern creature. Gradually he becomes a daring rationalist, an empirical scientist.[27] The most immediate heirs of this Columbus were the intellectual conquerors of the heavens. 'The memory of Columbus and Vespucci will be renewed through you', wrote the enthusiastic Lorenzo Pignoria to Galileo in March 1611 on hearing of the success of his observations of sun-spots, and added, 'and with even greater nobility, as the sky is more worthy than the earth'.[28]

These comparisons were not fortuitous. The earth and the heavens stood in close metaphorical relationship to one another. Both astronomy and navigation required travel, and although the Galilean astronomer travelled only with his eye, both resulted in the reduction of a part of the cosmos to cartography. Both assumed Nature to be transparent, something which in Galileo's terms could be 'brought in' by anyone with the eyes to see. Both, crucially, proceeded by the interpretation of signs.[29] Like Galileo, Columbus had read 'the book of nature' and, like Galileo, what he had found there was strikingly unlike what the established authorities claimed that he should have found. For Columbus, as for Galileo, the world was a text; but a text of a very special kind since its author was God Himself, a text which could only be read by means of rational hypotheses verified by experiment. As the Neapolitan man of letters, Giambattista Manso, observed in a letter to Galileo in 1610, 'Ptolemy had been judged to be a new Hercules beyond whose limits it was impossible to go'. In Manso's conceit, Ptolemy's text had been given the solidity of Scylla and Charybdis, the Pillars of Hercules. No one had dared venture out beyond the limits which it had set upon all possible geographical knowledge until Columbus – the new Odysseus – had landed in the Antilles, proving it to be false. In a similar manner, said Manso, Galileo too had travelled 'by routes previously unknown to the human intellect' so that, he concluded, 'you may count yourself almost a new Columbus' (*quasi novello Colombo*).[30]

Columbus could also be made to represent another turn in the argument against scriptural authority. The single eye-witness of a successful experiment can confound a system such as Ptolemaic geography, which was based solely upon conjecture. But it can also *confirm* an hypothesis grounded on reason which had seemed, in the first instance, to deny both sense-experience and the assertions of the canon. Copernicus had arrived at his vision of a heliocentric universe by means of mathematical calculations. These had seemed to support the view that, contrary to what appeared to be the case, the earth revolved around the sun, not vice versa. It was not, however, until Galileo's observations of the movement of sun-spots that this hypothesis had been confirmed experimentally. Galileo himself was very conscious that this was what had occurred. 'O Nicolas Copernicus', he makes the figure of Sagredo in his *Dialoghi sui massimi sistemi* (Dialogue Concerning the Two Chief World Systems, 1632) cry out across the century that has passed between them, 'what pleasure it would have been for you to see that part of your system confirmed by so clear an experiment'.[31]

Something very similar happens to the story of the discovery of America. Here, too, an initial hypothesis which is based upon a careful assessment of probabilities (or so it was believed) is finally demonstrated by experiment to be true. Only, in this case, Columbus is the agent of the verification of his own experiment, the Galileo to his own Copernicus. Like Copernicus, Columbus had begun with an hypothesis which seemed to contradict both sense-experience and canonical authority and which, like Copernicanism, had been savagely rejected by the defendants of orthodox scientific opinion. No matter for the moment that this hypothesis seemed to so many to be counter-intuitive for the very good reason that it was false, the consequence of shrinking the size of the degree by half, the outcome of selective reading in just those texts, Aristotle, Ptolemy, and the Arab geographer Al-Farhani, that Columbus's own experiment would prove wrong.[32] For the moment all that matters is that it is an hypothesis which, in the words of the eighteenth-century Scottish historian, William Robertson, had been arrived at 'from theoretical principles and practical observations'.[33] As earlier observers had recognized, the success of Columbus the scientist–navigator, had not been a fortunate blunder by a man who quite literally did not know where he was going. Instead it had been, in Humboldt's telling phrase, ' a conquest of reflection'.[34]

To give credibility to these claims, Columbus's religious concerns, even his passion for gold and his own glory, had to be discarded. In their place came a detached scientific personality. This personality was, as Kepler claimed, a man possessed of so many gifts that he 'keeps his readers uncertain whether to admire his intellect in divining the New World from the direction of the winds, more than his courage in facing unknown seas and his good luck in gaining his objective'. No hint here of the startled encounter with the 'Terrestrial Paradise'; no mention of the thesis that the world might, in fact, be shaped like a ball with a woman's breast on top. But then neither Kepler nor Manso were concerned with the discovery of America as anything other than a *discovery*, or with Columbus as anything other than a discoverer.

ii

By the time that Robertson came to write his immensely popular *History of America* in 1777, the historical reconstruction of the circumstances which had made the discovery possible, as with its probable consequences for Europe, had become subjects of widespread general concern. Robertson's work, as the long history of navigation which occupies the whole of Book I makes clear, is a contribution to the eighteenth-century debate over the place of commerce in the progress of European civilization.[35] For Robertson, Columbus's voyages, and to a lesser degree those of Vasco da Gama, constituted a turning point in the development of European civilization. In part this was due to the simple fact that these had enormously enhanced the scope of world trade, and made possible the final transition from largely agricultural communities to fully developed commercial societies; a claim which, as we shall see in Chapter 5, was given far greater weight at the end of the century by the Abbé Raynal. What concerned Robertson, therefore, was a history of science which could be closely linked to a progressive, if largely conjectural, history of society. To have brought about the final stage in the history of civilization, in Robertson's understanding of causation in human affairs, Columbus had to have been not the agent of a divine plan (as he had been for Las Casas), but the manifestation of the best that the European 'spirit' had reached at a particular and crucial historical moment. He therefore assured his readers that Columbus had been 'naturally inquisitive, capable of deep reflection', a man who combined 'the modesty of true genius . . . with the ardent enthusiasm of a projector'.[36] For Robertson, the history of Columbus's initial rejection at the hands of the Genoese, the English, the Portuguese and even, at first, the Spanish, made his personal biography an ideal subject for metaphorical transformation. All of those who will transform the world, must first struggle against the world.

In order to realize his scientific vision, Columbus, like Henry the Navigator before him, had been compelled to confront those who 'from ignorance, envy or from that cold timid prudence rejected whatever has the air of novelty'. Like Henry, who remains in Robertson's narrative a somewhat shadowy figure, Columbus is a modern before his time. And as with every good modern, the 'appeal to the authority of the Ancients' which his adversaries had drawn up against him, had made no impact on his 'determined philosophical mind'.[37] Columbus may not yet be a true scientist – Robertson does not require that he have either the mathematical or the technical skills which even Da Gama possessed – but he is a true scientific visionary who, having offered an incredulous Old World the prospect of a New one, had been greeted by uninformed bigots with the response that 'if there were really such countries as Columbus pretended, they could not have remained so long concealed'.[38]

This image of Columbus, so ironically false, as one whose achievements were based largely upon a rejection of traditional exegetical modes of understanding in favour of direct empirical confrontation with the natural world, rapidly become a commonplace. Once again, like Galileo, Columbus too had 'brought nature in', and a far larger portion of it than had ever been suspected. As one later champion of free inquiry, the Baptist minister and emancipationist, Robert Robinson (1735–1790), expressed it, Columbus and King Ferdinand, when confronted by those who argued on the authority of texts, had 'ventured to dissent, judged for themselves . . .'. And because this mythic Columbus had been fortunate enough to find in the equally mythic Ferdinand a powerful patron, his venture had avoided the sorry fate of 'Copernicus and Galileo, the fathers of modern astronomy', whose findings (or so Robinson seems to have believed) had remained buried by priestly bigotry for nearly a century. 'These,' Robinson warned sternly, 'are the fruits of denying the right of private judgement'.[39]

Obviously, however, this new Columbus could not be credited with an initial hypothesis based upon the (false) claim that, as Columbus himself had confided to his journal on his third voyage, 'the world is small and the water in it very little'.[40] It could not even be based upon the much less contentious belief in the possibility of a western sea-route to a greatly enlarged continental Asia. Columbus the determined philosopher could only have set out with the *intention* of discovering a New World. This Columbus is already present, albeit in a somewhat murky form, in Las Casas's narrative. When Las Casas described Columbus as having claimed to be able to discover 'another world', what he had in mind was either a western extension of Asia or one of the many islands with which medieval cartographers had littered the 'Ocean Sea'. But it is clear that when Columbus came before Ferdinand and Isabella, he was offering something more than a sea-route to China. He was offering them 'new' if unspecified domains and, crucially, lands which were hitherto 'locked in darkness' – to all that is but their aboriginal inhabitants who, because they were not yet Christians, lacked the power to see. For Las Casas, Columbus had clearly discovered the New World, not merely for the rest of Europe, but for the whole of mankind. These claims have some basis in Columbus's own account of his objectives and in his insistence upon his rights to political authority over the lands of which he had 'taken possession'. They also suited the image of Columbus the prophetic visionary, which Las Casas had been concerned to promote, as well as they suited the image of Columbus the scientific experimentalist. Having, Las Casas tells us, reasoned from 'authorities and examples and experiences, both of his own and others' (what these were Las Casas does not say)

> that there must exist lands in the Ocean Sea of which no man had had prior notice, he determined, to affront whatever dangers and labours that might befall him (which were many and such and so continuous that it is impossible to describe them in such a way that they would be believed) to unlock the locks which the Ocean had

closed since the Flood, and by his own person to discover another world.[41]

Las Casas, however, had been cautious. Columbus could easily have supposed that there might be undiscovered islands in the Atlantic because, as Las Casas points out, 'in his days ... the Cape Verde Islands and the Azores and a great part of Africa and Ethiopia' had all been discovered. Discovery, Las Casas suggests, was a feature of the age. Later generations, however, were not so moderate. The Abbé Raynal, for instance, claimed to believe that Christopher Columbus 'knew by instinct that there must be another continent, and that it was up to him to discover it'. The outcome of his determination had, in Raynal's view, been generally appalling, but the idea was 'one of the greatest which has ever entered into the human spirit'.[42] Even the more sceptical Edmund Burke who had a firmer grasp on the historical figure than most, claims that, although Columbus's maps were wrong, he 'undertook to extend the boundaries which ignorance had given to the world'.[43] By the second half of the eighteenth century, this Columbus had been successfully integrated into a genealogy of modern science.

iii

Columbus's success, as Kepler may have been the first to note,[44] could also be taken as evidence of a very different kind of scientific occurrence: that a false theory may lead to some quite startlingly unexpected results. As Thomas Spratt, the first historian of the Royal Society, observed in 1667,

> It is not to be questioned that many inventions of great moment have been brought forth by authors who began upon suppositions thought to be untrue. As it frequently happens to philosophers as it did to Columbus.

Provided, he believed, that such people had, as Columbus clearly had, the courage of their own convictions, they will in the end 'be guided to the truth itself'.[45] But for most of those who looked upon the discovery as a turning point in the history of European civilization, it was hard to accept that this had been the outcome of mere persistence in what was clearly, with hindsight, a false hypothesis. As Cornelius de Pauw, author of the *Recherches philosophiques sur les Américains* (Philosophical Researches on the Americans, 1769) and of the article on 'America' in the *Encyclopédie* argued, nothing so striking as the discovery of America could ever be the outcome of chance. No one could simply have stumbled by fortune and false reasoning upon a new continent. To accept such a proposition would have been to threaten the epistemological status of scientific discovery through experiment. On de Pauw's account, all peoples belonging to the same climatic zone and possessed of the same industry must come across much the same things in nature at much the same time, even if they have no knowledge of each other's existence, just as the Chinese and the Europeans had independently and with no cultural contacts between them discovered the compass, porcelain, printing and gunpowder. Discovery is a product of civilization. At any given stage in their development, all cultures will display more or less the same features. The agents of these 'discoveries' may be independent as far as their actions are concerned, but they are agents of a specific set of cultural laws. Columbus was just such an agent. Far from stumbling across America, claimed de Pauw, he had, in fact, 'invented' it seven years 'before the date of his first navigation in 1492'.[46]

In the figure of Columbus who had divined the existence of America, whether with the assistance of the Florentine cosmographer, Toscanelli, or from what he had been told by a ancient pilot he was widely thought to have met on one of his earlier voyages or, as Kepler believed, from the direction of the winds,[47] the scientific community and more generally all those who, in the seventeenth and eighteenth centuries wished to challenge the cultural hegemony of the 'Ancients', had created a culture-hero. In the words of the early nineteenth-century French historian, Jules Michelet, Columbus had become 'one of those five or six men' who were 'the heroes of the will' (*les herós de la volonté*) and who, because they alone had proved able to drag themselves out of the intellectual slime of 'the Gothic middle-ages'[48] had transformed the modern world. Together with Luther, Calvin, Vesalius, Servetus, Dumoulin, Cujas, Rabelais, Motaigne, Shakespeare and Cervantes – the list is Michelet's – Columbus, both in what he had achieved, and in the changes which had been effected as a consequence of his discoveries, had joined the ranks of the architects of the Age of Reason. These were the men who, because of their refusal to accept what Spratt had called 'the rubbish of the Ancients',[49] had become the creators of the modern world. They were, said d'Alembert, those who had 'raised a corner of the curtain which had hidden from us the truth',[50] and it was on their achievements that the new ordering of knowledge, of which his *Encyclopédie* was to provide a record, was to be based.

With the creation in the eighteenth century of a determinedly speculative and philosophical history, Columbus's discovery and his conception of that discovery became, as did the inventions of Galileo, Descartes and Harvey, not only an event in the history of science; it became also, and primarily so, an event in the history of the European consciousness. For the eighteenth-century historians – for Robertson, for Raynal, for Voltaire – Columbus was not merely a bold empiricist, he was as he had been for Las Casas and Oviedo, a man with a vision. This time, however, the vision is not one of gold nor of souls-to-be-converted; it is not even, particularly, a vision of new worlds waiting to be discovered. It is a vision of the new cultural order which would inevitably follow from the sudden widening of our geographical and anthropological horizons. Columbus, as Raynal said, had perceived a 'new order of things beyond the several discoveries whereas both the common man and the wise man had seen only the discoveries themselves'.[51] Raynal's Columbus had foreseen not only the existence of America, he had also understood something of what its discovery would mean both for its inhabitants and for the peoples of Europe. He had, in a sense, already anticipated that prolonged debate which began in the eighteenth century – and to which Raynal had himself had contributed – over the nature of the 'impact' of the Old World on the New.

iv

The image of Columbus, and with him the understanding of the significance of his discovery, would now in the last decade of the eighteenth century take a further turn. This was the work of Humboldt. For Humboldt, Columbus was far more of a real historical figure than he had been for any of his predecessors. He had read the early narratives – primarily the works of Las Casas, Oviedo, Acosta, and Peter Martry – and some of the later and more general histories such as those of Antonio de Herrera and Francisco Javier Clavigero, as well as Washington Irving's romanticizing biography. The extended and detailed account of the discoverer's life which he incorporated into that encyclopaedic history of the geography of America, the *Examen critique de l'histoire de la géographie du nouveau continent* (Critical Examination of the History of the Geography of the New Continent, 1836–9), and later, in a revised form, into *Kosmos*, Humboldt's philosophical history of the physical universe was, he claimed, an attempt to describe 'a representative of the ancient customs of Liguria and Spain'. Humboldt fully recognized that Columbus had been not so much a determined experimentalist as 'the unforeseen, almost involuntary, instrument of the discovery of the New World'.[52] For Humboldt the discovery was an event in world-history which had been inescapable. Not because sooner or later someone would have run into America if Columbus had not done so, but because the development of the human mind required, at this stage in its development, precisely *this* kind of experience. With the discovery of the New World, a new epoch – the 'epoch of Columbus' as Humboldt called it[53] – had begun in the history of the European consciousness poised 'on that uncertain border where the middle ages and the modern world merge with one another'.[54]

Humboldt's view of the historical process was, however, more evolutionary than that of many of his predecessors. Whereas the earlier historians of the discovery of America had seen the ages of man as discrete and self-determining, Humboldt preferred to use the same language to describe man's journey through time as he did his journey through space. The isolines and isotherms which bind together phenomena in the natural world had, he believed, their analogues in the temporal chains which bind together the lives of men. He was careful to locate each of the great events in his account of the progress of civilization within the context which had produced it. Genius for him, however remarkable it may be, is never a wholly isolated phenomenon, any more than a plant type or a rock formation can be wholly isolated from the vegetation or the geology which encompasses it. All of the significant moments in the progress of what he refers to as 'civilization' have been anticipated to some degree by previous moments. The seeds, to use another of his metaphors, germinated in one age are carried forward to another in which they finally bear fruit; just as every species of plant may travel along its individual isoline from one part of the globe to the next.

But there are still boundaries – the lines which separate one epoch from another – just as there are strata which divide one rock-formation from another. Columbus may now have been transformed into the instrument of an inescapable (if also entirely secular) process, but it was not a matter of indifference to Humboldt, any more than it had been to Las Casas, what kind of instrument he was.

Humboldt's Columbus is still the man whose 'creative thoughts' had given 'the unexpected thrust forward to the march of civilization',[55] still the man whose 'lucidity of spirit' had made his particular discovery possible, still the man, as he was for Michelet, who had succeeded where others might have failed because of the power of his will.[56]

But the kind of history to which he now belonged was very different from anything which had preceded it. For Humboldt history was a function of the environment. Men are the products of the climates, rock-formations, and above all the vegetation by which they are surrounded. Humboldt's plant geography, his 'natural physics', had been intended to demonstrate the lines which link not only the different species, but also the varying configurations of what he sometimes called 'the empire of man'.[57] Once these lines had been drawn, he believed, it would be possible to distinguish clearly between those features which could be used to unite 'states and neighbouring nations' and those which 'present to their commerce and communication obstacles more powerful than the mountains or the sea'.[56] His *Vues des Cordillères et monuments des peuples indigènes* (Views of the Cordillères and of the Monuments of the Native Peoples) of 1810 was, he explained, an attempt to present 'in a single work the gross monuments of the indigenous peoples of the Americas, and the picturesque views of the mountainous countries those peoples inhabit', in the hope that he might thus be able 'to bring together objects whose connectedness cannot escape the wisdom of those who are given to the philosophical study of the human spirit'.[59]

Unlike plants, however, men – even the as yet unformed Amerindians – are capable of transcending the conditions imposed upon them by the natural world. Columbus's voyages are the culminating incident in the history of one such moment of transcendence.

Both the *Examen critique* and *Kosmos* are histories not so much of man's acquisition of knowledge about the cosmos, as of his perception of it. *Kosmos*, in particular, that 'mad fancy', as Humboldt described it, 'of representing in a single work the whole material world',[60] corresponds to Humboldt's own conviction that all the sciences, natural and moral, could be understood as a single unified whole. As Mary Louise Pratt has said of him, Humboldt's objective was to re-invent America in order to create a 'new kind of planetary consciousness'.[61] His ambition, he claimed, had always been to become a physicist 'as Bacon called for in the *Sylva Sylvarum*'.[62] 'I am trying,' he wrote to Joseph Banks as early as 1797, 'to penetrate the secrets of organization and to bring the sciences together'. *Kosmos*, written nearly fifty years later, was to be both the fulfilment and the dissemination of this project. This massive work which gripped the citizenry of Weimar with what Humboldt called 'Kosmos-fever' was, he told a friend, originally to have been entitled simply *The Book of Nature* – the 'sort of thing one finds in the Middle Ages by Albertus Magnus'.[63]

In the context of this project, Columbus, the agent of the transformation of the human spirit, is not so much a daring rationalist – indeed, as we have seen, the truth-value of his geographical claims is largely irrelevant – as he is the sensitive and precise observer of nature. The story of the discoverer's struggle with the monarchs of Europe and their ignorant cosmographers, though still treated as exemplary, is of little immediate significance. Columbus's vision is not one of the probable existence of a new world, it is instead an image *of* that world. It is a vision based neither upon reading nor upon inspired scientific conjecture. It is one based upon an intuitive poetic perception of the natural world. For Humboldt, Columbus was a man who had responded, as all good experimentalists must, to 'the mere contact with great natural phenomena', but he had instantly transformed those intuitions into 'the perceptions required for accurate observation', and he had achieved this despite the disadvantage of the 'entire absence of any preliminary knowledge of natural history'.[64]

Like most eighteenth-century historians of science, Humboldt saw histories in terms of instructive (or subversive) genealogies. And just as both Robertson and Raynal had located Columbus somewhere on a line which ran from Euclid through Copernicus, Kepler and Galileo to Newton, so Humboldt placed him on one which ran from Petrarch and Bembo at one end, to Buffon and Goethe at the other, the two great poets of the natural world who had made possible the literary–scientific investigations of the early Romantics, of which Humboldt himself was an exponent. The full power of Columbus's descriptions of the New World may now, Humboldt admitted, be available only to those 'acquainted with the ancient power of the language of that time'. But it was evident, even through the opacity of Columbus's somewhat lumpen prose, to discern the force of his response to the natural world, and that his 'simple love of nature' had enabled him to 'comprehend every individual object which was previously unknown to him'.[65] What Humboldt had done by so re-adjusting the image of Columbus's achievement, was to appropriate him as one of his own intellectual ancestors. Humboldt is not interested in Columbus the 'projector', because Humboldt himself had no such projects to offer. He was concerned with him as the 'discoverer', the 'namer'; above all, he was concerned with him as the man who had mapped and made transportable the very startling newness of the New World. This, for instance, could have been an account of Humboldt and Bonpland's own journey:

On arriving 'in a new world under a new heaven' he [Columbus] noted carefully the form of the land, the physiognomy of the vegetation, the habits of the animals, the distribution and variation of the earth's magnetism.[66]

The historical Columbus, the Columbus who had famously heard nightingales singing in Hispaniola, had, of course, done none of these things.

Like Columbus, Humboldt too had reduced the dimensions of the globe, for he too had brought the New World home to the Old. Climbing up the slopes of Chimborazo in Venezuela, then believed to be the highest peak in the world, Humboldt passed through climate after climate, vegetational stratum after vegetational stratum. From this he could, he said, offer a 'profile of a great part of the world'.[67] Profiles, like isolines, could be used to contain and stratify the globe. They could be used, too, to dissolve in the imagination, as Humboldt's own acts of attachment had done, the seemingly limitless distances which separated the New World from the Old.

In 1806, Goethe drew a sketch for Humboldt's *Naturgemalde der Tropenlander* (Physical Portrait of the Tropics) which he claimed to have found of the greatest interest, but in need of some visual representation. Goethe's sketch, printed in the *Allegemeine geographischen Ephemeriden* in 1813, was, he said, an attempt to represent the respective heights of the highest mountain ranges in the two continents. But it was also a striking icon of Humboldt's entire scientific project. For in Goethe's drawing, the ocean which separates Europe from America has been erased. In their place at the bottom of the scene is a stone slab inscribed with Humboldt's name. And, Goethe explained, 'in order to show those men who have climbed to the highest heights in both parts of the world, I dared to place little figures on both peaks'. Standing, therefore, just below the summit of Chimborazo is the minuscule figure of Humboldt himself. Standing on the other side, on the top of Montblanc, is the famous physicist and Alpinist, Horace-Benedict de Saussure. Floating between the two men, 'in those regions where, a few years before, only the imagination of mankind was able to venture',[68] Goethe has drawn in 'according to his own indication' the balloon piloted by his friend and Humboldt's, the celebrated balloonist Louis Joseph Gay-Lussac. (See figure 5.)

v

Humboldt's Columbus and Humboldt himself also shared another feature in common. They both – and this surely is the point of the long suggestive analogies in both the *Examen Critique* and *Kosmos* – belonged to transformative moments in the progress of human civilization. Their objectives and achievements were clearly dissimilar. But it was evident that, just as Columbus's voyages had prefigured Humboldt's own, so the fifteenth century had prefigured the early nineteenth century. During Columbus's lifetime and that of his immediate successors, the drive of curiosity, which in Humboldt's schema had replaced Divine Providence as the motor of history, had generated many of the scientific

5.   Drawing by Goethe showing the relative elevations of the mountains in the New and the Old Worlds from the *Allegemeine geographischen Ephemeriden*, 1813.

concerns which would only finally be resolved in Humboldt's own day. 'In a careful study of the original works of the earliest historians of the *conquista*,' he wrote in *Kosmos*,

> we often discover with astonishment . . . the germs of important physical truths. At the sight of a continent in the wide waste of waters, far removed from other lands, many of the important questions which occupy us in the present day presented themselves to the awakened curiosity . . . questions respecting the unity of the human race, and its derivations from a common normal type; the migrations of nations, the relationship of languages . . . the possibility of the migration of particular species of plants and animals.[69]

But this 'Age of Columbus' possessed another distinctive feature, without which none of this initial and disparate curiosity could have brought about the changes which Humboldt had attributed to it. It belonged, he wrote,

109

to those rare epochs in the history of the world, in which all the efforts of the human mind are invested with a determinate and common character, and manifest an unswerving direction towards a single object.[70]

This, then, was an age which was remarkable not merely for number or even the kind of its achievements, but for the fact that its agents displayed the same unifying tendencies which Humboldt himself had established as the mark of the great – and, above all, the modern – scientist.[71] And Columbus could be made its master-figure, because he more than any other of his contemporaries, or so Humboldt professed to believe, was 'not content to gather together isolated facts; he combines them, he seeks for their mutual relationship, and boldly raises them to the level of general laws'.

Humboldt, however, did not, as we have seen, believe in the existence of isolated historical phenomena. An age's distinctive properties, although seemingly unlike anything which had preceded them, could, in fact, only be the outcome of long periods of gestation. In *Kosmos*, where the narrative of Columbus's life is tied directly to a meta-narrative about the evolution of the universe itself, he therefore provided a detailed account of the pre-history of the 'Age of Columbus', which ran from the crusades and the early voyages to the East to the re-discovery of the classics. It is a history described, as with all such narratives, in terms of the convergent point of a series of intellectual genealogies. One of these links Roger Bacon to Nicolas Scotus, to Albertus Magnus and Vincent of Beauvais, and finally to Francis Bacon; another traces a descent through the nominalists, Duns Scotus and William of Occam, to Nicholas of Cusa, Ramus, Campanella and Giordano Bruno. Each of these men had cast 'long beams of light . . . which we may trace through the whole of what has been called the dark ages'.[72] And each of them, as the metaphor claims, was able to illuminate one or another aspect of the natural and moral world. But because none of them (with the possible exception of Roger Bacon, whom he called 'the most comprehensive genius') had ever engaged in the kind of direct observation of nature which Columbus (and Humboldt himself) had made the subject of his investigations, their 'scholastic' philosophy could offer ultimately only forms. Ultimately theirs was, Humboldt claimed, a philosophy

deprived of ideas, deprived above all of the notions which, because they are born of a more intimate contact with the natural world, are capable of substantially enriching our intelligence.[73]

These new scientific heroes differ from their predecessors precisely in that they, who are the beneficiaries of a science which brings them into 'intimate contact' with nature, can grasp not merely the particulars but also the whole. In Columbus's world,

> The scattered images offered to the contemplation of the senses, notwithstanding their number and diversity, were gradually fused into a concrete whole; Terrestrial nature was conceived in its generality, no longer according to mere presentiments or conjectures floating in various forms before the eyes of fancy, but as the result of actual observation.[74]

Columbus, however, is not alone. The age to which he had given his name had also produced powerful transforming agents in other areas of 'the political and moral life of Europe': Luther's reformation, the discovery of the Laocöon and the Belvedere Torso, Michelangelo, Da Vinci, Titian, Raphael, Holbein and Dürer, were only the most significant of these. But since, in Humboldt's view, it is the changes in our physical world which most powerfully affect our sensibilities, it is the discovery of America which constituted 'the first link in the immeasurable chain of these fate-fraught events'.[75]

If this 'Age of Columbus' was to be made to bear such tremendous historical significance, the discovery of America could not, as had so many other useful discoveries, be merely an event – however significant – in a history which was only a history of science. Columbus, in Humboldt's account, had brought into existence a world in which man's achievements, instead of being, as they had always been in the past, 'purely scientific', were now elevated to become part of what he called the 'dominant character of the age, its distinctive tendency'.[76] For the belief in the unity of the sciences, and the conviction which all historians had had, since the sixteenth century, that the discovery was so singular an event as to constitute a 'species of new creation', meant that like Galileo's proof of the heliocentric theory, like the invention of printing, it had to be an event in the history of man's moral understanding.[77] It was for this reason that in 1655, Georgius Hornius, one of the first historians of the new philosophy, had given it a prominent place in the history of moral philosophy.[78]

The Columbine vision was now represented not merely as a triumph for experimental science, but also as a radical shift in man's understanding of his relationship both with his fellow men and with the natural world. A new world of European moral and social understanding had begun with the discovery of the New World of America. 'We may record,' wrote Humboldt, how, since that grand era, a new and active state of the intellect and feelings, bold wishes and hopes scarcely to be restrained, have gradually penetrated into the whole of civil society.[79]

This, too, is the thrust of Michelet's famous remark that

Two things belong to this age [the sixteenth century] more than to all its predecessors: the discovery of the world, the discovery of man.[80]

For both Michelet and Humboldt, the discovery of America constituted a transformative stage in what Humboldt called 'the progress of all nations towards the attainment of an elevated mind and system of morality'.[81] 'Never,' he wrote, 'has a purely material discovery, by extending [man's] horizon, produced so extraordinary and lasting a moral change'.[82] As an event in other contiguous histories, the discovery of America became not simply, as it had been for Gómara, a turning point in human history as isolated as the Incarnation. Instead, it came to form part of an age marked by similar achievements in cosmology, philosophy, aesthetics, law, economics: 'one of those rare epochs', in Humboldt's words, 'in which all intellectual endeavours possess a common character and all are directed towards a determined gaol'.[83] This age, which Michelet had called the 'Renaissance', was marked not by a set of conveniently spaced dates, but by a continuous series of events which, taken together, constituted the beginnings of modernity, 'les temps modernes'. 'The sixteenth century,' wrote Michelet, 'in its widest and proper limits, goes from Columbus to Copernicus to Galileo, from the discovery of the land to the discovery of the heavens',[84] and the 'clarifying beams' of this age were the discovery of 'printing, antiquity, America, the Orient and the true system of the world [Galilean astronomy]'.

vi

But just how had all this come about? For Robertson, Raynal and Smith, the answer had been an uncomfortably mechanical one: commerce. The discovery of America, and of the sea-route to India, had hugely extended the range and nature of the ancient trade-routes. It had not only brought about the completion of the final stage in the development of European civilization from agricultural communities to commercial societies. It had also opened up the possibility of greater communications between the now significantly greater number of the races in the world.

But for Humboldt no such explanation was available. Concerned as he was with the circulation of life through those isotherms, isolines, isodynamics and isogonics with which he had encircled the globe, the relationship between natural and moral agency had to be intelligible in terms of the perceptual relationship between how we understand ourselves and what we know of the physical world we inhabit. 'In the great chain of causes and effects', as he said in the *Essai sur la géographie des plantes* (Essay on the Geography of Plants, 1807), 'no material, no activity can be considered in isolation'.[85] It was, he argued, simply unthinkable, therefore, that a culture should remain unchanged by the recognition that for centuries it had lived in ignorance of the very existence of half the globe it inhabits.

Humboldt was not the first to come to this conclusion. Erasmus, Cardano and Campanella had all, in their very different ways, had similar intuitions. And in 1793 Condorcet, in his *Esquisse d'un tableau historique des progrès de l'esprit humain* (Outline of an Historical Account of the Progress of the Human Spirit), had argued, in an historical account which was not unlike Humboldt's own, that

It was only in this epoch that man could know the world he in-habited; study, in every country, the human species modified by the sustained influence of natural causes or social institutions; observe the products of the earth or of the seas, at every temperature and in every climate. . . . The knowledge of these things could bring new truths to the sciences and destroy accredited falsehoods.[86]

Humboldt's view of the place of America in the development of European society was, however, far more dramatic than that of any of his predecessors. Unlike Erasmus or Cardano, unlike even Condorcet, he was convinced that the discovery of America had 'multiplied the objects of knowledge and of man's contemplation'[87] to the point where he had been driven to adopt a new mental stance to cope with the information now available to him. In Humboldt's view of causality, scientific change is the consequence of an intellectual response to a 'sudden increase in the stock of ideas', a response which, in turn, would become the agent of new patterns of 'intellectual and moral effects'.[88] And just as the landscape 'determines the imagination and aesthetic sense of peoples', so the range of their knowledge of the world deter-mines their moral history – what Humboldt's brother, Wilhelm, called *anthropologie*.[89]

Humboldt's claim was that perceptions may themselves be con-stitutive of moral change. It is the contemplation of 'the objects of man's knowledge' which alters his conceptual habits. There was, he argued, a natural history of man's moral awareness, just as there were natural histories of every other aspect of man's existence. In the *Essai sur la géographie des plantes*, he provided a brief account of what such a history might be like. It would, he said, be divided into three stages: the 'acquisition of natural laws', the 'events of the world which have suddenly widened the extent of the horizon and observation', and finally 'the discovery of new means of perception'. Each of these stages leads ineluctably to the next. The causal link between them is provided by the kind of aesthetic experience which Humboldt himself had often encountered when, 'in the middle of these researches into the natural world, we prepare ourselves for an intellectual joy, a moral liberty, which will strengthen us against the blows of destiny'.[90] All three would be combined in the truly remarkable individual who would thus, once he had reached the final stage, be able to 'pursue freedom in a hitherto untried path'.[91] Columbus of course was such a one, as were those other great fifteenth- and sixteenth-century masters of natural representation, Michelangelo, Leonardo, Raphael, Holbein and Dürer.

vii

Humboldt's implicit sensationalism required no account of the mechanisms of intellectual and conceptual change. It also allowed him to make one further, and more dramatic, claim on behalf of the discovery of America. For Humboldt, this had marked a turning point, not only in the range of 'objects of contemplation' known to man, or even in the means of communication which made knowledge and human understanding possible; it had also brought about a radical transformation in the very methods by which knowledge was acquired. Humboldt believed that until the discovery of America the intellectual progress of (European) man had been determined by his capacity to respond to 'external occurrences'. His mind was thus constrained precisely by what he knew about his natural environment. But once America had been added to the 'objects of contemplation' now available to the European scientific gaze, the intellect 'henceforth produces . . . grand results by its own peculiar and internal power in every direction at the same time'.[92] Once, that is, it had grasped the significance of its collective encounter with the New World, the human intellect had begun to operate in new and distinctly modern ways.

But although the discovery might have altered all our mental worlds in ways which were unprecedented, it had not brought the process of discovery to an end. The 'century of Columbus', he wrote in the *Examen critique*, by suddenly extending the sphere of our knowledge, has given a new release to future centuries. It is the property of discoveries that as they touch upon the collected interests of society, they increase both the circle of conquests and the terrain left to conqueror. Feeble souls believe that at each epoch humanity has reached the culminating point of its march forwards. They forget that as they advance, so the field left to cover reveals itself to be still yet greater, bounded by a horizon that recedes without end.

By thus extending 'the circle of what is known', the sudden presence of America had also 'opened further the prospect of what still remains to be overcome'.[93] For the scientific discoverer, the intellectual conqueror, there can be no end to the quest. Science constitutes a form of conquest and of possession. But the objects it seeks to possess are infinite. The plea of Alexander the Great that we should all 'leave something still to conquer', cannot, Humboldt said solemnly, 'apply to scientific discoveries, to the conquests of the intellect'.[94] The modern world which Humboldt inhabited was no longer one of simple linear progression. It was one of an atemporal creativity; of, in his own metaphor, an ever-receding but perennially visible horizon. In this modern world, the Humboldtian vision of the unity of the sciences is to be found not, as had been the case in the 'Middle Ages', in chronology, in those multiple, instructive (and sometimes subversive) genealogies with which *Kosmos* is littered; it is to be found in physiognomy, in a global physics which will match Schiller's vision of an aesthetic empire, where men will be led to a new and most lasting union 'beyond the state'.[95] The discovery of America had been instrumental thus in freeing man from his past and placing him in direct contact with nature. If, as Humboldt had claimed, the European mind was now capable of producing 'grand results by its own peculiar and internal power in every direction at the same time', its final role had been to bring traditional history to an end. For the scientific discoverer, the intellectual conqueror, there can be now no end to his quest. However it may be measured, charted, sampled or described, the horizon of our understanding must continue to recede for the rest of human time.

CHAPTER FOUR
The Savage Decomposed

Mon idée seroit donc de décomposer, pour ainsi dire, un homme
Denis Diderot, *Lettre sur les sourds et les muets*

i

If America had merely been different from Europe, if its discovery had been only a spur, however remarkable, to mankind's development away from inspired conceptualization to true scientific understanding, then, as Jean de Léry had observed, 'Asia and Africa could also be named new worlds with regard to us'.[1] But America, which was unmistakably, sometimes shockingly, 'new' in ways that neither of the other continents were, belonged also, as they did not, to the collective human past. America was still, in John Locke's celebrated phrase, 'in the beginning'[2] of the whole world, and its inhabitants, unlike the Asians or the Africans, had seemed at first sight to live in the 'Golden Age of their customs'.[3]

America was new in both senses of the word: new in relation to geological and human time, and new in relationship to us, the European observers. This is the paradox of Rousseau's savage Caribs. They are contemporary with the reader, yet they belong to a period of human infancy. It was a paradox for all those who saw in this new land the image of a world which man, in his progress from the state of nature to civil society, had had to abandon. They, these 'savages', are not like us as we are now, the argument went, they are like us as we once were. Thus, as the European vision of the world moved westwards, so it moved also inexorably backwards. The great debate in the eighteenth and nineteenth centuries over the literal newness of America, the claim that its animal and plant life had been arrested in its development, or were immature – that pumas were lions which had never evolved, Amerindians men who had never matured into civil beings – records some of the confusions which this paradox involved.[4]

The conjunction of time and space meant that Latour's 'immutable mobiles' – including the traveller's narratives – now had to travel through both dimensions. The Brazilians whom Montaigne had met at

Rouen had brought with them to Europe not the image of a new world but, as their observations make clear, only the infancy of *his* world. By the end of the eighteenth century, this journey had become a familiar one. 'The traveller–philosopher,' wrote Joseph-Marie Degerando in 1800,

> who sails to the farthest corners of the Globe, travels, in fact, along the road of time. He travels in the past. Every step he takes is a century passed. The Islands he reaches are for him the cradle of human society. The peoples whom our ignorant vanity despises are revealed to him like ancient and majestic monuments from the origins of time, monuments which are a thousand times more worthy of our admiration and respect than the famous pyramids which line the banks of the Nile.[5]

In order to sustain this kind of comparison between new worlds and their 'old' inhabitants, both the simultaneous newness and the antiquity of America had to be kept always in focus. There were many ways of achieving this, but the most sensitive, most complex and, for my purposes, the most illuminating, was in the field of language.

ii

'Language is the instrument of empire', as the Spanish grammarian Antonio de Nebrija had told Queen Isabella, in that same *annus mirabilis* of 1492. To conquer and, above all, to convert, to transform cultures into some semblance of your own, relied in the first instance upon speech. From the day that Columbus unfurled his banners on 'Guanahani', the question had arisen of whose language would triumph in the new worlds he had now taken for Castile, by an act which was itself almost wholly linguistic.

The struggle for political and cultural control in America was also, at a crucial level, a struggle for linguistic supremacy. The first Spanish and Portuese settlers and the first missionaries had accepted the need to understand the native languages. What we know of American linguistics we owe largely to a group of missionaries, most of them Franciscans, working in the first half of the sixteenth century. Even pre-contact records, Mexican screen folds and Inka *quipus*, were admitted as evidence for land-claims before Spanish courts in the early part of the century. But as the real difficulties of transforming complex, and varied, Amerindian cultures – with equally complex and varied languages – into ones that were Christian and European grew more apparent, a sometimes bitter struggle developed over the legitimacy of using Indian

118

languages for instruction, and hence over the inherent worth of those languages. On one side of this conflict there were those, for the most part members of the religious orders, who claimed, as did for instance the Jesuit historian, José de Acosta, that not only were the autochthonous American languages fit vehicles for acculturation, but that as they were the only possible road into the unsettling minds of the Amerindian peoples, they were also the only possible means to true evangelization. No people, he argued, will willingly adopt the religion and the culture of another, unless it can be persuaded of the desirability of what it is being asked to accept in terms which are immediately and powerfully intelligible to it. On the other side were the regular clergy, and increasingly, the crown and its agents, who shared the view that the belief systems of a culture were too closely tied to the language spoken by that culture for any form of instruction to be possible in any other tongue. 'Speaking Christian' came to mean speaking Spanish, or possibly Latin. These men also shared the belief that the progress of the Castilian empire, as Nebrija had suggested, was inextricably bound up with progress of instruction in Castilian.

Both sides recognized the power of language, and both knew that, when such things as cultural and religious understanding were at stake, language could contaminate as easily as it could ennoble. The fact that in certain regions of America, in the Andean highlands and the province of São Paolo, the indigenous languages were frequently used, despite their supposed deficiencies, not merely for purposes of religious instruction, but also in daily conversation, and not only by Indians but also by Europeans, created a spectre of a settler culture in the process of gradual 'nativization'. Languages could contaminate in other ways too. No one, it seemed, could ultimately hope to escape the acculturation which language acquisition seemed necessarily to imply. To translate, in particular, the sacred texts, even the catechism, into any tongue other than a 'Christian' one was not merely to run the risk of introducing probable solecisms so that, as one Franciscan pointed out, 'the congregation of the Saints' came out in Quechua as 'the merriment of the Saints'; more significantly it was, in some sense, to alienate those texts altogether. By the end of the seventeenth century, the Castilian crown had introduced legislation to prevent the use of all Indian languages for the purposes of evangelization, because it was deemed to be impossible, 'even in the most perfect of them . . . to explain well and with propriety the mysteries of the Holy Catholic Faith'. And in 1727, the Portuguese outlawed the use of Tupi for any purposes whatsoever.[6]

Underpinning this debate, however, was a far broader dispute over the relationship between language and the orgin and development of societies. All the participants in the battle over the worth of Amerindian languages agreed, *mutatis mutandis*, on one premiss: that language was the prime indicator of rationality, that what a man spoke was, to a very large degree, what a man was. And consequently, that one immediate and obvious point of entry into an alien culture was through its speech. In the eighteenth century, as we shall see, the discussions over the languages of the 'primitive', the 'savage', the 'barbarian', became a key register in which theories on the evolution and development were established – as well as the relative worth and hence possible commensurability of Amerindian societies.

None of this is surprising. The Hellenistic Greeks who bequeathed to modern Europe the concept of a single human species and the term with which to describe it – *anthropos*, 'Man' – also bequeathed to us the first term which was capable of making distinctions within that species. The term was *barbaros*, 'barbarian'. And a barbarian was, before he was anything else, one who was a babbler, one who spoke not Greek but only 'barbar'. The close association in Greek thought between intelligible speech and reason made it possible to assume that those who were devoid of *logos* in the one sense were probably also devoid of it in the other. For most Greeks, and for their cultural heirs, the ability to use language, together with the ability to form societies, became the indicators of rationality, those things which could truly distinguish men from other animals. Only men possess reason and only men, or so Aristotle claimed, possess as tongues organs which are sufficiently broad, loose and soft to be able to form intelligible sounds at all.[7] At the most fundamental level it might be possible to say that those who do not speak like us do not conceptualize like us, and those who do not conceptualize like us, are *not* like us.

It is little wonder then that the shock of the encounter with America should so often have been registered in linguistic terms. 'You know what I call the language of this land?' 'Barchilon' asks the astonished Justino, in Quiroga's *Dialogos de la verdad*,

> the most outrageous gibberish that has ever been used in all the world. See what land you are in, that everything that you dare to think or say requires a daring which competes with that of Hell itself.[8]

Let us now go for an imaginary walk in the woods of French Canada in the first decade of the eighteenth century. Here two men are engaged in a heated debate. One of them is a Frenchman, Louis-Armand Lom d'Arce, a sometime soldier of fortune and the self-styled – since his father had sold the title to settle his business debts – Baron de Lahontan. The other is a Huron, called by Lahontan 'Adario', a 'savage of good sense' and one 'who has travelled', notably to France, where he has had the opportunity to see Europeans in their natural environment, and to New York where, to judge by what he tells Lahontan, he had lengthy discussions with the English settlers on the conflicting claims of Anglicanism and Catholicism.[9] The subject of their dispute is the relative merits of French, that is 'civil', and Indian, that is 'savage', society. Lahontan is attempting to persuade his 'savage' interlocutor of the superiority of his world. Adario, for his part, who did not much care for what he had seen of France, is determined to defend the values of what he frequently refers to as 'the woods'.

Lahontan's *Dialogues curieux entre l'auteur et un sauvage de bon sens qui a voyagé* (Curious Dialogues Between the Author and a Savage of Good Sense Who Has Travelled), which was first printed in 1703 as a supplement to his *Nouveau Voyages* and *Mémoires de l'Amérique septentrionale* (New Voyages and Memoirs of North America), became enormously popular.[10] Lahontan himself was frequently regarded as an unreliable charlatan, a man who professed to find the life of savages far superior to anything to be found in Europe yet spent all his energies attempting to regain his family's title and lands. In December 1693 he was forced to flee from Canada to Portugal and spent the next seventeen years wandering through southern and central Europe. His books were published under somewhat murky circumstances, and he was even denounced as a literary fiction. 'I assure you,' wrote Leibnitz (who knew and claimed to like Lahontan) to his friend Friedrich Guillaume Bierling in 1710, 'that the Baron de Lahontan is a real man, not a fiction and that his travels are as authentic as he is'.[11]

But his accounts of his life in Canada, coming as they did from a man who had had prolonged contact with both the Huron and the Algonquin, and who was also a member of the minor nobility with a fluent, if not exactly elegant, style, suited the purposes of many of those *philosophes* looking for compelling and detailed models of man's pre-civil existence, which they could transform for their own ends. Here was a literate eye-witness of the virtues and the life-styles of the 'savage' writing in a recognizably 'philosophical' idiom. Voltaire and Rousseau borrowed heavily from him. Indeed almost every *bon sauvage* of Canadian origin created by succeeding writers owes something, and frequently everything, to Adario. Leibnitz was so persuaded by Lahontan's tales of a tribal existence of peaceful co-operation and family love without the benefit of government, laws or arms, that he claimed that they had demonstrated the falsity of Hobbes's account of the origins of society by proving that 'men are neither sufficiently driven by their good nature, nor sufficiently compelled by their wickedness to acquire a government and to leave the state of nature'.[12]

Adario is the embodiment of the virtues of life in the state of nature, yet because of his travels he is equipped with a detailed knowledge of European culture and a fully developed European vocabulary. His critique of French society is in many respects familiar enough. He reviles the French for the unnecessary luxuries they crave, for their frivolities and their disdain for all that they have not created and cannot, therefore, fully possess. His two main preoccupations, however, are with the nature of European religious belief and with the law. And since, as becomes clear in the course of the dialogue, for the civil man these are things which are dependent upon the manipulation of texts, at the heart of much of what Adario has to say on these subjects is a set of observations on the place of language in the structure of human society.

Underpinning all the criticism which Adario levels against the world which the figure of Lahontan in the *Dialogues* (whom I shall call 'Lahontan') attempts to press upon him are two familiar claims. The first is based upon a clear and self-evident distinction between what is natural and what is artificial, between the law of nature (the *ius naturae*) and the purely human law (the *lex humana*). The savage understands that some aspects of all men's lives are inescapably the products of culture. The Huron himself hunts with a bow and arrow. He wears rudimentary clothes. He lives in *cabanes* of his own manufacture. But he never acquires more than his self-consciously simple life demands. And he orders his life, not by any artificial code, but only according to the dictates of Nature which he can understand, as can all men, by the simple use of unfettered reason. From Adario's viewpoint, to confuse or equate the artificial and the natural, to claim, as the fictional Lahontan persists in doing, that what is self-evidently the product of human convention has, in fact, the force of natural law, is to retreat into a world of one's own making where the rule of reason is replaced by that blind adherence to received opinion which the Christians call 'faith'. For Adario the world is a simple transparent place. His understanding of God is deist, in that it supposes a direct correspondence between what is and what can be seen. By the time Lahontan came to write his *Dialogues*, this had already become an easily recognizable image (there were, of course, many others) of the non-European 'savage'. Placed upon the rack to force him to reveal the whereabouts of his treasure, the 'Montezuma' (in historical fact, the Inka Atahualpa) of Dryden's play the *Indian Emperor*, written in 1665, is lectured by a priest on the truthfulness of Christianity. Montezuma (an Anglican Whig in disguise), who argues by reason alone, consistently gets the better of his opponent. Finally the priest, driven into a logical corner, turns from argument to command. 'Renounce your carnal reason and obey,' he tells the Aztec. But Montezuma, like Adario, like every subsequent *bon sauvage*, knows that:

> The light of nature should I thus betray, T'were to wink hard that I might see the light of day
>
> (Act V. Sc.ii.)

To the Indian Emperor and those like him, the Europeans' social world and the precepts which underpin their religious beliefs, even if they were to be given a more sympathetic mouthpiece than Dryden's priest, are founded upon a false assumption: that God's design for the world cannot be properly understood through his works and that a great part of how we behave and what we choose to believe is dependent, not upon the operation of our rational minds, but upon the authority of a few. These few claim access to a special form of knowledge which is not only not of this world, but is, in many significant respects, a direct contradiction of what we can know about that world through the use – all 'savages' are good Lockeans – of our senses. Those few, the 'Jesuits' as Adario persistently calls them, peddle self-evident absurdities which only the mentally blind could possibly believe. Hence the outrage of Voltaire's imaginary 'Huron' l'Ingénu (many of whose attitudes as well as what few Huron words he utters are borrowed from Lahontan) when he is confronted by the ludicrous image of a well-meaning English Jansenist called 'Gordon' who attempts to explain to him the difference between the various Christian sects. 'It is an absurdity,' he cries, 'it is an outrage against the human species, an effrontery to the supreme and infinite Being to declare:"there is a truth which is essential to Mankind and God has hidden it"'.[13]

The priests who thus fill mens' minds with obscurities, to the point where they are no longer able to see the world of nature as it really is, are the real creators of evil. For the natural man, as for Socrates, evil is only ignorance, and the deepest, most insidious form of ignorance is the false claim to knowledge.

Adario, like the Indian Emperor, like l'Ingénu, like Diderot's Tahitian sage (whom we shall meet again in the next Chapter), is a fairly conventional mouthpiece for an argument in favour of natural religion. The second of his claims, however, is one for the centrality of language in the civil man's construction of the world. For what links both 'religion' in the first part of the *Dialogues* to 'law' in the second is precisely the way in which, for Lahontan, both are determined by the word.

For natural man, for Adario, humanity is a moral property. The difference, as he puts it, between men and beavers is an innate capacity to recognize what is good and what evil, and the unswerving will to act on that recognition. For 'Lahontan', however, the difference is between those creatures who do, and those who do not, possess the capacity to create. For him man is an animal who 'stands upright on his two feet, who knows how to read and write and who has a thousand other abilities'.[14] Here 'Lahontan' is merely repeating, and Adario inverting, an ancient paradigm: the claim that all nature exists only potentially, that it is man's special skills – his *techne*, his *scientia* – which allow him to reveal its actuality, and that man is *by nature* a creator of artificial worlds. But the point here is that for 'Lahontan' man's supreme invention is not agriculture or navigation, it is, instead, language. More specifically, it is the capacity to create texts, for it is the text which will allow him to order his moral and social world without the need for reflection or for those acts of individual understanding which, for Adario, are constitutive of man's moral nature.

The attempt by the fictional Lahontan to convert Adario begins, as it must, with an appeal to the word. The truth of Christianity, 'Lahontan' tells Adario, has been written down. This is a religion based wholly upon the understanding of a set of texts. The mere existence of the Bible is itself proof of what it contains. But, replies Adario, all that this 'Bible' contains is essentially meaningless without the faith that sustains it. Yet it does not itself offer any clear or compelling reason for adopting that faith. 'These Holy Scriptures which you quote every time as the Jesuits do,' he says,

> depend upon that great faith which the Good Fathers are constantly dinning into us ('nous rompent les oreilles') but that great faith cannot be anything other than a persuasion. To believe is to be persuaded; to be persuaded is to see a thing with one's own eyes, to recognize it by clear and solid proofs.

Adario, who is a good Cartesian, knows that texts are inert. As he discovered in New York, they can be interpreted in a thousand different ways. The English he had met had claimed that their version of the Scriptures – which was wholly at variance with anything he had been taught by the Jesuits – was clearly the only true one. As for the Jesuits, 'out of five or six hundred sorts of religion [they claim] that there is only one good and true one, and that's their own'. In Adario's eyes this is clearly all nonsense. 'If I tell you,' Adario continues,

that they [the account of the Creation and the Redemption] are more likely to be fables than the truth, you will reply with arguments from your Bible. Now, the Scriptures, you once told me, were found three thousand years ago and printing is four or five centuries old, how then can you be so certain of so many different events over so many years?

Both the Bible and the Jesuit *Relations* are books, and as books neither would seem to possess the truth-value which 'Lahontan' seems to be claiming for all forms of textuality. 'Now,' insists Adario,

if we see, with our own eyes, lies in print and things other than the way they are set down on paper, how should I believe in the truth of these Bibles which were written so many centuries ago, translated from so many different languages by ignoramuses who had no understanding of their original meaning or the liars who have changed, increased or diminished the words which we find today.

'Lahontan's reply is, of course, an appeal to the status of this particular text. How, he asks, can you place the Jesuit descriptions of Canada, 'these bagatelles', on the same level as the 'Holy Writ which has been composed by authors who do not contradict one another'.[15] At this point, Adario's and 'Lahontan's mental worlds become fully incommensurable and dialogue, which has up until this point been strained, ceases to be possible altogether. For 'Lahontan' the truth of the Bible depends upon the status of its (supposed) author. For Adario, by contrast, the proof of authorship would have been the self-evident truthfulness of the Text. Had God been responsible for it, its meanings would have been blindingly simple. But, in fact, he declares indignantly, this Bible is more filled with obscurities and contradictions than any Jesuit account of Huron life. No deity of the kind 'Lahontan' has been trying to describe could possibly be responsible for such a work. As a moral tract, as an account of the Natural world, it is worthless and Adario, who can no more abandon his natural reason than Dryden's Montezuma could, will have nothing to do with it.

Adario's claims for the supremacy of reason over revelation – and by implication, for observation over interpretation – belong in part to the dispute which we examined in Chapter 2, over the status of the eye-witness. But they belong also to another, equally prolonged, similarly inconclusive, argument over the origin of language and its place in the development of human society. This is at least as old as Plato, but in the seventeenth and eighteenth centuries, as the exploration of the Americas, and subsequently of the Pacific, exposed Europeans to an increasingly wide variety of different cultures speaking a bewildering range of languages, it became a subject of wide theoretical concern.

iii

In 1866 the Linguistic Society of Paris declared that the dispute over the origin of language was now dead.[16] As Giambattista Vico had caustically observed in 1725, it was a subject in which 'the number of theories held matches the number of scholars who have investigated it'.[17] We *can* never know who uttered the first words or why or what kind of words they were. If we accept, however, the premiss that speech is what distinguishes men from beasts, then the understanding of the origin of languages is clearly central to any understanding of what the human mind is. Speculation over the origin of language was, therefore, not so much a search for real historical knowledge, as a way of writing a 'conjectural history' of man's cognitive powers and of human society.[18]

In such a history, the first language was, of course, that given by God to Adam. For most Christians, this was something of an embarrassment, since languages had generally been considered to be conventional in origin, whatever the contingencies of their individual creation, since the days of Aristotle. 'Every man', as Locke had famously noted, 'has so inviolable a liberty to make words stand for what idea he pleases'.[19] The Adamic view, like the Platonic, ascribed the existence of a necessary connection between words and things. For a Platonist, human agency is very largely eliminated and the word 'donkey' is said to express the essence of some part of what it was to *be* a donkey. On this view, of course, a *history* of language would be of no value in tracing the development of the human mind, much less of human society.

The myth of the building of the Tower of Babel, however, and the subsequent 'confusion of tongues' allowed for a complete break between the Adamic and post-Adamic periods in human history. There were some, such as the grammarian Bernard Lamy, who believed that traces of an *Ursprach* could still be detected in a number of non-European languages. For him its 'energy and harmony', still echoed in the 'intervals of breathing' in the poetry of the Persians, the Tartars, the Chinese, the Arabs, the Africans, and 'many of the peoples of America'.[20] But by the eighteenth century,[21] anyone who took any serious interest in the Adamic language had to admit that all they could say about it was mere conjecture. The language of Adam only had one certain property – universality – and that, as Leibnitz concluded, could best be reproduced by mathematics and symbolic logic.[22]

All actual languages were generally recognized to be post-Babel. Language-use, it was argued, provided a map – or rather a series of different maps – of the human mind precisely because language was a human invention, a product that is, of culture.[23] It was mutual agreement which alone ensured that the same word stood invariably for the same thing. And if all languages were conventional they had also to be transparent. Words related directly and unmysteriously to the objects in the speaker's mental world. On Locke's account, just as ideas had their origin in sensations, so the lexicon had its origin in individual human needs.[24] As the number of the objects in a person's mental and sensational world increased, so too did his vocabulary. The 'savage' clearly inhabited a social world of restricted complexity whose function was limited to meeting the barest needs of survival. His languages were, therefore, thought to be correspondingly simple. No American Indian, claimed Locke, could count above a thousand, because Amerindian languages were 'accommodated only to the few necessities of a simply and needy life unacquainted with Trade or Mathematics'.[25] As James Beattie later observed of some similarly Hobbesian communities, the Scottish Highlanders: 'We cannot imagine that those whose garments are but a rag and whose lodgings a hole should effect superfluities in their speech'.[26]

These itinerant inhabitants of the Americas who served contemporary Europeans as spokesmen against their own cultures, refer constantly to this aspect of the conjectural history of language. For the savage's understanding of European culture is severely restricted by the limits of his speech. He simply cannot understand those things for which his society has no words. And invariably the things for which he has no words are precisely those things for which none of us, as humans, would in our 'natural' state have any need. As Lahontan, who provided his *Nouveaux Voyages* with a vocabulary of Huron, observed (a point which Adario stresses in the *Dialogues*), the native inhabitants of Canada

> are ignorant of the ceremonial and complimentary terms and of a number of verbs which Europeans employ to give force to their discourses. They only know how to speak in order to know how to live. They have not a single word which is either useless or superfluous.[27]

These anti-lexica, these lists of terms which savages did *not* have, grew longer and more complex as the Europeans' knowledge of 'savage' cultures grew more detailed. They could be used either to reflect on the poverty of the savages' cultures or on the unnecessary, and malign, richness of ours. But they were always used in the same way. Words were matched against things. If the things were there so, too, it was assumed, would be the words. The Parisians who encountered the Tahitian Aotouru whom Bougainville had brought back with him were, so Bougainville tells us, shocked by his inability to learn French. Most Europeans, they pointed out, had little difficulty in acquiring the language after only a few months residence in the country. Aotouru stayed for nearly a year and still could only utter a few isolated words and phrases. But, as Bougainville tried to explain (an explanation which Diderot put to a rather different use in the *Supplément*),[28]

> those foreigners have a grammar similar to our own, moral, physical, political and social ideas identical to ours ... while the Tahitians possess only a limited number of ideas which refer to the simplest and most limited societies, and to needs which are reduced to the smallest possible number.

To have learnt French with any degree of proficiency, he continued, they would have had to create 'a world of primary ideas before they would be capable of learning the terms in our language which apply them'.[29] But, complained Bougainville, few Europeans seemed able to grasp the point. Nor, before the end of the nineteenth century, were there many who demonstrated much interest in Lafitau's observation that our languages and those of the American Indians might have such wholly different structures as to make such simple analogies of this kind meaningless.

Bougainville's claim that equivalents for the crucial terms employed in civil society cannot be found in the language of the savage, because such terms only acquire their meaning within that society, had, however, found a place in the counter-history of civility to which Adario, and Diderot's Orou (if not Bougainville's Aotouru) and every *bon sauvage* who touches on the subject belongs.[30] It is not merely, as Locke had argued, that natural men do not need such words as law or treason, faith or deceit. They do not even have access to them – any more than, as we shall see, they have access to abstractions or universals – because in the natural world of Tahiti or of the American forests such concepts simply do not exist. Aotouru, says B in Diderot's *Supplément*, could have told the Europeans nothing about his native land because, 'he would not be able to find in his language any terms which corresponded' to the *ideas* which the Europeans might have.[31] As Voltaire's L'Ingénu mockingly observes, no Huron has ever been converted to Christianity because in his language there is no word for 'inconstancy'.[32] Their language and his were simply incommensurable.

But not only are there crucial lexical differences between civil and savage languages; there are also radical differences in the uses to which such vocabularies as they do share in common are put. The savage, whose contact with nature is unmediated through any form of artifice, uses speech for the sole purpose of describing what is palpably 'out there'. As the Jansenist Gordon recognizes in his cell, the Huron 'sees things as they are, instead of the ideas which are given to us in our infancy and which make us see our lives as they are not'.[33] L'Ingénu believes only what he has good inferential reasons for believing. His speech is transparent and cannot, therefore, be used, as can the languages of civil men, to deceive about the nature of reality. The gift of lying is, as Voltaire's Inka princess Alzire laments in her struggle to confront her would-be conquerors, 'an art of Europe. It is not made for me'.[34] European languages are not only better equipped to deceive than savage ones; they also, like the Europeans' sexual, religious and social beliefs, have the capacity to attribute, in the words of Diderot's Tahitian sage, 'an arbitrary character to things'. The savage's discourse, by contrast, is only about the true, the given, nature of the world.

The Lockean account of the origin of language in sensation and need operates, of course, only at the level of the single term – of *parole*. For most seventeenth- and eighteenth-century language-theorists, however, the origin of human speech – *langue* – was to be found not so much in specific needs as in the passions.

Only the desire – or the need – to communicate passions, and specifically those complex passions which arise only within society, could explain the transition from a simple word/object relationship to the complex structures of formal speech. When, according to Rousseau, – in one of those heuristic tales of which he was so fond – the first men from different families came face to face for the first time they cried out – if they lived in the south, where life was easy – 'aimez-moi'; and if they lived in the north, where life was altogether tougher, 'aidez-moi'.[35] In both cases it was a passion, the passion for communication or the passion for survival, which first compelled man to create entire phrases.

It was, then, passion which, in the words of César Chesneau Du Marsais (author of the article on 'Accent' in the *Encyclopédie*), 'drew forth the first voices'. But for most, including Rousseau, those voices did not in the first instance speak. They sang. Song, music and the dance, those immediate, unreflective expressions of the passions, preceded articulate speech. 'Poetry, song and language,' wrote Condillac, 'all share a common origin'. From this he concluded that 'the earliest expressions were tropes . . . extremely figurative and metaphorical'. Laws, religion and the *chanson des gestes* which constituted the histories of early peoples were, he believed, all sung in the open to the assembled society, 'in order to awaken in the citizens the sentiments of love, admiration and emulation'.[36] The difficulties that contemporary singers had in making their words understood was, mysteriously, not a problem for early man, since the harmonic nature of his world ensured that the prosody of speech and the melodic line were identical. Traces of these early configurations, or so some claimed, could still be detected in the structure of Latin.

In his early state, then, man's speech habits are harmonious. He speaks, sings and dances in one seamless act of communication. This, perhaps, is why although Aotouru found it difficult to learn French, he was a passionate devotee of the Parisian Opera. It was, observed Bougainville, 'the only one of our spectacles which he liked because he was passionately fond of dancing'.[37] There was, however, another reason for supposing that the earliest, and the most primitive languages, were poetic; or, more explicitly, metaphorical. For primitive men, as for 'modern savages', explained Moses Mendelssohn in 1764, individual ideas originate as 'images'.[38] The view such persons have of the world is just that – a *view*. 'Our mind is a moving picture,' observed Diderot, in his *Lettre sur les sourds et les muets* (Letter on the Deaf and Dumb) of 1751,

> from which we paint ceaselessly . . . the mind does not go step by step like expression. The brush executes only in the process of time what the painter's eye embraces in a flash. The formation of language demanded the decomposition.[39]

This claim, that the formation of language proceeds by the 'decomposition' of an initial whole, and the subsequent reconstruction of a fully logical language from the components of the original speech-act, is a transposition to the linguistic domain of the resolutive-compositive method employed in Galilean physics.[40] It seemed highly likely that if speech was a mirror of the human mind, then it should be formed in accordance with the same principles which had been used so strikingly to 'unlock the secrets of nature'.

But it seemed equally likely that men in their cognitive infancy would attempt to resist that decomposition; that in the first act of language-creation, they would attempt to devise a speech which would capture the image *as* an image. Primitive man and 'modern savages' were thought therefore to retain in their speech some of the immediacy of the eye's original imaginative and cognitive reach. Metaphor has many of these properties, and the predominance of metaphor in the formal languages of some Amerindian societies, in particularly Quechua, was believed by those like José de Acosta, to be evidence of the truth of this theory.[41] The eloquence of American 'savages' became a literary commonplace from Lahontan, who was so impressed by the speeches of the Iroquois tribal leaders that he translated one in full in his *Nouveaux Voyages*, through Chateaubriand to such later popularists as Fenimore Cooper.[42]

It was also believed that if, in this way, primitive languages could capture entire images, they might also be able to express entire, if uncomplex, verbal structures in a single word. The Canadian Indians, explained Pierre Louis Moreau de Maupertuis in 1756, 'whose language is not yet formed can confuse and express at the same time the pronoun, verb, substantive, adjective and noun, and with a single word say, "I have killed a great bear"'.[43] Such non-linearity shared something with the original harmony between man and the natural world, by suggesting the presence of what Rousseau called 'the sovereign intelligence which sees at a glance the truth of all things'.[44]

Linearity, however, is a necessary condition of true thought as opposed to unstructured reflection. 'As this happens,' wrote Condillac of the process of decomposition, 'we can observe what we do in thinking, we can render account of it ourselves; we can consequently learn to conduct our reflection. Thinking, therefore, becomes an art, the art of speaking'.[45] Primitive man had no access to this art. He was a poet, possibly, but a poor philosopher. The gulf which separated him from civil man was immense; so immense that Leibnitz even wondered if the languages of 'America . . . and the extremities and distant places of Asia and Africa' were not so very different from those of Europe 'by the entire quality of speech, not to mention body, that one would say it is another race of animals'.[46]

The crucial step in the move away from this primitive 'ideal speech-situation' towards the language of reflection, is the creation of abstractions and universals. This marks a decisive stage in the history of the development of man's cognitive powers. It marks the recognition that the natural world possesses an intelligible order governed by a body of immutable laws, that there exist qualities not immediately accessible to the senses, and that the same transparency which characterizes the relationship between a concrete noun and a palpable object also characterizes the relationship between abstract nouns and abstract qualities. It is also the stage through which all Europeans and most of the non-European higher cultures – those of the Arabs, Turks, Chinese,

Japanese, and Indians – who were generally regarded as civil beings, but very few Africans or Amerindians, were thought to have passed. As Antonio de Ulloa, who knew not a word of it, confidently declared, Quechua was a language which 'approximated most closely to the speech of children'.[47]

Civil man, then, came increasingly to possess languages which were rich in abstractions and general categories. The savage, on the other hand, still living largely through his senses, persistently failed to grasp the principle of genera. In his *History of America* (1777), William Robertson declared, when speaking of the Amerindians, that 'the mind of man, while still in the savage state' recognizes only such objects

> as may be subservient to his use, or can gratify any of his appetites, attract his notice; he views the rest without curiosity or attention. Satisfied with considering them under that simple mode in which they appear to him, as separate and detached, he neither combines them so as to form general classes, nor contemplates their qualities apart from the subject in which they adhere. . . . Thus he is unacquainted with all the ideas which have been denominated *universal*, or *abstract*, or *of reflection*.[48]

As many travellers had observed, Amerindians had innumerable names for trees, but no single word which could translate the term 'tree'. 'If one oak was called A,' Rousseau pointed out,

> another was called B; for the first idea that one derives from two objects is that they are not the same, and it often takes a long time to notice what they share in common; therefore the more limited knowledge was, the more extensive the dictionary became.[49]

Like Bougainville, Rousseau recognized that no one could possibly have 'imagined or understood' such terms except in the context of a complex philosophical, and hence by definition, civil culture. For, after all, he remarked acidly, 'our philosophers, who have been using them for such a long time have considerable difficulty understanding them themselves'.[50]

For most Europeans, however, understanding abstractions was a necessary condition of civilized life. Underpinning the quarrel over the suitability of native-American languages as a means of conversion and acculturation was precisely the supposed absence of such concepts amongst most such languages. Christianity, after all, was heavily dependent upon universal categories. If some non-Europeans possessed no terms for such basic concepts as 'God' – not to mention such terms as 'Trinity', 'sacrament', 'virginity', and 'immaculate conception' – then indoctrination would be at best difficult and at worst conceptually dangerous. As the Franciscan Antonio de Zúñiga despairingly told Philip II in 1579, 'among them there is no language sufficient to explain the mysteries of our Holy Catholic Faith, because all lack the vocabulary'.[51] The same argument could also be applied to their political systems. 'What,' asked the Italian Jesuit, Giovanni Maffei, 'can you make of societies whose languages lack the very sounds L. R. and F. and could not therefore say *Lex, Rex, Fides* even if it could have been explained to them what these terms meant?'[52]

Maffei's irony may, perhaps, have been intended. But the very real difficulties which most missionaries experienced in learning Amerindian languages deepened the sense of their alieness. A conviction that all languages had to conform to the formal structure of Indo-European speech, that to constitute true languages at all they had, at some level, to abide by the 'modes, tenses or order of rules and agreement' set down by Quintilian, did not facilitate matters.[53] The earliest missionaries to Mexico and Peru, while they had great respect for what they saw as the poetic qualities of Nahuatl and Quechua, composed grammar books and dictionaries which did their best to force these languages into the grammatical structures of Latin. Little wonder that those, like the Jesuit Martyr, Jean de Brebeuf (1593–1649), found that it was simply impossible to make the many compounds of which Huron is composed conform to any set of Indo-European syntactical norms. It was, he finally concluded, as different in structure 'from our European language as heaven is from earth'.[54]

There was also the question of the multiplicity of tongues. If language was conventional in origin, it was not only a measure of the cognitive power of the mind of its user, it was also a measure of its users' abilities to co-operate with others of their kind. Amerindian languages were not only both difficult and unfamiliar. There was also a very large number of them. Communities separated by a few kilometres of rain-forest sometimes spoke mutually incomprehensible dialects. 'The configurations of the land,' Humboldt reasonably supposed, 'the force of the vegetation, the fear that mountain peoples in the tropics have of exposure to the heat of the plains, hindered communications'. And it was this which was responsible for the 'astonishing variety of American languages'.[55] But few eighteenth-century language-theorists looked to such obvious, and deterministic, explanations. Most sensed in the diversity of Amerindian languages some distinctive, and corrupting, feature of the New World. Fragmentation, like the primitiveness of the language forms, was further evidence of the recent origins of all things American. Some, Lafitau and de Brosses among them, had hoped that a somewhat over-simplified philology might bring a degree of coherence to what seemed to be a potentially endless proliferation of language-groups. To Antoine Court de Gébelin, the author of the most extensive analysis of the 'Primitive World' in the eighteenth century, such plurality, despite the 'apparent variety of these languages diversified to infinity so that they seem to deny the possibility of any analysis', could be seen, on examination, as only a manifestation of a deeper unity. A detailed study of Amerindian languages – for which he provided some of the materials – would, he believed, reveal an inner similarity between all of them, thus offering further proof of that 'beautiful principle that ALL is ONE in the Universe; a great and sublime truth, so consoling for men'.

Few of those who encountered Amerindian languages directly, however, were much inclined to be consoled by them. For those who were faced with the difficulty of attempting to learn and communicate in them to their seemingly obdurate and unintelligible speakers, they frequently seemed to be merely an expression of the hopeless confusion of Amerindian social and political life.[56]

iv

The conjectural history of language, which goes from simple terms to complex ones, from metaphorical utterances to logical ones, from the unified speech-act to the decomposed language of the syllogism, is the history that Adario, the savage critic of all that 'Lahontan' has told him about European society, is seeking to invert. In Adario's narrative it is not the savage but the civil man who is the unthinking victim of his passions. For Adario, universals and abstractions cannot be the work of rational minds, for reason operates only with what clearly is. Instead they are the phantasmagoria of the imagination, for only the imagination is able to conjure up abstract connections between things, connections which do not exist in nature and cannot be comprehended by the observer's 'innocent eye'. 'You give all,' he complains therefore to 'Lahontan', 'to the imagination and almost nothing to that beautiful part of ourselves which makes us reason'.[57] It is precisely on the fertile and deceptive imagination of civil men that the Gospels and those other codes by which Christians rule their lives have made their imprint, so that now 'reason no longer has the power to move their minds'.[58] So long as the savage's discourse was fixed upon the substantial world, he possessed a greater clarity about the nature of the real than civil man could hope to acquire. The savage, as Herder later observed (drawing on the information provided in Peter Kalms' *History of Pennsylvania*), his ear undiluted by imperfect thoughts and unperplexed by written symbols, hears perfectly what it hears: it eagerly takes in words which indicate determinate objects, and are more satisfactory to the mind than volumes of abstract terms.[59]

In order to become 'civil', however, we have, at some point in our history, chosen to privilege the understanding which the language of science brings with it over the perceptual and moral certainties which governed our primitive state. Herder was willing to concede that the creation of universals had been 'very useful', but 'considered in itself, and according to the nature of things, it affords not a single perfect and essential idea, not a single intrinsic truth'.[60]

Adario's view, though cruder and untroubled by the relative merits of the 'science of metaphysics' is roughly similar. In his eyes the moral world inhabited by men like 'Lahontan' is wholly composed of linguistic tags, and because of this it is governed by those who have acquired the power to dictate what those tags shall mean. The Huron, says Adario indignantly, may have no term for 'God', but 'Lahontan' is a fool if he believes that they cannot therefore possess the concept of a supreme deity.[61] The savage's ignorance of abstractions, Herder would later observe, precludes the possibility of the term 'deity', but he *lives* as if he had one and 'goes to the land of his fathers with more tranquillity than many word-learned sceptics'.[62]

The final appeal of all those who peddle in empty abstractions to order and to compel others to their will, is made not to nature, to the visible and, in the savage's view, knowable world. It is made instead, as 'Lahontan' had made it, to a text. For the final stage in the natural history of language is, of course, the transition from speech to script. For all European social-theorists, since the early Middle Ages at least, the invention of writing had been seen as the crucial transition into an ordered social world. A literate world is one which does not require that each generation re-invent the discoveries of the previous, and it is the only world in which cultural and scientific progress is at all possible. The development of the script was also thought to have proceeded by stages which matched those through which speech itself had passed. The earliest nations, claimed Vico, 'thought in poetic characters, spoke in fables and wrote in hieroglyphs',[63] since hieroglyphs, like myths, like those early composite languages described by Maupertuis, were believed to represent the images which lay behind the word, rather than the words themselves. The second stage was symbolic writing; the third was the alphabet. All these follow the same process away from initial cohesion towards linearity which speech itself had followed.

Only the alphabet, which is the supreme instance of the coextensiveness of time and space – a system wherein there is one symbol, that is, for each unit of *sound* – detached the whole process of recording from its prior dependence upon the senses. Only an alphabetic script could adequately record abstractions and universals. Furthermore as societies grew more 'civilized' and their languages ever more dependent upon universalization, so they increased both in complexity and variety. Only an alphabetic script, as Antoine Yves Gouget observed in 1758, could represent 'that infinite variety of acts and deeds, which circulate within civil society'.[64] Since alphabets are wholly artificial semiotic systems, and require for their creation 'a double convention', as Rousseau put it,[65] they are also proof of a very high degree of social cohesion. Men have to agree not only on the meaning of words; they also have to agree on their representation.

Again, evidence to support this conjectural history could be found both among the Ancients and among the more technologically sophisticated 'primitive' peoples. Mexicans employed what most Europeans who had never seen them believed to be hieroglyphs. These, claimed Rousseau, 'correspond to the passionate language (*langue passionée*) and already suppose the existence of society and of those needs created by the passions'.[66] The Peruvians possessed, or at least so Maupertuis supposed, a primitive symbolic script, which located them roughly 'where the Chinese were at the time of the Flood'.[67] While the Chinese themselves were believed to have pushed symbolic writing to the very limit where it seemed to stand on the edge of alphabetization.

European attitudes towards writing were, however, at best ambiguous. Writing was the supreme technological feat. But it also threatened transparency by making repeated interpretation possible. There is a tradition of hostility towards the text which goes back, at least, to Socrates's observations in the *Phaedrus*.

> For this I believe, Phaedrus, is the evil of writing, and in this it closely resembles painting. The creations of the latter art stand before you as if they were alive, but if you ask them a question, they look very solemn and say not a word, and the same is true of written discourse. You could imagine that they spoke as if they possessed sense, yet if you wish to understand something they say, and question them about it, you will find them always repeating the same story. (275 D–E)

On this account, writing destroys the human capacity for conversation, it exposes the speaker's words to false interpretation since every text is, as Socrates goes on to say, 'tossed from hand to hand, both among those who understand it and those for whom it is entirely unsuited'; ultimately it threatens political liberty which depends upon persuasion, rather than force. For later critics, who also thought of reading as a necessarily silent and solitary activity, writing seemed also to have driven out the human intimacy which speech required. 'You say,' Adario accuses 'Lahontan',

> that our women are stupid, because they do not know how to write love-letters to their friends as yours do. But should they learn to write, all that would replace their present intimacy would merely be *lettres galantes* carried upon an eternal silence.[68]

In this account, writing is seen not as the triumph of human rationality and co-operation, but rather as the final stage, of which 'decomposition' had been the first, of the history of the detachment of language from the person. 'Words on paper,' wrote Bernard Lamy, 'are like a dead body laid upon the ground'.[69] By removing tonal variations – and of course the possibility for spontaneity – which are features of oral cultures, writing, claimed Rousseau, 'freezes' a language; it makes it 'cold and monotonous',[70] and pushes it towards the condition of algebra, and what Rousseau regarded as Leibnitz's absurd attempt to create a universal language.[71] Furthermore it was recognized by theorists as diverse in their ends as Rousseau and Smith, that writing was not only the consequence of a need to capture universals, and hence convey knowledge, it was also a response to the creation of property. The quest for property and the development of commerce prompted men to discover a common pattern in several mutually incomprehensible languages, and the means to transcribe them all by a single system of notation. So long as men remained at home or in the public spaces provided by the ancient Republics, or in those uncomfortable Alpine villages of which Rousseau thought so highly, or the Canadian forests, they had no need of a script. In commercial societies, however, languages become privatized, as do needs. Speech changes so that it not only loses its musicality but also its range and its persuasive power. The limits of the Greek *polis*, claimed Rousseau, had been marked by the carrying distance of the human voice. The same is true of the Iroquois or the Huron or the Carib village. The limits of all civil societies, by contrast, are marked by the decrees of their rulers, decrees which, like the words with which all Europeans have seized those lands which are not naturally theirs – like Columbus's letter and the plaque that Bougainville leaves behind on Tahiti with the words 'This land is ours' – are inscribed in texts. Civil men, claimed Rousseau, are another species of barbarian, and whereas the earliest men had met and cried to one another 'aimez moi' or 'aidez moi', the master phrase in the absolutist state is 'donnez moi d'argent', which is an appeal not to the persuasive power of speech but only to force; and it requires not soothing rhetoric but 'placards on the street corners and soldiers in the houses'.[72]

Adario and Orou are part of this same counter-history. They, too, know the humanity of the spoken word and distrust and revile the text. 'You attach the names of Vices and Virtues to actions which are not susceptible of any morality,' says Orou. And the only reason why those names remain attached over time is because they are set down in writing.[73] Without writing, they would not survive the telling. 'These are *books*,' Adario cries of both the Bible and the European's law codes. And books can have no authority beyond the authority with which you chose to invest the written word. 'Ha! Dammed writing,' he concludes, 'pernicious invention of the Europeans who tremble before true chimeras which they represent to themselves by twenty-three little figures'.[74]

For Civil men, written words are magic tokens in the same way that ritual objects are. This is why the Aristotelian, whom Voltaire's space-travelling giant Micromegas (a rational 'savage' in another form) meets on earth, believes that the Greek terms used by Aristotle are themselves a source of knowledge, although he has no idea what they mean.[75]

Adario, by contrast, 'reads' only in the Book of Nature which, of course, is not only the sole authoritative text, it is also, like speech itself, indeterminate. In the end Adario tells 'Lahontan' to leave him and his fellow beings in peace. The writings of the Europeans, together with their *writing* itself, can only bring the corruption which Adario – 'qui a voyagé' – has seen for himself in France and New York.

Adario and Orou are both fantasies, but they represent a characteristically eighteenth-century attempt to confront an elaborate history of humanity, which privileges the capacity to control through translation not only thought, but the external world itself over un-mediated understanding; and in so doing, implicitly seeks to replace nature by culture. As Derrida long ago pointed out, the fact that by making language 'the force of rupture with nature' Rousseau 'had *naturally* installed an order which was radically distinct from the natural order',[76] makes clear that there can never be any sense in which the counter-history can ever over-rule the history. The same is true of Adario as it is of any of these savage critics of the European speech-habits and their social analogues. The savage remains locked forever into his own linguistic universe. He has been driven forward by his 'discoverers' and up the temporal scale, to confront a world he finds abominable. But it is also, as he sometimes recognizes, a world that will one day be his own. He can only hope to escape it, as Adario does, by returning to the

6.   Frontispiece to the Baron
de Lahontan's *Nouveaux
Voyages dans l'Amérique
septentrionale*, 1703.

woods. Only there can he hope to live for a while unmolested. Adario has
taken a long, hard and informed look at the goods on offer in European
societies, and rejected them for what he recognizes to be the far harder,
but also the far more virtuous life in the Canadian woods; a life without
rulers, laws or the printed word. His society, however, as the readers of
the *Dialogues curieux* could not have failed to be aware, is in the process
of being absorbed into a European one. His life, and his language, like
the lives and languages of the other Amerindian peoples – like the lives
and language of the Tahitians – are themselves in the process of being
colonized.

The frontispiece to the *Mémoires de l'Amérique septentrionale* is decorated
with an emblem. An almost naked Indian holds up an arrow and a bow

– the only instruments he possesses – and stands with one foot on a crown and sceptre, the other on a book. The book is the book of the laws. Framing this image is the legend, *Et Leges et Sceptra Terit* ('I trample upon the sceptre and the laws') (see figure 6). This is, as Lahontan explains, an image of the natural freedom which he, unlike his fictional alter-ego, would willingly exchange for the life of the Europeans perpetually compelled to 'bow their knees before those who sacrifice the public good to their particular interests'.[77] The unintended irony is that while this savage, clearly Adario himself, may be able to leave 'Lahontan' behind, he has, unlike poor Aotouru, learnt how to speak excellent French. He has been able both to describe his world in sufficiently compelling terms to confound 'Lahontan', and to mount a fierce attack on European society. He is already half colonized. His is the discourse of one who has set himself up against a world which he knows he has every reason to fear. He knows, too, that his America is about to be transformed, and transformed with the help of Lahontan himself, sometime soldier in the French army in Canada.

CHAPTER FIVE
Domestic Tigers in the Jungle

Inventa primus secuit qui nave profundum
et rudibus remis sollicitavit aquas,
qui dubiis ausus committere flatibus alnum
quas natura negat praebuit arte vias.
Claudianus, *De raptu proserpinae*

i

'We respected our image in you,' says the ancient Tahitian sage of
Diderot's *Supplément au Voyage de Bougainville* (1773), as he berates the
departing French explorer Bougainville and his crew; berates them for
the inconsistent brutality of their behaviour, their stubborn refusal
to follow nature's self-evident laws, their 'inutiles lumières', their
unthinking gift of those things the Tahitians most do not require: the
knowledge of crime and the fear of illness.[1] For all this the visiting
Frenchmen remain human. It is even possible to carry on a meaningful
conversation with them. But, as the Tahitian also knows, once we make
any serious attempt to go beyond that common image, once we make
any attempt to understand the cultural complexity which makes 'them'
fully human, we are lost. As the speaker called B in the dialogue which
occupies a large part of the *Supplément* remarks, 'all we carry with us at
birth is an organization similar to that of other beings, similar needs
which draw us towards the same pleasures and a common aversion to
pain'.[2] Beyond the limits of the senses, however, there are no useful
indicators, no immediate or evident means of making the other's
behaviour intelligible.

Diderot supplies Bougainville with an Aumonier, a man who sub-
scribes, unthinkingly, to all the European sexual mores, and who is
driven by every human sexual passion. Each night in the *cabane* which
the thoughtful Tahitians provide for him, this unfortunate is visited by
four beautiful women all begging him to 'honour' them. Each night he
succumbs, each night crying out for his broken vows and lost 'virtues'.[3]
Diderot is playing here with a stereotype: the wanton, effortlessly
available savage such as Vespucci's 'lascivious' Carib women who, he
claimed, had given themselves readily to every member of his crew.
The crucial difference is that Diderot's Tahitians are strictly moral
utilitarian beings. It is not simple pleasure which drives them, much

141

less frustrated love for the Aumonier; indeed they take no interest in him as a person at all, it is procreation with which they are concerned. They clearly experience and – if the Aumonier's nightly inability to resist is anything to go by – give pleasure. But the arguments they offer the tortured Frenchman are couched wholly in terms of the production of children. Thia, the youngest of the Taihitian women, pleads with the Aumonier:

> Honour me in my cabin and among my family. Raise me to the level of my sisters, who now mock me. Asto, the eldest, already has three children. Palli, the second one, has two, but Thia has none at all. Stranger, honest (*honnête*) stranger, do not refuse me. Make me a mother.[4]

For his part, the Aumonier, although he is driven by the same pleasure principle as they, cannot understand why the Tahitians should *act* as they do and consider such behaviour 'natural'. Similarly the Tahitian, Orou, husband to one of the women and father to the other three, utterly fails to make the Frenchman understand that sexual desire is natural because it is the necessary condition for procreation, and that therefore it *should* never be resisted. In the state of nature, action follows directly on passion, since that is what passion is *for*.[5] Both Orou and the Aumonier remain locked in their own cultural worlds, although for Diderot Orou's world should be fully comprehensible to any rational being, while the Aumonier's mental landscape, littered as it is with the worthless debris of unexamined customs, is closed to any but those who already inhabit it.

But for all his adherence to false beliefs, the Aumonier comes in the end to recognize that these people are happy in ways which he has never experienced. What he fails to understand is that for him to enjoy such happiness he has to abandon 'his soutane, his state, his vows'. And were he, in fact, to do so, were he, that is, to abandon his Frenchness and remain on the island, he, like Léry's Norman translators, could never again hope to return to Europe. As B says at the end of the dialogue, we can only ever be what we are where we are. 'Let us imitate the good Aumonier, a monk in France, in Tahiti a savage'.[6]

The *Supplément au Voyage de Bougainville* – together with Montesquieu's *Lettres Persanes* (1721), Voltaire's *L'Ingénu* (1767), François Delisle de la Drévetière's, *L'Arlequin sauvage* (1756) (which, said Rousseau, was his favourite play) to take only a random sample – belongs to a recognizable eighteenth-century genre. It is a genre in which the 'savage', natural-man and child-of-nature, reverses the traditional order of travel. Now it is not we, the perennially itinerant Europeans, who visit him, but he who visits us. In Europe, confronted by the self-evident folly of European customs, this 'savage' finds himself, as do Montesquieu's Persians (natural-men in another garb) 'in another universe'.[7] Remote, yet like all good fictions persuasively real, the savage is made to speak from the position of a culture which could never have been his, a culture which could never have existed at all, a culture which has been fabricated by the simple procedure of stripping away whatever the author most disliked about his own. Both author and reader remain firmly at home. As the character named A in the *Supplément* remarks, with Diderot's characteristic self-irony, the views attributed to the old Tahitian do, indeed, sound remarkably European.[8] B's reply that this is only because it is a translation from Tahitian into Spanish (which, for some reason, Orou is said to understand) and then into French, is merely an ironic subterfuge. It is a tacit recognition of what Rousseau told d'Alembert, that 'those who wish to describe strange customs have to take great care to adapt their work to ours'.[9] But it is also the case that the full persuasive force of the savage's voice depends precisely upon its transparency. It cannot survive translation into the speech of civil man for, as we have seen, that speech is by its nature unable to convey the simple truths which constitute the savage's view on the world.

But the various voices in the *Supplément*, wilfully contradictory and intentionally evasive though they are, are not only a critique of all European norms. They are also a contribution to a specific and enduring eighteenth-century argument against colonization and the inescapable cultural annihilation which colonization was thought to involve. It is an argument about the integrity and ultimate incommensurability of all cultures, an argument about the destructive potential of migration, and about the reliance of 'Enlightenment' and civility upon diversity.

ii

The most sustained of Diderot's observations on European colonialism are to be found in his contributions to the Abbé Raynal's *Histoire philosophique et politique des deux Indes*.[10] This, which first appeared (without any assistance from Diderot) in 1770, rapidly became a bestseller. It also became, in subsequent editions, a kind of mini-*Encyclopédie* with unsigned contributions by a number of minor *philosophes*. It was hugely popular in the years immediately before, and during the French Revolution, to which it made a significant ideological contribution. (It had, said one of its critics, aroused in all its readers a new brand of fanaticism, 'the fanaticism of liberty'.)[11] By the mid-nineteenth century, however, the *Histoire* had ceased to find many readers. Since then it has frequently been described as little more than the work of a popularist, and dismissed as nothing other than a compendium of contemporary knowledge about the European colonies in America and India. It is true that the text of 1772 lacks much stylistic interest. It is also true, as Frédéric Grimm remarked, that, despite its title, it had very little to do with philosophy, and that its politics were 'more in accordance with established politics than with justice'.[12] Raynal had, in fact, begun his career as a hack in the service of Choiseul, and much of what he says in the work is contradicted elsewhere by what the other contributors, in particular Diderot and Pehcmeja, have to say.[13]

But like Bougainville, Raynal himself merely provided Diderot with a literary context. His contributions to the *Histoire* (which appeared in their final form in the edition of 1780) are not only the most extensive, they are also the most sustained and by far the most original parts of the book. If, in the words of Diderot's own riposte to Grimm, Raynal's work finally became 'the book which I love and which the kings and their courtiers hate, the book which will give birth to Brutus',[14] this is almost entirely because of Diderot's own presence in the text.

The Diderot who is the interpolator of the *Histoire des deux Indes*, takes up the theme of the Diderot, supplementer of Bougainville's *Voyage autour du monde*. As in so many of Diderot's works, these texts derive much of their imaginative power and cogency from a tension between two different modes of existence. In this case, there is on the one hand the image of the truly civilized life, the life at the side of Sophie Volland, the life of rational action and aesthetic contemplation; yet this is also a life which is characterized by luxury and superfluity, by 'boredom and the disgust of exhausted joys'.[15] On the other hand, there is the life of moral rectitude, of the harmoniousness but, at the same time, the threatening sameness of the existence of the 'savage'. It is a tension which cannot ever be resolved. Indeed Diderot makes no attempt to resolve it. It may perhaps be fanciful to imagine that he chose to contribute to the *Histoire*, not because he believed it would make the French into so many Brutuses, or because he believed that the image of the American Indian would serve to arm them ideologically for the revolution which, like Voltaire, he knew must one day come; but because so much of it, like Bougainville's *Voyage*, seemed to point in directions quite unlike those he wished to take.[16] If incommensurability was his theme, then the best way to capture that was in a language which he uses again and again, most strikingly in those two remarkable dialogical texts, *Jacques le fataliste* and *Le Neveu du Rameau*; a language which is built upon the opposition between discordant unreconcilable voices. The presence of Raynal's own text, with its mass of detail, its severe, but by no means entirely condemnatory, view of the European colonization of the Americas, and of the European slave trade, provides a constant reminder of the realities of what is actually *out there*. It is a world against which Diderot can pit his own image of what the European has done to America and, as we shall see, what the experience of going to America had done for the inhabitants of Europe.

Like his Tahitian, and in common with most eighteenth-century social-theorists, Diderot held that it was possible to identify in all human behaviour a common core. We are all Hobbesian to the extent that we all share the same basic needs. It is this 'mutuality of wants' which, as Tom Paine told Raynal in 1782, first unites individuals who share a common plot of ground into a 'nation'. But there, he concluded, 'the progress of civilization has stopt'.[17] We all, that is, possess the same basic mental machinery. We are all capable of identifying our interests, and we all ratiocinate in much the same way. We all, too, share similar, if not identical 'prejudices', a term which Diderot sometimes uses in the conventional Enlightenment sense of an obstruction to clear understanding, but sometimes, as the Roman jurists did, to describe the pre-established building blocks out of which any subsequent cultural knowledge has to be constructed, what Gadamer has labelled the 'fore-structure of knowledge'.[18]

But none of this gets us very far in the understanding of cultures other than our own. We may all be rational agents, but none of us, in the real worlds in which we live, ever make fully independent rational choices. For we actually live in societies which limit and determine the range of choices which are open to us. And all societies are artificial, not natural. The brief history of nearly all our customs, says B in the *Supplément*, can be reduced to one exemplary tale: 'there is a natural man, and on top of this natural man an artificial one has been placed. And a civil war has broken out in the cave which will last all his life'.[19] Or, in the terms Diderot uses again and again in his political writings: all mankind is governed by three codes: the natural, the civil and the religious.[20] The human societies in which we must all – even the poor Tahitians – finally come to live, are constructed by customs (*moeurs*) and custom is the unreflective obedience ('un soumission générale et un conduite conséquente')[21] to the second and third of these laws, frequently in violation of the first. We all necessarily live lives in the shadow of the unresolved struggle between nature and artifice. Only peoples like the Tahitians (and possibly the Iroquois whom Bougainville had also known) as they now are, but soon will cease to be, live purely and simply according to the law of nature.[22]

For Diderot, cultures are aggregates of *moeurs*, each of which constitutes a 'national character' (*esprit national*). Each one of these, he believed, is composed of two elements, one, which seems to be dependent on climate, is fixed, the other – which Hume, who had no patience with climatology, called 'the moral' – is variable and allows for variations over time.[23] Like Montesquieu, Diderot had some difficulty with the determinism of climatic ascriptions. He was prepared to believe that no matter how a people's social world might change, they remained in some sense what their environment had willed them to be. Look, he said, at the Indians, the Indians of 'Indostan', a people who have suffered for centuries at the hands of a tyranny by comparison with which even the Spaniards might seem benign, yet they still remain 'douce, humaine, timide', incapable of revolt, their only vice being their timidity.[24] The same was true of the attempts which all Europeans had made to reconstruct in America the worlds which they had left behind them. Try as they might to remain Frenchmen or English or Spaniards in the tropics, sooner or later the environment would reclaim its empire, and 're-establish things in their proper order, and with their natural names, although with those marks of change (*alteration*) that every great revolution leaves behind when it has passed'.[25]

But, like Montesquieu, Diderot saw in the environment only a limiting condition. It is the Indians' gentle nature, not their cultural performance, which they owe to their 'climate'. The complete collapse of a culture which had once rivalled that of the Egyptians, and to which the Greeks had gone to learn their science 'in the days before Pythagoras', is entirely to be attributed to the barbarism of India's Mughul rulers.[26] The environment into which an individual is born provides him only with certain natural dispositions. In some climates some peoples are inventive, capable of a high degree of civil organization and the construction of enduring civil societies. In others they are more unstable, given to nomadism, short of memory, fickle and imitative. Diderot was as disinclined as was Cornelius de Pauw to believe that 'treatises on philosophy' could be produced in the 'Torrid Zone'.[27] The inhabitants of the tropics, however close to nature they might be, could not be suspected of too much creative imagination. As Antonio de Torres, one of Raynal's most sympathetic Spanish commentators, observed, such peoples as the Amerindians 'very easily understood the idea of the drawings which were given to them by Europeans'. Moreover they were able to reproduce them with wonderful accuracy, turning out Flemish Madonnas in a mass of brilliantly coloured birds' feathers. But nothing would persuade him that there might ever be a Copernicus among the Brazilian Indians, any more than there might one day be a Newton among the Mongols.[28] Imitation and invention are two separate mental activities, and while the former might easily be performed by the races who lived on the edges of the temperate zones – on the edges of the known and civilized world – the latter was only possible to those who lived firmly within it.

For Diderot, however, the environment does not seem to have been a force which operates in some as yet undiscovered manner upon the human mind, as it was ultimately for Montesquieu, and would be again for Herder. Differences were too marked *within* any given culture or nation for that to be plausible. As Hume, whose essay on national character Diderot must certainly have known, remarked, 'No one attributes the difference of manners in WAPPING and ST JAMES to a difference of air or climate'. It was also the case, as he pointed out, that national characters did not follow natural climatic boundaries. The French on one side of the Pyrenees, Hume noted, were very unlike the Spanish on the other. And, as the Jews and the Armenians had clearly demonstrated, it was fully possible to transplant nations, and with them their national characteristics, from one climate to another.[29]

Unlike Hume, however, Diderot was not prepared to jettison the notion altogether, since a wider, more general definition of 'climate' could be made to include the land, and a love of the land, that 'vibrant and powerful emotion' which was 'the primal core of society', and which might plausibly be identified as the principal force behind love of 'patrie'.[30] Yet for Diderot, climate, even in this extended sense, operated only at the level of the needs and desires we all share. It may make men gentle, as it did with the Indians or, as it has done with the Tartars, make them fierce or, again like the American Indian, disinclined to hard labour. But the full force of the 'national character' is 'moral' – it belongs, that is, to *mores*, to the civil and religious law, the habits and customs, the *habitudines* which constituted, in Pascal's celebrated phrase, 'a second nature which destroys the first'.[31]

If each character, each culture, is the product of a distinct environment and is built up from a complex pattern of norms, no two will ever be alike. There may exist conglomerates of cultures united by a common cultural ancestry. Like most eighteenth-century social-theorists, Diderot acknowledged the existence of a cosmopolitan environment which reached from Russia to Greece and which might be called 'Europe'. As a Frenchman, he had a civil and religious existence which was sufficiently like that of a Englishman or an Italian for him to have no difficulty in understanding these peoples. But he recognized that faced by a Huron or a Tupinamba, he could have no discernible access to the mental worlds of those men; nor would they have any access to his.

There was also for Diderot, sceptic and relativist though he (frequently) was, a marked and substantive difference between 'civil' and 'savage' societies. Like most theorists who had thought about the problem of civilization, Diderot accepted that the distinction 'civil'/ 'savage', as a distinction between patterns of behaviour, was at one level a distinction in time. Since the first decade of the eighteenth century, it had become a commonplace to think of the distances between peoples in space as capable of expression in terms of distances in time. This meant that *all* cultures could, at some level, be made comparable and hence, or so it was believed, commensurable. One of the consequences of the Cartesian revolution had been that analogy and homology had become the accepted methods of scientific inquiry. By the time Buffon came to write in 1749 the section on man with which he opened his great *Histoire naturelle*, he could confidently declare,

> For all that we are able to reflect upon the origin of our under-standing (*connaisance*) it is obvious that we can only acquire such knowledge through the means of comparison. That which is absolutely incomparable is also entirely incomprehensible.[32]

Here the reader, the interpreter of a canon of texts, has clearly been replaced by the observer, and all possible understanding, necessarily limited, as Buffon admits, has been made dependent upon the supposed impartiality of the observer's gaze. The earliest and most influential attempt to use cross-cultural comparison of the kind that Buffon had in mind was Joseph François Lafitau's, *Moeurs des sauvages amériquains comparées aux moeurs des premiers temps* (Customs of the Savage Americans Compared with the Customs of the Earliest Times, 1724). To Lafitau, the Huron and the Iroquois he had encountered during his years as a missionary in northern Canada, seemed culturally to be another form of Spartan or Lycian. Extensive comparison between the customs of these peoples had revealed to him that they shared a common symbolic, political and linguistic universe. Lafitau expressed this in terms of what he called a 'symbolic theology'. This is far removed from Diderot's directly naturalistic language of needs and desires. But what unites all such theories is the place on their relative scales of time where 'we', the civil being, stands. For Lafitau, no less than for Diderot, the savage has an identity only in so far as he has a meaning, and he has meaning only in so far as he has a determinate and measurable relationship to 'us'.

Lafitau had demanded that all savage peoples should be judged on their own terms, instead of, as they had been by all previous authors, 'by our manners and customs'.[33] Yet his entire work, as he himself noted, had been precisely to locate the American Indians in relation to a specific European past. To do that, he not only had to disregard the savages' *own* past, he also had to equate the modern Huron with the ancient Spartan in a way which did nothing to sustain the autonomy of the Amerindian's culture. 'Seeing them according to their own customs' meant, in his historical practice, only applying the appropriate measure selected from one of ours. This had, it is true, some real cognitive benefits. Most of the things for which Lafitau has been praised by unhistorically-minded modern anthropologists, such as Van Gennep, derive from this technique: the recognition of the fact that kinship vocabularies could vary from culture to culture, of the importance of relative age in descent systems, or of the existence of rituals which come very close to Van Gennep's celebrated *rites de passage*. But it remains the case that Lafitau's comparative method subsumes two or more unrelated cultures beneath a single, culturally specific, gaze.

The same is largely true of the *Histoire des deux Indes* itself. Here two wholly unrelated geographical areas with myriad largely unrelated cultures are treated as if they possessed a common identity, because Columbus believed that he had found one when in fact he had 'discovered' the other.[34] For Lafitau, what linked the Huron and the Iroquois to the Spartan and Lycian had been a complex theory of cultural migration; the belief, as Diderot somewhat mockingly described it, that 'all peoples, subject as are all other bodies, to centrifugal force, [are] constantly dragged from the poles to the equator'.[35] In the *Histoire* what links the peoples of America and 'Indostan' is, as we shall see, commerce.[36] But commerce is itself a mode of operation which relocates everything on the 'savage' periphery' – including the savages themselves – in relationship to the 'civil' centre.

This conflation of place points also to the crucial distinction between the civil and the savage state. In so far as it develops from a primitive and untutored set of responses, 'national character' may be 'natural'. But what it develops into – the love of location, 'patriotism', that 'affection dominante' – belongs very clearly to the sphere of culture. The 'love of place' which characterizes all civil societies becomes in turn a preoccupation with time. Civil men, Diderot believed, lived in perpetual suspense between the recollection of their past and anxiety about their future. For Diderot, as for most of his contemporaries, human societies are in essence constructions over time. In common with all human artifacts, they correspond to the principles for scientific representation set out in Descartes's *Discours de la méthode* (Discourse On Method), and they all, therefore, proceed from the simple to the complex.[37]

The most direct cultural analogy for this process, other than Descartes's rules for representation, is language; for language is not only a necessary instrument of sociability, it was also – as we saw in the last

Chapter – believed to be structured as human societies are structured, so that Rousseau, like Aquinas before him, had difficulty in deciding which preceded which.[38] Like language, the human society begins as a single undifferentiated unit, the family. Like language, this primitive association, whose origins are natural (the urge to procreate) and whose collective activities are limited by the restricted physical capacities of its members,[39] evolves by a process of linearity. As we have seen, natural language, in Diderot's account, develops by the initial 'decomposition' of a natural and unified *Ursprach* – the first cluster of instinctive cries – into the components of true speech: the structures of verb, noun, adjective, pronoun, etc. And just as it is possible, in the imagination at least, to strip away what constitutes 'civil' man in order to reveal the natural man beneath, so it is possible to discover beneath even the most complex philosophical discourse, the original, Lockean sensational linguistic impulse. 'Take a word,' wrote Diderot (significantly in his article on 'Incomprehensible' in the *Encyclopédie*), 'Take the most abstract. Decompose it. Decompose it again, and it will dissolve in the last instance into a sensational representation'.[40] The components which go to make up civil society are created in a similar fashion. Savage societies – and it is clear from Diderot's account that he understood savages to live in some kind of society – are a response to the dictates of what he and Rousseau often referred to as the heart. They are merely the aggregate of our instinctive human responses, the capacity of what Diderot called 'the mechanical movement which precedes all deliberation' to recognize and respond to the needs of others.[41] Civil society 'decomposes' these instinctive responses into formal patterns, into codes of laws which will protect all the members of the community, even in circumstances when, through passion or self-interest, the 'mechanical movement' is prevented from operating. Just as savage societies were ones in which it was possible for a man to say in a single word 'I have killed a great bear' so, as Adam Smith claimed, they were communities in which it was possible for a man to be simultaneously a warrior, producer, statesman and judge.[42] The 'decomposition' of speech, the codification of a body of laws and the division of labour are all the determining features of a civil society. They make for difference, as well as for discord. The 'un-decomposed' savage, so to speak, can experience none of these things. He cannot, so Smith tells us, even perceive significant differences in the world that surrounds him. The 'small incoherences which in the course of things perplex philosophers' are opaque to him. He is capable of responding to the 'magnificent irregularities' of nature, but his response to these things is only awe mingled with superstition. He has no use for human curiosity and therefore does not experience the 'sentiment properly called *Wonder* that is the source of philosophical enquiry'.[43] Because of this, his world remains undifferentiated within itself and therefore impervious to change.

What terrified Diderot, as much as it did Smith, about the truly 'natural' state, was precisely the sameness which his Neapolitan critic, Francesantonio Grimaldi, using a theatrical metaphor often employed by Diderot himself, called 'the mask which makes [each man] exactly like his fellow'.[44] The savage might lead a happy life, in that it was one bereft of the impulses which derive from any but the most basic needs. But he also led a remarkably monotonous one. Unlike Rousseau, Diderot could never quite escape from the thought that life in Utopia – Canadian forests, Pacific islands, or Alpine villages – would be a pretty bleak and unmodulated experience. And much as he disliked Rousseau's most excitable critic, Simon Linguet ('n'est il qu'un declamateur', he once told Grimm),[45] he could not have failed to agree with him on this point, that all men not only 'wish for houses, responsibilities, manufactured goods', but that ultimately 'we even *need* them'.[46] Needs, the great building-blocks out of which sociability is constructed, are themselves culturally determined, and grown exponentially as the society. Diderot may not have shared Linguet's confidence in the ultimate progress of western civilization, but one part of him at least valued highly the plurality which only that civilization seemed able to bring. From his writing-desk he could see that, within a Europe beset by a miserable populace concerned exclusively with survival and the restrictive power of established religion, 'the progress of Enlightenment is limited'.[47] Beyond the limits of the civilized world, however, no 'Enlightenment' was possible at all. If he admired the stoicism which the savage, Canadian, Indian, Tahitian, or 'Brames' seemed to possess, he seems also to have shuddered at the conditions which made it necessary. As with so many of Diderot's more brilliantly perceptive insights into the human condition, his recognition that the kind of life that may of necessity accompany our highest moral aspirations might not be much to our liking, owes much to the language of contrast and conflict in which all his observations on the nature of civility are cast.

Civil societies are complex because they have developed linearly. In contrast to the restricted range and essential homogeneity of all the elements of which savage societies are built, every civil society is composed of a multiplicity of individual elements. And each one of these elements arouses in man a sense of instinctive attachments, attachments to the workplace, to the individual city or to the soil itself. It is these collective sentiments which Diderot gathers together under the heading of 'patriotism'. 'Show me,' demands Rousseau in *Emile*, 'the good man who owes nothing to his country?' It is not a matter of indifference where you are. A man who is a slave in Geneva may be a free man in Paris. 'Do not say therefore,' Rousseau continued,

'What does it matter where I am'? It matters that you should be where you are able to fulfil your obligations, and one of these obligations is an attachment to the place of your birth.[48]

All civil men, in Diderot's view, are driven by such patriotism. One of the necessary conditions of this is a life lived in continuous time, a participation in the process of linearity itself. In civil society there can, therefore, be no significant present tense, because the 'patriotism' which constitutes the social identity of all its members is dependent upon the constant accumulation of associations. That is, we are all, as we were indeed for Aristotle, in a process of becoming. 'The memory of his innocent pleasures,' wrote Diderot of civil man, 'ceaselessly embellishes the image of his cradle, and this image then . . . leads him back to his homeland'.[49] But if such men have no present, the savage has neither obvious past nor imaginable future. By the eighteenth century, it had become a commonplace to appeal to the savage's supposed inability to look beyond the satisfaction of his immediate wants as a sign of his unredeemable inhumanity. Even Raynal himself is supposed to have observed to Linguet that, ' "I am not hungry" is what they say to anyone who wishes to employ them'.[50] They cannot imagine – since their imagination is constrained by the narrowness of the human worlds which they inhabit – what will befall them from one day to the next, even if those are always the same things. 'Such is still nowadays the extent of the Carib's foresight,' claimed Rousseau, 'that he sells his cotton bed in the morning and comes weeping to buy it back in the evening'.[51]

In common with many eighteenth-century critics of civilization, however, Diderot turns this argument around. An indifference to the miseries which tomorrow will inevitably bring had always been part of the Stoic claim to auto-sufficiency, *autarkeia*. But here *autarkeia* (Diderot, after all, had been Shaftesbury's translator), the claim that the source of all pleasure and of the good lies within each individual, is made to account for the one emotion, 'patriotism', whose external manifestations might be thought of as wholly communitarian. For, Diderot argues, if we seek inner tranquillity, then clearly we have also to escape from the demands of time. This the 'savage' succeeds in doing. For only he who 'plays at each moment of his life with the pleasures and the goods that he brings with him', only he, who cannot remember yesterday and refuses to sacrifice present goods for an easy old age, knows that the sources of all pleasure lie within himself. Along with Shaftesbury's perfectly happy man, Diderot's savage can claim that 'My own concern is with truth, reason and right *within* myself'. Where the condition of the savage differs crucially from that of Shaftesbury, is that he, the savage, a creature of instincts, is concerned with pleasure rather than with the abstractions of truth, reason and right. The tranquillity of the Stoic, however, comes from having confronted 'friends dropping off, accidents and calamities impending, diseases, lameness, deafness, loss of sight, of memory, of parts' – to cite Shaftesbury's own list[52] – precisely those things which an active memory and constant premonition tell us threaten all our lives. The tranquillity of the savage, by contrast, comes not from intellectual recognition, but from the simple refusal, or inability, to recognize the very existence of such calamities. It is not *autarkeia*, but happy ignorance. And since the savage is thus able to escape the demands of *time*, he is similarly placed to escape from those of place. For the savage alone knows that 'sa patrie est partout'.[53]

iii

The savage, placeless and also timeless, may be, then, the only truly happy man. But Diderot recognized that civil society is a state that awaits us all. It is a claim to which he returns again and again. We cannot ever escape from the time/space continuum and yet remain fully human since for each of us these are the co-ordinates which make our worlds. 'All civilized (*polices*) peoples,' wrote Diderot, 'have been savages; and if left to their natural impulses all savage peoples are destined to become civilized'. Just as there is something gross and imbecile about the infantile adult, so there would be something gross and imbecile about the savage who ultimately failed to respond to the demands of civility. In the end, the kind of happiness the savage enjoys is simply not our human lot. But, or so Diderot seems to imply, no real-life savage ever did resist the civilizing process. If nearly three hundred years after their 'discovery' the Indians of America remained in a state of near imbecility – and Diderot had largely been persuaded by de Pauw that they had done so – then this was because of the tyrannies to which they had been subjected since their lands had been invaded.[54] The same held true of the Indian under Mughal rule and the Black African. Like Condorcet, Diderot looked forward to the day when the deleterious effects of European colonization would be reversed and Condorcet's cosy image of the grateful savage waiting for his European 'brothers' to lead him with reason and encouraging words to full Enlightenment, might become a reality.[55]

But the space/time continuum *is*, ultimately, a continuum. And if we are bound as a species to move up it, we are also, as individuals, at liberty to move down it. What we can never do, however, is return fully to our primitive condition. The refusal to understand this, said Diderot in his critique of Helvétius's *De l'homme*, was Rousseau's great failing. None of us can 'return to the woods' (although Rousseau had, in fact, never suggested that one could) if only because, for us at least, the woods are no longer there. Even those at Ermenonville, where Rousseau spent his last days, depended for their existence upon the goodwill – and the gardeners – of the Marquis René de Girardin.

The only possible human solution lay elsewhere, in a midway world, 'in a kind of society which is half civilized half savage'. Helvétius, Diderot went on, had been right 'to locate the happiness of social man in mediocrity', for although it is clear that the cabin is a far more comfortable home than the cavern, it was by no means certain that the palace was a necessary improvement on the cabin – especially if, as was invariably the case, it had had to be constructed at such enormous human cost. Diderot's belief was that it should be possible to redefine civilization as a middle period, compatible with our inescapable need for improvement, but yet 'less remote from the savage state than one might imagine'.[56]

Diderot took much the same view of both 'savagery' and 'civilization' as he did of the passions which, to so many eighteenth-century theorists, seemed to be the overwhelming threat to all possible forms of civility. There are, he argued, whole areas of our lives which are inaccessible to reason. To suppress them, even to redress them by countervailing interests, was to lose a great and primordial part of what it was to be human. 'Desire,' he wrote in the *Eléments de physiologie*, 'is the offspring of the organism, the offspring of happiness and unhappiness, of good living and of evil living'.[57] Man was a complex creature, far too complex for any one part of his being to be suppressed. To wish to do so was to fall into the same trap – in the name of reason rather than faith – into which the Church had always tried to lead its believers. 'It seems to me,' he wrote in the *Lettre sur les sourds et les muets* in 1755, 'that one must be at once inside and outside oneself. One must perform the roles simultaneously of the observer and the machine that is being observed'. The mind and heart must seek an equilibrium between the chilling abstractions of pure reason – the 'frigidity' of a Locke, as his friend Beccaria phrased it[58] – and the degradation of Rameau's Nephew.[59] It might even be possible, he believed, to imagine a colony quite unlike any that had ever previously existed, in 'some remote corner of the world', which would lie between the condition of the savage and what he referred to sarcastically as 'our wonderful civil state, an environment (*milieu*) which would retard the progress of the children of Prometheus, ... and which would fix civilized man between the infancy of the savage and our present decrepitude'.[60] One might even argue that, as the savage becomes necessarily more civilized, and the civilized man increasingly disenchanted with the world he has created for himself, so that he seeks to 'return towards his primitive state', the two should meet at some midway point where a more than transitory state of happiness is possible, 'where the happiness of the species resides'.[61] In the *Entretiens sur le fils naturel*, written in 1757, Diderot had even conjured into existence on the island of Lampedusa in the southern Mediterranean, 'far from the land and in the midst of the waves of a sea', just such 'a small band of happy men'.[62] In the more sombre context of the *Histoire philosophique et politique*, however, there would seem to be little hope for any such solution unless, as we shall see, it was to be the nascent United States. The problem was to decide who it was who was to say when the midway point has been reached and, more urgently, who was to arrest these compensating movements of progression and regression, and how was this to be effected. It is at this moment in the argument, with this crucial but unanswerable question hanging in the air, that Diderot introduces the menacing mediatory figure of the traveller/colonizer.

iv

We shall return to him. What matters here, however, is the claim that because each society grows out of our natural bundle of needs, desires and prejudices, in climatic and environmental conditions which are wholly dissimilar, all cultures must be, at least initially, incommensurable. True, Diderot is less pessimistic than some – less pessimistic, for instance, than Herder – about the possibility of cross-cultural understanding, and more insistent upon the moral obligation which each new and unfamiliar culture places upon us. But he is equally certain that we simply *can* have no immediate or intuitive understanding of other worlds. We may all once have been savages, but having now become one or another species of civil men, we can no more hope to understand the savage as he understands himself, than we can hope to understand other civilized cultures – the Indian or the Chinese – which are remote from us not in cultural time but in space. Our own immediate pasts may be more or less accessible through careful historical reconstruction of the kind Diderot's collaborator on the *Encyclopédie*, Jean d'Alembert, had called for, but we can never hope to know anything about our pre-civil state.[63] The cross-cultural analyses performed by the likes of Lafitau and de Brosses, Court de Gébelin and, later in the century,

Degerando and Volney, while interesting as regards the body of data they provided, could never be anything other than conjecture. To hope, as Lafitau had done, that modern Amerindian 'savages' might provide an insight into what even the classical world was like was (once his theory of migration had been removed) to disregard the huge changes which take place within all societies – even those of the Huron and the Iroquois – as they develop.

Similarly, and perhaps more strikingly, we cannot hope that the savage will ever understand *us*. Orou's incomprehension before the Aumonier's insistence on his need to preserve his 'virtue' is only a heuristic device intended to mock the moral imbecility of the Frenchman's sexual beliefs. The Tahitian cannot understand them because there is nothing to understand. But, in a more sombre mode, Diderot also observed that 'the savage, who, on seeing for the first time one of our great buildings, did not admire it as evidence of our power and our industry, but only as a extraordinary phenomenon of nature, would be a man of good sense'.[64] Without access to cultures which both knew how to build and had the need for such things, what else, after all, *could* he have taken it to be? We, too, might be forgiven for making similar mistakes. What we do, however, which the savage does not, and for which there can be no forgiveness, is to misunderstand what is in nature. To kill a Tahitian for 'stealing', as Bougainville's crew do, is not, as the sage explains, to misunderstand the nature of exchange, which is cultural. It is, instead, to violate the laws of reciprocity and generosity which, since these depend upon the recognition of our common humanity (*nôtre image en toi*), are natural, and therefore transparent.[65]

Diderot's ambition had been, in the words of his first biographer, Jacques-André Naigeon, to create a 'natural and experimental history of man',[66] which would constitute a refutation of the materialism of Helvétius and Buffon; a history which would explore the conflict between the apparent homogeneity of the physical make-up of the species and the huge diversity of behaviour of which its individual members were capable.[67] In the context of this vast and necessarily incomplete project, culture was perceived as acting as a restraint upon the naturally dispersive passions and desires which, for Diderot, were a constitutive feature of what he called 'les actions des particuliers'.[68] Distinctive, holistic and incommensurable though it may be, a culture, however, only ever holds the individual as a member of a group. Every civil man or woman may, if he or she so choses, follow Rousseau into the woods. Cutting oneself free from one's cultural moorings in this way may be a difficult, but it is by no means an impossible, task. Few, however, make the attempt. Even Rousseau's woods were provided for him and at no great distance from Paris. But there is one recognizable human type who finds himself sliding inexorably back down the scale of civility: the traveller.

Like Montesquieu – who, in the *Lettres Persanes* has Usbek declare, 'Happy is the man ... who is a stranger to every land but the one in which he was born'[69] – Diderot too did not much approve of travelling. For the traveller, who is terminally deracinated, whose objective is not inner tranquillity, but the pursuit of gain, is the very antithesis of the Stoic. How, he makes A in the *Supplément* inquire, could Bougainville, who had been a mathematician, the epitome of the self-absorbed, self-sufficient thinker, exchange that life for the 'active, punishing, wandering and dissipated profession (*metier*) of traveller'?

If all cultures are, at best, only commensurable with extreme difficulty, then nothing can be gained by leaving the place in which one was born. The savage who, as the perfect 'inward man', to use Augustine's phrase,[70] is at home everywhere, knows this. 'Happy is the Tahitian,' exclaims B, who, unmoved by 'fantasies from across boundless oceans', is content to 'stay where he is'.[71] Not only is the savage's world simple and stable, it is also wholly self-sufficient. Aotouru, the Tahitian whom Bougainville brought back with him to France and who was horrified, rather than astonished, by what he could see of Europe, never ceased sighing for his native land. 'And I am not surprised,' retorts B on being told this, for 'Bougainville's journey is the only one which has given me any taste for a country other than my own'.[72]

Diderot's disapproval of travel belongs to an ancient European tradition, one which locates the source of all civility – which is, after all a life lived in cities (*civitates*) – in settled communities, and which looks upon all modes of nomadism as irredeemably savage. All men, other than pilgrims, who leave their native homes are suspect. And pilgrims, of course, put themselves, in de Certeau's words, to 'the test of travel', only in order that they may return home purified. Their objective is the return itself, not the journey. Crossing the ocean was an act contrary to nature, for the gods – or God – had filled half the world with water precisely in order to keep humans apart. 'The first who dared to cleave the deep sea with a ship constructed by his own hand,' wrote the late fourth-century poet Claudianus – the lines which provide the epithet for this Chapter – 'and with his crude oars stirred the waters; he who dared unfurl his sails to the breath of the uncertain winds, opened up with his art, routes which nature had denied to men'.

There is, said Diderot, 'no state more immoral than that of the continual traveller (*voyageur par état*)'. He who travels constantly resembles 'a man who owns a huge house and who, instead of remaining by the side of his family, wanders constantly from room to room'.[73] In part, Diderot's attack on errancy belongs to a common eighteenth-century concern with population growth; for travellers, or so Diderot claimed, leave no progeny.[74] But it is only partly that, since the kind of traveller Diderot has in mind – the 'voyageur par état' – is a particular being; one who, like Bougainville, is also, potentially a colonist. Not only is he driven to visit every room in his house, he must also take possession of each one of them. And although Bougainville himself makes no effort to establish a colony on Tahiti, he leaves behind him for the next French arrival – and to the disgust of the Tahitian sage – a plaque inscribed with the words: 'This Land is Ours'.[75] Like the Columbus who hoped to transform an archipelago by re-describing it, like Balboa, who claimed the Pacific Ocean by bathing his feet in it, this traveller assumes that mere presence, and a simple verbal assertion, can be transformed into possession.

The 'voyageur par état' will carry home with him as his 'immutable mobiles' his claims to possession, however wicked these might seem to those whose lands they really are. What he carries *out*, in Diderot's account, is only a long list of human vices:

> tyranny, crime, ambition, misery, curiosity, I know not what restless-ness of spirit, the desire to know and the desire to see, boredom, the dislike of familiar pleasures – these things men from all ages have carried abroad (*expatrié*) with them, and will continue to do so.[76]

All that 'the audacious attempts' of Columbus and Vasco da Gama have achieved, Diderot concluded, was the creation of a hitherto unknown form of fanaticism, a fanaticism for discovery. Ever since the first Portuguese voyages in the fifteenth century, men from one pole to the other have gone off in search of 'some islands to ravage, peoples to despoil, subjugate and massacre'.[77]

Such traveller/colonists are generally to be found among those who seek to fulfil ambitions for which their native land offers no scope. They are, that is, the products (or the victims) of what no civilization can avoid: the inescapable gap between ever-increasing human needs and the society's capacity to meet them. Happiness for the children of Prometheus, as Helvétius had pointed out, was a 'machine which has constantly to be rebuilt'.[78] Just as the savage is always content with his lot precisely because it *is* his lot, so these travellers are forever dis-contented with theirs because they are theirs. It is one of the measures of the distances which lie between the savage and the civil condition.

Such men, Diderot believed, carry with them 'in the bottom of their hearts the germs of depredation' which under another sky and far from the public gaze grows 'with inconceivable fury'.[79]

For many eighteenth-century observers, migration and, *in extremis*, deportation, appeared as the only solution to the growing number of the dissatisfied and socially restless beings which every advanced commercial society seemed destined to create. Some of the promotional literature of the period hinted that migration of this kind might even turn out to be a stage in the natural growth of modern societies. Once, that is, a society had reached a point at which needs and desire had far outstripped the potential for even minimal satisfaction, then nature would provide new lands. The discovery of America by Europe at just such a point in its development could, therefore, be interpreted as, in part at least, providential. On this account, discovery and colonization became a natural impulse, much like the impulse which was supposed to have driven men from the woods on to the plains, to abandon hunting for pastoralism and pastoralism for agriculture. The Marquis de Chastellux, for instance – author of a widely read account of a journey through North America in 1782 – argued in his *Discours sur les avantages ou les désavantages qui resultent pour l'Europe de la découverte de l'Amérique* (Discourse On the Advantages and Disadvantages For Europe of the Discovery of America, 1787) that nature might have provided a 'species of rapid rotation', which drew inwards towards its centre all those who are capable of satisfying their needs within their own communities, but flung away 'from its sphere of activity' all those who were not. In this way the 'metropolis is delivered both from their disquieting activities and their despair, which is as dangerous to their compatriots as it is to themselves'.[80]

Diderot clearly did not share this view, but neither was he inclined to underestimate the 'speed and inconceivable fury' which drove the dispossessed, the land-hungry, the gold-greedy and the simply avaricious, overseas. The whole colonizing process was vitiated from the start by the 'atrocious motives' of the first settlers, and by the recognition that such initial acts of possession as Columbus's or Bougainville's can only ever be transformed into reality through the destruction of an entire society, and frequently through the destruction of a society which had at least the *potential* for developing into something far finer than any civil society then available. It was all a matter of where you started from. The savage started from nature. Left to his own devices he might finally come to create something close to a true civilization, as many of Diderot's contemporaries (if not Diderot himself) believed the Inka had done. But as fifteenth-century Europeans had only been able to start from a position of largely irredeemable corruption, the record of their peregrinations could only ever be a dismal history of devastation. 'About two centuries after the depopulation of Europe into Asia,' said Diderot, summarizing that history, 'there came the migration into America. That revolution reduced all things to chaos, and mixed in among us the vices and the corruptions of every climate'.[81] Just as Montesquieu's Persian, Rhedi, viewed the invention of the compass from the point of view of the American Indians as 'absolutely pernicious', so Diderot looked upon the compass and the sailing ship as instruments of cultural ruin.[82]

Even those who may have gone to America for other more benign reasons than those of the habitual colonist, inevitably suffered the fate which befell all immigrants. For in order to travel you must, of necessity, leave something of yourself behind. The metropolis is where that self-defining, self-creating 'esprit national' is generated. In abandoning it, the traveller is compelled to become another kind of being. 'I will accept that there are very few exceptions,' wrote Diderot. 'The greater the distance from the capital, the further the mask of the traveller's identity slips from his face. On the frontier it falls away altogether ('Il tombe sur la fontière'). 'From one hemisphere to another,' he continued,

> what has he, the traveller, become? Nothing. Once past the equator a man is neither English, nor Dutch, nor French, nor Spanish nor Portuguese. All that he preserves of his homeland are the principles and prejudices which authorize or excuse his conduct.[83]

Travel, 'les expéditions de long cours', have 'reared a new generation of nomadic savages . . . those men who visit so many countries that they end by belonging to none . . . these amphibians who live on the surface of the waters'.[84]

The faceless European traveller has, in a sense, reversed the journey which his ancestors once made. By travelling through space he has gone backwards in time, by going from Europe to America or India or the Pacific he has also gone from civility to savagery. But this decomposed natural man is not the 'savage' whom Bougainville had met. All great revolutions, as Diderot said elsewhere, change ineradicably the human and social landscapes over which they move. The principles and prejudices which the mask of civility inevitably leaves behind clutters the mind of the new savage quite as much as it did that of the old civil man. For what lies hidden beneath civil man is no longer natural man. Time and the civilizing process has changed the whole person. Decomposed civil man is what Diderot nicely calls the 'domestic tiger who has returned to the jungle'.[85] Greed, the 'soif d'or' which is the one thing the *bon sauvage* does not know, is also the one thing the civil man cannot ever unlearn. And with the thirst for gold comes, too, the thirst for blood.[86]

The only possible exception to this dismal rule was the English. For uniquely, the English had been driven overseas not by greed, nor even by the wish to impose their beliefs upon others. They had gone in pursuit of liberty. Whereas all the other races of Europe had exported the worst, the English had driven out the best; and whereas the Spanish, Portuguese and French Creoles in America had now become 'more or less degenerate'[87], the English–Americans had sustained and developed their concern for liberty. As Chastellux in *De la Felicité publique* (On Public Happiness, 1772) remarked, theirs was an America which had been 'peopled under the auspices of liberty and reason'.[88] It was even possible for Diderot to ignore the Indian massacres and the expropriation of Indian lands which, as others less friendly to the new United States could point out, were every bit as bad as those committed by other Europeans in other parts of America. The Thirteen Colonies may not have been the societies of planned miscegenation which he had half envisaged for America. But in their political constitutions and their social objectives, they came very close to being the kind of midway station between savagery and civility of his imagination. Here was virtue without enthusiasm, and in the half mythical person of the Quaker it was possible, from a distance at least, to see a transitional figure between the ancient republican and the modern merchant. The United States was clearly not Utopia. But then Diderot had little time for utopias, and if it was not the ideal society it was, at least, an attainable optimal society.

All other Europeans, however, 'have ... shown themselves, indistinguishable, throughout all the countries of the New World'.[89] They had, in effect, become not savages, but what Diderot had defined elsewhere as 'barbarians', those who have been cursed by 'that sombre disposition which makes man inaccessible to the delights of nature or art and the sweetness of society'.[90] 'Savages' exist only in a particular cultural milieu, but 'barbarians' are with us always, no matter how civilized we become.

These new barbarians travel outwards to the lands inhabited by free and innocent 'savages'. There a conflict occurs which underscores, once again, the incommensurability of all cultures. Columbus and his men, on arrival in the Caribbean, are carried ashore by the unsuspecting Indians. They are dressed in the finest cottons, given food to eat and hammocks in which to rest. At this moment the Spaniards are satisfied, their claws, one might say, sheathed. Hold this moment, Diderot tells his reader, for it will not last for long, and now remember what the Indians in this little scene do not know; the slaughters, the pillage and the massacres that are soon to follow. 'Let us recall', the passage ends with a leap from imaginative recall to moral condemnation, 'that moment of discovery, that first encounter between two worlds, in order to truly detest our own'.[91]

v

Travel decomposes civilized man. Colonization ultimately only destroys cultures which, although they may know no law codes, 'no civil nor criminal justice', and although their members may live in huts and wear no clothes, are like those of the innocent Caribs, probably in most significant respects superior to our own. Out there on the frontier, the natural man and the domestic tigers fight their unequal and ultimately disastrous battles. But Diderot, like Montesquieu, also knew that the metropolis could never be fully insulated from the consequences of the processes of overseas expansion which it had itself initiated. Chastellux's vision of a safe, sanitized haven for the potentially destructive forces within European society ignored the fact that, remote though America was, it was still socially, culturally and politically, linked to Europe. And the routes which had carried the colonist out would also allow his vices, his 'tyrannies and his cruelties', to seep back into the mother-land. You cannot, as Montesquieu had observed, practise tyranny abroad while remaining free at home; of this, as he had demonstrated, the Spanish Empire in America was the paradigmatic example.[92]

For Diderot, however, the experience of travel, of discovery and finally of colonization, was not exclusively a political or even a moral concern. It was also, as was every aspect of the human experience, a psychological and, ultimately, an aesthetic one.[93] Something other than tyranny had seeped back to Europe after the settlement of the Americas, something which comes close, though he is never very explicit, to being the inescapable detachment and disenchantment which finally befalls every 'voyageur par état'.

The Greeks, Diderot noted, invested all natural phenomena with a sense of wonder, transforming every stone, mountain, tree and wood, into a personalized magical force, the force which aroused admiration and curiosity. But when the moderns arrived in America 'a nature which was totally new remained mute beneath the Spaniard's impassive gaze'. Why, asked Diderot, had America never suggested to any European, wonders of its *own*? Why, that is, were all Europeans seemingly so 'infatuated by their dream of antiquity' as to have been driven merely to transport to the New World the wonders of the Ancient, the Amazons, the Fountains of Eternal Youth, the eternally ageless Hyperboreans?[94] In Europe these things, fantastic though they might have been, belonged nevertheless to an understanding of nature. They had originated in the Greeks' direct encounter with their world. Out there in America, however, detached like the poor travellers themselves from the particularities which had generated them, they became mere fantasies, idle stories, curios as culturally meaningless as Aztec drinking bowls and armadillos would be in Europe. As Diderot said elsewhere of the painter's not dissimilar problem of representation, 'when the truth of nature is forgotten, the mind fills with actions, positions and figures which are false, affected, ridiculous and cold'.[95] The answer to his initial question was that no European had set out with any intention other than to 'discover' – to uncover precisely what the canon of authorities had taught him *must* exist somewhere in the world, but which had, so far, eluded him. These forms of immutable mobility, as we have seen in Chapter 1, also served to achieve the kind of attachment to the known, the possibility of which Diderot was asking them to renounce. To stand, so to speak, conceptually and imaginatively naked before the unknown would, as least for those early Spaniards, have been unthinkable. Putting nature aside seemed to be the only strategy for dealing with a nature which was so wholly other. And not merely was conceptual nakedness an impossible option but, as Diderot himself had noted, so too was almost any kind of direct cultural exposure to the threatening presence of the undescribed and unreconstituted 'new'. 'Nothing,' he wrote,

> is so bizarre than to see a Europe transported and reproduced, so to speak, in America, by [replicating] the names and shapes of our towns, by [imitating] the laws, customs, and the religion of our continent.[96]

For Diderot, however, the answer to the question why the colonist behaved in these unimaginative and bizarre ways was to be found in the very process of which the early discoverers were a part. For Raynal, himself, it may have been the case that 'the discovery of a new world alone could provide food for our curiosity',[97] but for Diderot – his interpolations, once again, running directly counter to the argument of Raynal's original text – the very reverse is the case. Prolonged travelling wearied the imagination, and reduced the traveller's capacity for wonder. Since Plato 'wonder', *admiratio*, had been thought of as the origin of philosophical and scientific thought. It was primitive man's wonder at the night sky which had first driven him to map and understand it. Without wonder, we experience no need to question. 'Wonder,' (*admiration*) said Descartes, who in *Les passions de l'ame* (On the Passions of the Soul) provided the most influential and extended early-modern account of this process, 'is a sudden surprise of the soul which causes it to apply itself to consider with attention the objects which seem to be rare and extraordinary'. The power, or as Descartes would say, the 'use' of wonder lies in the fact that it 'causes us to learn and retain in our memory things of which we were formerly ignorant'. A certain amount of wonder then 'disposes us for the acquisition of the sciences'.[98] It is also, Diderot claimed, fantasy, the corollary to wonder, which by unsettling the mind becomes the prime source of 'that infinite diversity of laws and customs' which characterizes all civilized societies.[99] The savage, by contrast, is entirely untroubled by the cultural imagination which generates such restless desires.

Descartes's notion of wonder – and all subsequent theories of the sublime which Diderot shared – are defined in terms of a set of responses made by the subject, and of that subject's relationship to his or her faculties.[100] It must, therefore, be the case that the agent's own individual capacity to experience wonder may – indeed must – diminish as the shock of the new is reduced. Familiarity may not always breed contempt, but it does breed indifference and detachment, and with it the failure to *see*. The traveller, John Mandeville or Marco Polo, who goes out once and then returns home, returns precisely with what Mandeville called a book 'of the marvels which I had seen in diverse countries'.[101] Diderot's traveller, by contrast, is not a man to wonder. He does not travel in order to experience and to record, to make his own world wider through contact with others. Instead, as we have seen, he leads a dissolute life cut off from the normal ties of family and the normal social bonds. Unrestrained by laws and customs he is, ultimately, an identityless being. He (no woman could ever, or would ever wish to, attain such a state) also experiences wonder in diminishing degrees as he wanders. As the mask of his identity slips away, so too does his capacity for imaginative response to novelty. In time, the diminution of his imaginative powers, like the collective tolerance for tyranny and cruelty, seeps steadily back from the periphery to the centre, from the colony to the metropolis.

Navigation and long sea voyages may have had the effect of familiarizing people who once believed that their cultures were the only possible measure of all things with a diversity of human types of which they had no previous experience. But the outcome of this had not been tolerance or the erosion of superstition, but rather a decrease in the capacity for imaginative response. 'The difference of cults and of nations,' wrote Diderot, 'has familiarized even the grossest minds with a spirit of indifference for the objects which would once have startled their imagination'.[102] Diderot was prepared to accept that because of the oceanic discoveries European customs had, to some degree at least, become deregulated and religious hatreds had cooled. But accompanying these unquestionable goods was another kind of loss:

> the variety and multiplicity of objects which our industry has presented to our minds and senses have diminished the affections of man and have weakened the energy of all our sentiments.

The travel of a few has thus left us all ultimately the poorer. The imagination, as Diderot had said elsewhere, borrowing a metaphor from d'Alembert (or d'Alembert from him), allowed us

> to raise a curtain and to reveal to men a hitherto unknown, or rather ignored, corner of the world which they inhabit. He who is [thus] inspired is sometimes uncertain if the thing that he declares to be there is a reality or an chimera, if it has any existence outside of himself. He is then at the furthest limits of the energy of the nature of man, and at the extremity of the resources of art.[103]

The traveller and the discoverer have blurred the boundaries between the natural and the artificial. They have revealed to the general gaze an increasing number of unknown and neglected corners of the world. But for them the act of discovery, the raising of the cloth, does not have the power, as it would have for the true artists, to move them towards the limits of their 'natural energy' and over into an act of human creation.

It is not merely the case that no one now visiting the Taj Mahal or the Grand Canyon or St Peter's is likely to be infused with anything very much more wondrous than a strong sense of *déjà vu*. It is rather as if – and the image was a familiar one in the eighteenth century – the capacity for wonder had a finite capital life which the great voyages of exploration had seriously diminished. It had also, and more damaging still, increased our tolerance of the sufferings of others. For the understanding of suffering requires not only the recognition of the humanity which the observer shares with the sufferer, it requires also a leap of the imagination. The intrusion of the American world into the Europeans' imaginative and cognitive space had made this leap possible now only for those enlightened few who could still keep the existence of a universal benevolence firmly within their imaginative grasp. Because of this, Diderot declared of the Americas, we had in the end no alternative but to 'curse the moment of their discovery'.[104]

vi

Diderot's claim that the discovery of America had brought with it not only the miseries inflicted by the gold-greedy and the land-hungry, but also the disenchantment and the disengagement which permitted those miseries to persist, despite the active resistance of such heroes of humanity as Las Casas, belongs, as we have seen, to a familiar European language which represents travel as inimical to true family life, to civility, even to the propagation of the species. It is also an inversion of the kind of language which, as we saw in Chapter 3, linked the discovery of America with the creation of the modern world, and with the final stage in the evolution of what by Diderot's time had come to be called 'civilization.'[105] Diderot does not deny that the discoveries are a crucial factor in the triumph of the modern. What he does deny is that that triumph has been an unmixed blessing to humanity. The argument, however, is not that we can now undo the damage that has been done, much less that we can – or would ever wish to – go back behind the fifteenth century. It is that we have to accept that the modern world simply *is* a place of disenchantment and limited benevolence. Just as modern man lost his instinctive poetic imagination as he learnt to think in terms of universal abstract concepts so, as his mind becomes increasingly familiar with what had once been called the 'variety of the things' – the *varietas rerum* – he had to accept that he had lost that sense of wonder which had driven him to attempt to *understand* the phenomena he could both see and describe.

Alexander von Humboldt came to similar conclusions. He, however, was not concerned with the diminution in our capacity for benevolence. He also dismissed the claim (which he attributes to Edmund Burke) that the great astronomical discoveries had been first prompted by a sense of wonder, as the product of a 'vicious' (and characteristically Anglo-Saxon) empiricism. Had Burke been right, he argued, 'the illusion of the senses . . . would have nailed the stars to the crystalline dome of the sky'. The impulse to science, true science, comes instead from the recognition of the 'general view which allows us to recognize in the particular plant or animal, not an isolated species, but a form linked in the chain of being to other forms living or extinct'.[106] And this process, as we have seen, he believed to have reached both its apogee, and some kind of crisis point, in the fifteenth and sixteenth centuries. 'The powerful age which we here seek to describe in regard to its influence on the development of cosmic ideas,' he wrote of that 'grand era',

> gave to all enterprises, as well as the impression of nature offered by distant voyages, the charm of novelty and surprise, which begins to

be wanting in our present more learned age in the many regions of the earth which are now open to us.

The age to which he belonged, he reflected, had lost the pace with which, in the early-modern period, the 'Age of Discovery' had transformed human culture beyond recognition. Human knowledge, as we have seen, now moved forward not from epoch to epoch, but 'henceforth produces grand results by its own peculiar and internal power in every direction at the same time'. 'Our more deeply investigative age,' he continued, 'finds in the increasing riches of ideas, a compensation for the lessening of the surprise which the novelty of the great and imposing natural phenomenon once called forth'.[107] In the place of wonder, which for Humboldt, as for Schiller (Humboldt's' 'immortal poet') and for Goethe, was a purely aesthetic response with no particular philosophical, much less scientific, pay-off, came understanding through the patient accumulation, description and quantification of data. 'The good observers,' he wrote to Geoffroy St Hilaire in 1836, 'who like Ehrenber, Purkinie, Valentin and Corda spend some four or five hours a day in front of the microscope . . . finally come to see the same thing'.[108] Science is no longer the inspired endeavour of a few great individuals. It is, instead, a work of co-operation among many: 'slower', Humboldt would say, than the work of the isolated geniuses of the past, but far more certain. The image of the scientist at his microscope, which for Christiaan Huygens some two-hundred years before had been itself the image of the discoverer of 'New Worlds',[109] now replaces the inspired navigator of Kepler and Giambattista Manso's imagination.

Both Humboldt and Diderot had seen, in the sudden and massive increase in our knowledge of other worlds which the discovery of America had entailed, a significant change in the ways in which we respond to our own. But their conclusions also point up the differences between the objectives of the late Enlightenment and those of the early Romantics. For Humboldt, the exchange of the pace of wonder for the development of a unified scientific vision, a gaze which would slowly reveal the underlying analogy between all things, human as well as natural, had, in the long run, been an unalloyed benefit to man.

For Diderot, by contrast, the discovery, settlement and colonization of America threatened the possibility of further imaginative response to difference, threatened to reduce us all to the citizens of a single invariable culture. Colonization shared this in common with the practices of Humboldt's 'good observers': that it could, with time, patience and sufficient force, make the incommensurable commensurable. But it could only ever do this by lessening and finally, perhaps, even eliminating the gap which lay between ourselves and the 'other', by making the other entirely like us.

This terrifying process was by no means complete, and perhaps, given the tendency of the settlers to decline into lasciviousness and luxury under the influence of the climate of the New World, might never be. Yet the European empires in America were already vast conglomerates, over-populated and over-extended. Like so many modern cities, they were 'monsters of nature', which nature seeks always to destroy.[110] 'Every colony,' wrote Diderot, 'whose authority rests in one country and whose obedience in another, is in principle a vicious establishment'.[111] Empires become, of necessity, societies divided between masters and slaves, and communities which are so divided are bound one day to irrupt into unparalleled violence.[112] Ever since antiquity such fissures had been a recognized threat to the political viability and cultural homogeneity of all empires. The situation in the European Atlantic colonies, however, since they embraced such widely disparate cultures over such vast areas, was far more acute than anything which the Greeks or the Romans or even the Arabs had had to face. Was it really possible, Diderot asked, even with modern technology, 'to rule peoples separated from the metropolis by immense oceans, as if they were subjects bound by the same sceptre?'[113] Clearly the answer was no. Sooner or later, as the English had already discovered, these distant colonies will respond to a 'violent desire for self-government'[114] – an argument which may have persuaded Turgot of the desirability of a complete French withdrawal from America.[115]

But it is not only the political and economic consequences of distance which make all empires unworkable, monstrous and unnatural societies. It is also, as we have seen, the obligation they impose upon all their members to travel, to transport themselves further and further from the metropolitan centre where civilization alone is possible. For the colonists the only hope of regeneration lay in the creation of new independent metropolises. And the only way this could be achieved was through miscegenation. This is what is happening on Tahiti as Bougainville and his reluctant Aumonier leave the island. But here, as the sage makes clear, the seeds already quickening in the wombs of the women of Tahiti, will bring forth only monsters. The language, as with all languages of colonization, is explicitly sexual. The visiting Frenchmen on Tahiti may be said to have reversed the one curse which America was believed to have visited upon Europe: syphilis.[116]

Diderot was not always so pessimistic as the voices he had created. In the *Histoire*, he constantly holds up the possibility of sex as a form of liberation. Not only, as with the Tahitian Orou, is sex a mode of understanding – perhaps, in the absence of a common language, the only mode of understanding – which can pass between distant and incommensurable cultures. It is also the only means to bring into being the new society which alone can resolve the conflicts which those misconceived empires have created. Young men and women, he fantasized, should now be sent to the Americas, and 'through consanguinity the foreigners and the natives of the place would have made a single and common family'. There, he said wistfully, there would 'have been no weapons, no soldiers, only large numbers of many young women for the men, and many young men for the women'.[117] He had even hoped that the Portuguese crown's legislation of 1755 (which had attempted to put an end to the slave-trade, and to curb the worst abuses of the colonists) might arouse sufficient confidence in the Indians of Brazil and Paraguay as to 'draw the savages from their forests', and that, 'a complete confidence might imperceptibly develop between the Americans and the Europeans so that with time they might come to form one people'.[118]

For Diderot recognized that cultures (*les moeurs*) do change over time, sometimes (*pace* Rousseau) for the better. In his sexually liberated, miscegenated world, neither European nor Indian, but fully 'American', men would be uniquely placed to benefit from civilization without being corrupted by it. They would also be able to see the evident superiority of European technology to which the 'imperious and imposing tone' of the 'masters and usurpers' had blinded the Amerindians. Such a society would thus have achieved what all eighteenth-century dreams of commercial harmony had aimed at, a union 'between men with reciprocal needs'.[119]

Diderot knew full well that his single family was, and would remain, an illusion. Even in those parts of the world, such as Tahiti, where the Europeans still had the opportunity to create such societies, they would never have the vision or the will to put them into action. In the end, and like the imaginary state poised half-way between savagery and civility, the miscegenated society could only ever be a device by which to measure the failures of European civilization.

vii

On this account, the discovery of America, 'the most significant event for the human species in general and for the peoples of Europe in particular',[120] would seem to have been an unmitigated disaster for mankind. In 1782, however, Raynal suggested to the Académie de Lyon that they offer a prize for the best essay in answer to the question of what had been the advantages, and what the disadvantages, to Europe of the discovery.[121] On the face of it, the 1780 edition of his own *Histoire* would seem to have demonstrated overwhelmingly that it had been a disadvantage. Yet for both Raynal and Diderot, and for most of those, including Chastellux, who wrote essays for the prize, there was another side to the story, one which made travel into a virtue, and which might yet for all the miseries it had inflicted upon mankind, transform the history of European colonization: this was commerce. As Mandrillon, who was one candidate for Raynal's prize, observed, if the new commercial societies of the eighteenth century had not actually been created by the discovery of America, they had certainly been molded by it. It was the Spaniards, however, who had least understood the nature of the enterprise on which they had embarked.[122] If only, he lamented, they had 'made liaisons with the Indians in accordance with the laws of humanity', they could have gone on to create what he, like Las Casas before him, saw as Columbus's project for a 'Castilian Utopia' in America, rather than the destructive giant that the agents of the Castilian crown had erected after Columbus's departure.[123] Mandrillon's vision was overly optimistic, but part of his synoptic, and conjectural, history of the exploration and conquest of the Americas was also shared by both Diderot and Raynal.

Commerce – and the *Histoire des deux Indes* is, in large part, a history of commerce – had, Diderot believed, gone a long way towards the peaceful erosion of the older 'prejudices' which had traditionally separated the various races of men. Already, he believed, 'the fanaticism of religion and the spirit of conquest, those two causes of disturbance in the world, are not what they were'.[124] But this was due to commerce, not colonization. *Le doux commerce*, in Montesquieu's famous phrase, was responsible for 'making men gentle' since it involved far more than the mere exchange of necessities. Ever since the days of Aquinas, the exchange of goods and the acquisition of the knowledge and understanding of a common humanity had shared a single vocabulary. Trade demanded communication, and communication finally brought understanding. 'Letters, the tongue of the world', as Tom Paine informed Raynal,

> have in some measure brought all mankind acquainted, and, by an extension of these uses, are every day promoting some new friendship. Through them distant nations become capable of conversation.[125]

Commercium had always been more than mere trade. But in the eighteenth century, the merchant, once despised because of the non-military profession he pursued, came to be seen as the agent of the transmission of civilization. Commerce, as Mandrillon put it, 'made men more communicative and humane'.[126] Merchants, wrote Diderot, should now have 'a noble idea of their profession'. Although it was still pointless to ask the majority of them as they actually were to have trust in each other, the trust that was required if the whole system was to function at all, the day was not far off when 'credit' would come to replace 'honour' as the motivating force within all societies.[127] Since commerce operates through the mechanisms of mutual co-operation rather than domination, it is in the interests of the merchant that everyone should benefit from his labours. Commerce, as one of Raynal's commentators put it, is 'the science of the needs of others'.[128] Unlike the colonist who merely exploits – and exports – whatever the colony has to offer, the merchant develops. Under the beneficent hand of the merchant, technology is transformed from an instrument of European oppression into the agent of material improvement and universal enlightenment. 'I ask myself,' wrote Diderot,

casting a imaginary eye over the plains of 'Indostan', who dug those canals? Who drained those plains? Who founded those towns? Who gathered together, clothed and civilized these people? All the voices of all the enlightened men who live among them, cry out in reply: it is commerce, it is commerce.[129]

Commerce, 'the new arm of the moral world',[130] as he called it, was certain one day to become also the agent of a new world-order, a new empire, based not upon power, but upon reciprocity. 'Everywhere,' he wrote in the first of his contributions to the *Histoire des deux Indes*, 'men have made a mutual exchange of their opinions, their laws, their customs, their ills and their remedies, their virtues and their vices'.[131] And as empires based upon reciprocity could only ever be ones were mutually beneficial to all their members, the tyrannies practised by the Europeans in America would one day vanish, and in their place would come a new international order. 'A war among commercial nations,' he wrote in a remarkable passage,

is a fire that destroys them all. The time is not far off when the sanctions of rulers will extend to the individual transactions between the subjects of different nations, and when bankruptcy, whose impact can be felt at such immense distances, will become an affair of state . . . and the annals of all peoples will need to be written by commercial philosophers (*commerçans philosophes*) as they were once written by historical orators.[132]

The metaphorical shift from the orator to the philosophically informed commercial historian is significant. For the ancient world, whose claims to a universal moral authority Diderot distrusted intensely, had been dominated by the range and power of the significant speech-act. As we have seen, the ideal speech-community of Rousseau's imagination was one which was only as extensive as the limits of the most powerful human voice. The community of the 'commercial historian', by contrast, is global, and the means of communication he has at his command – the written word and the exchange of goods – will be used to construct societies far more complex, and ultimately far more humane, than the constraining oligarchies of Rome or Athens. In the new empires of Diderot's imagination, reciprocity would replace domination. Cultures which had once been wholly incommensurable would come to be, if not yet wholly commensurable, certainly capable of that degree of mutual understanding which would finally make a truly 'New World' a possibility.

viii

Fluid and ultimately porous though Diderot's cultures may have been, they were also thought of as integral and discrete. It is only possible, as we have seen, to travel in one direction. As with Léry's Norman translators, any possibility of return has been pre-empted by the journey itself. At best he (or she) who has undergone the trial of travel will be condemned, like Gulliver, to perpetual isolation from those who had once been his fellows. Diderot's vision of incommensurability, however, was underpinned by the concept of a providential order in which all humans should be in harmony with nature. The writer who came closest to sharing these views is Kant's pupil, Johann Gottfried Herder (1744–1803). It might seem odd to link Diderot the cosmopolitan to Herder, the supposed father of German nationalism. Diderot's attack on colonialism in the name of the inevitable incommensurability and the necessary integrity of all cultures stops well short of any kind of exclusivism. It is also the case that Herder's ultimate appeal to religion as a form of knowledge which could unite all peoples would have sounded very odd indeed to Diderot. But then it is also overly crude to describe Herder as a 'nationalist', since his concept of a 'People' (*Volk*) makes not more claims to the political entitlement which a 'nation', in the modern sense of the term, must surely possess, than does Diderot's *patrie*.

There is, however, a sense in which Herder, who never mentions the *Histoire des deux Indes* although he had clearly read it,[133] carries Diderot's arguments to the point at which they become, in effect, a rejection of the whole argument (which Diderot had no wish to challenge) for the unity of the human race.

For Herder, as for Diderot, colonialism is an evil because it reduces, or threatens to reduce through human, and thus artificial, means, the number of cultural variants that exist in the world. That is an evil because plurality is part of the way the world is constituted. For Herder, as for Diderot, travel is a source of moral corruption because it violates Nature's intentions, which are always to preserve things in their original state. 'Nature,' he wrote, in what is perhaps his best-known work, the *Ideen zur Philosophie der Geschichte der Menschheit* (Outline Of a Philosophy Of the History Of Man), 'has not established her borders between remote lands in vain'. But whereas for Diderot the 'voyageur par état', the savage nomad, is a menace to those he encounters, for Herder, such an assault upon nature can only result in the mental and physical collapse of the assailant. 'The history of conquest,' he observed,

as well as of commercial companies and especially that of missions afford a melancholy and in some respects a laughable picture.... We shudder with abhorrence when we read the accounts of many European nations, who, sunk in the most dissolute voluptuousness and insensible pride have degenerated both in body and mind and no longer possess any capacity for enjoyment or compassion. They are full-blown bladders in human shape, lost to every noble and active pleasure, and in whose veins lurks avenging death.[134]

This last assertion was meant to be taken literally. Europeans in America, he claimed, quoting the Swedish botanist, Peter Kalm's, *Natural and Political History of Pennsylvania* (1768) mature more rapidly and die younger than they do in Europe. This phenomenon has nothing to do with the environment since the same source confirmed that the native Americans, whose rate of maturation was thought to be notoriously slow, sometimes lived to be very old indeed.[135] Exactly what the mechanism is by which nature produces such effects Kalm does not say. But it clearly follows from its very existence that not only can no people hope to transport its own culture intact to another world, neither can it mate with an autochthonous one to produce a new hybrid culture. The only possible mode of transplantation is for the traveller himself to go native. 'But how few,' Herder lamented, 'such people are there'. All those who fail to assimilate in this way find themselves, sooner or later, the victims of a superior nature. 'And does not Nature revenge every insult offered her?' he asked.

Where are the conquests, the factories, the invasions of former times, when distant foreign lands were visited by a different race, for the sake of devastation and plunder! The still breath of climate has dissipated and consumed them, and it was not difficult for the natives to give the finishing strokes to the rotten tree.[136]

The extravagance of this claim, in the aftermath of the creation of the United States and on the eve of the Independence wars in the Caribbean and South America (the *Ideen* was written between 1784 and 1791), may now seem absurd. But Herder's image of the degenerate colonist finally succumbing to the influence of nature is a function less of any observation about the real world than it is of his belief in the utter impenetrability of all cultural forms. 'The idea of every indigenous culture,' he claimed, 'is confined to its own region'; so confined, that the possibility of communicating just what it is becomes seemingly impossible. For the 'European has no idea of the boiling passions and imagination which glow in the negro's breast; and the Hindu has no conception of the restless desires that chase the European from one end of the world to the other'.[137] We are all, Herder believed, in the same position as the 'King of Siam' who, on being told about ice and snow, declared them to be non-existent. Like Diderot's savage who thought that Paris was merely an unusual natural feature, the Siamese, who had no possible access to extremes of cold, could only dismiss such things as the ravings of foreign travellers. Literally nothing that does not come within the range of our own cultural experience, and hence within range of our own language, can have any meaningful existence for us.

Herder's claim for both incommensurability and incomprehensibility went far further than any previous argument in favour of cultural integrity. Such extensive claims had also to be grounded in an entirely new vision of social development. Diderot, as we have seen, operated well within the limits of the traditional Hobbesian, Grotian model of sociability: according to this model all societies have their beginnings in the general recognition of the desirability of an escape from the state of nature. They grow and develop in order to satisfy human needs which in turn increase 'as the patterns of our lives have increased and become more perfect'.[138] This process, despite innumerable local variations, is universal and universally recognizable. Although Herder accepted that all communities began in this way as 'savage', and although he speaks of savagery as a single uniform state, and ascribes to all human beings common methods of understanding, he rejects the claim to which all seventeenth- and eighteenth-century social theorists (including Rousseau) subscribed that social evolution was ultimately the outcome of the rational calculation of interests. Such a theory, since it made of all men the agents of mere rationality, was, he believed, inherently implausible. 'I find myself unable to comprehend,' he wrote in *Auch eine Philosophie der Geschichte zur Bildung der Menschheit* (Yet Another Philosophy Of History, 1774), 'how reason can be presented so universally as the single summit and purpose of all human culture. Is the whole body just one big eye?'[139] Like Hobbes and the modern natural-law theorists, Grotius and Puffendorf, Herder believed that self-preservation was 'the first object of every existing being'.[140] But this, he claimed, had led not to the war of all against all, and thus to the evolution of societies based upon utility. It had led instead to a natural state of immobility. 'Everything,' he wrote, 'from grains of sand to the solar orb, strives to remain what it is'. War is not man's first condition. It is instead the consequence of the growth of human desires. Given enough space and enough resources, all peoples develop such radically different needs that 'what is a matter of indifference to one man, to another is an object of desire'. So long as humans follow their own natural instincts and remain where they are, there can be no cause for conflict. But humans are the only animals who are capable of violating the natural limits of their territories. Once outside their natural habit men soon fall to fighting over resources. War is thus, said Herder, inverting the Hobbesian paradigm, 'the offspring of necessity, not the legitimate child of enjoyment'.[141] Similarly, he claimed that society, when understood as the simple extension of the family unit to include 'a band of sworn friends', or as communities that are held together by the relationships, husband/wife, parent/offspring, friend/friend, is natural.[142] But all government is an artifice.[143] Rather than having been devised, by either contract or by covenant, to provide the means of exit from an irredeemable state of nature, it had instead been the act of a few men, who by a process he confessed to find unintelligible – 'the most obscure phrase in the human language'[144] – had succeeded, he said, echoing Hobbes, in inspiring men 'to submit their understanding, their abilities, nay frequently their lives . . . to the will of one'.[145]

Just as Herder rejected the possibility of any interpenetrability between cultures, so he rejected what seemed to him to be an implausibly uniform view of human social evolution. His attack on what in effect amounts to the whole basis of the eighteenth-century 'Science of Man' begins where much of his argument for cultural singularity, and many previous claims for cultural homogeneity, begin; that is, with language. Perhaps Herder's best-known work, beside the *Ideen*, is his early *Abhandlung über den Ursprung der Sprache* (Treatise Upon the Origin of Language, 1770). In this he set out to refute the theory (which we discussed in Chapter 4) that languages are created and develop as a function of, and in response to, the user's increasing social needs. What neither Rousseau nor Condillac had been able to explain, argued Herder – what, indeed, no previous language-theorist had ever attempted to explain, although Condillac had clearly seen that it was a problem – was *how* the first men had progressed from sounds to words, and from words to phrases, phrases to sentences, and so on. Similarly neither Rousseau's nor Condillac's conjectural histories of the acquisition of language had been able to provide any mechanism which would explain *how* one got from one stage to the next.[146] It would be no use crying out in need, 'aidez moi', to take Rousseau's example, if there were not a sufficient number of other persons similarly inflicted who had all had the same idea at the same time.

The same objection, argued Herder, in the *Ideen*, applied equally to the traditional accounts of the evolution of society which operated with similar discrete, independent stages or epochs, and in particular to Puffendorf's 'Four Stages Theory'. This explained the evolution of society in terms of changing means of production, from hunter-gatherers to pastoralists to agriculturalists and finally to the commercial society, each one of which was seen as a response to a change in the structure and complexity of the needs of the society. Apart from the empirical fact that few human societies actually followed this pattern, and that there is little evidence to suggest that agriculture *is* superior to pastoralism, there is, argued Herder, simply no mechanism which can possibly account for the shift from one state to the next.[147]

For Herder, therefore, there could be only one explanation for the seemingly inevitable changes in human speech and human modes of association: they are, in some sense, innate.[148] When applied to language, this claim was hardly startling. The critiques which Smith, Ferguson, Millar, Filangieri, Grimaldi and Linguet had all directed against Rousseau's theory of language, for instance, were based on similar observations. What Adam Ferguson in the *Essay On the History of Civil Society* (1767) listed as man's 'disposition to friendship or enmity, his reason, his use of language and articulate sounds', are all attributes, not adjuncts, of the self. They are thus, he said, 'to be retained in his description, as the wing and paw are in the eagle and the lion'.[149] But Herder also claimed that just as we inherit our language-knowledge from our forebears so, too, do we inherit our social and cultural understanding from them. The imagination which, like Diderot, he believed to be 'the least explained of all the powers of the mind', rather than reason, was the instrument of social and cognitive change. And the imagination, the 'knot that tied body and mind together, the bud, as it were, of the whole sensual organization'[150] has to be, to some degree, innate. Although Herder, like Shaftesbury, recognized that the scholastic notion of 'innate ideas' could never be resuscitated, he believed nevertheless in the continuing existence of 'a predisposition to receive, connect and expand certain images and ideas', something which came very close to being a cultural analogue of Shaftesbury's 'moral sense'.

This move effectively reduced the power of all human agents to shape successfully their own social and cultural ends. No matter what we do, we are all isolated as cultural groups within a given 'mind set', what he called variously 'opinions', 'fancies' and 'mythologies'. These can and do change over time, but each changes in its own, untransferable way. The impulses for modification, the imaginative grasp of contingency, are transmitted from parent to child, along with the expressive tools, the language, in which these changes can be made intelligible.

Having thus detached the process of change from any direct causal link with the temporal, Herder was now free to attach it to the spatial. The imaginative grasp – and it is that which determined cultural form – inevitably varies from region to region, as indeed it must from one mode of production to another. 'The shepherd', as he phrased it, 'beholds nature with different eyes from those of the fisherman or hunter'.[151] Language, too, must vary from culture to culture. 'A new language,' he claimed, 'must arise in each new world, a national language in each new nation'. The diversities of human cultural types can be accounted for, and determined over time, by the diversities of environments. Since men are unique among animals in being globally distributed, it would be unnatural to suppose that an Eskimo *could* have any cultural features in common with an African, particularly if cultural traits have now to be thought of as, in some sense, genetically transmitted.[152]

The way is now open for a vision of a deterministically pluralist universe, which has turned the entire Enlightenment image of relative incommensurability around. Underpinning Herder's social theory is the persistent image of nature as a harmonious whole with which we tamper only at our peril. And, if our cultural habits are genetically transmitted, not only must they be in harmony with the particular environment to which nature has assigned us, they must, in a quite specific sense, be a *part* of that environment. The natural world which has shaped men's culturally diverse forms was clearly in place before 'the artificial ends of great societies' came into being. 'How wonderfully,' Herder exclaimed,

[has Nature] separated nations, not only by woods and mountains, seas and deserts, rivers and climates, but most particularly by languages, inclinations and characters, that the work of subjugating despotism might be rendered more difficult, that all the four quarters of the globe might not be crammed into the belly of a wooden horse.[153]

The Trojan Horses which seek to subvert this naturally plural world are, of course, the European empires. 'Nothing,' Herder wrote, 'appears so directly opposite to the ends of government as the unnatural enlargement of states, the wild mixture of various races and various nations under one sceptre'. The use of force and economic interest may temporarily have 'glued together' the world's empires into 'fragile machines of state', but underneath this apparatus, they are all 'destitute of internal unification and sympathy of parts'.[154] Sooner or later they will all collapse into their natural constituent parts, as had the Athenian, the Persian, the Mughal, the Roman, and the Empire of Charles V. Whatever colonies these leave behind struggle on to preserve lifestyles long since abandoned in the metropolis until, as we have seen, they are finally subsumed by whatever cultural form nature had originally designated for that particular environment.

But, for Herder, it is not only empires which are doomed in this way. So too, is the Enlightenment's ambition for ultimate human perfectibility through reason, for what Benjamin Constant in 1815 called the 'égale repartation des lumières'.[155] Since on Herder's account culture (*Kultur*) and enlightenment (*Aufklarung*) must be interchangeable terms, 'Enlightenment', a standard imposed by one culture upon another, could mean nothing. 'The history of mankind,' he wrote, 'is necessarily a chain of socialness and plastic tradition'.[156] Within this chain, each individual culture will come to its own individual and unique 'Enlightenment' in its own time and in its own way.

The last claim is the most striking, most radical of all. For Herder was also prepared to argue that the same was true of that other human good the Enlightenment had hoped would one day follow in the wake of the European colonizers, once the massacres and the butchery had finished, and more enlightened rulers had replaced the Gothic monarchs of the early-modern world: universal human happiness. 'Human nature,' wrote Herder in *Auch eine Philosophie der Geschichte*, 'is not the vessel of an absolute and unchanging and independent happiness, as defined by the philosophers; everywhere it attracts that measure of happiness of which it is capable'. Even the image of the thing we call happiness itself 'changes with each condition and climate'.[157] 'It would,' he declared, 'be the most stupid vanity to imagine that the inhabitants of the World must be Europeans to live happily. Should we ourselves have become what we are out of Europe?'[158] This was a strikingly novel assertion. Ever since Aristotle, in the first book of the

Nichomachean Ethics, had managed to establish *eudaimonia*, commonly, if inaccurately, translated as 'happiness', as precisely a *universal* good, all European social thought had worked with the assumption that this was the one constant and invariable human objective. Now, Herder was claiming, the European colonizing process which had begun with the discovery of America had finally revealed that it, too, had been an illusion. And if, as human beings, we are not alike in our understanding of happiness then, in a profound sense, we are not alike in anything. All we can hope to do is to recognize from afar the projects of others as the possible ends for beings whom we recognize as men and women like ourselves.[159]

As Isaiah Berlin has pointed out, this is not, as has so often been claimed, a form of relativism.[160] Cultures for Herder remain absolute within their own compounds. Any attempt to understand one in terms, relative or otherwise, of another is to misunderstand the fundamental and insurmountable incommensurability which they all share. This is what, for Herder, makes 'ethnocentrism' of any kind so absurd. The European claim to have invented the arts and sciences, he wrote, is as ludicrous as the belief of the 'madman of Piraeus' that all the inventions of the world must be Greek simply because he lived at 'a confluence of these inventions and traditions'. 'Steer thy frigate to Otaheite,' Herder contemptuously told Bougainville,

> bid thy canon roar along the shore of the New Hebrides, still you are not superior in skill to the inhabitant of the South-Sea islands who guides with art the boat he has constructed with his own hands.[161]

We all do our own things in our own ways, and the things that we do are all different things.

On this account, there can be no common cultures, no common beliefs or certainties which we can all claim to share by virtue of our common humanity. There cannot even be a common set of descriptive terms upon which we could all agree. Herder accepted that at some deep level, there might be such a thing as 'human nature' which would allow us instinctively to recognize the 'other' as one of 'us'; but this did nothing to help us understand human beings as they are currently constituted, and nothing at all to make the particular life-ways of the other commensurable with our own. Herder was one of the earliest, and remains perhaps the fiercest, opponent of the comforting argument that in order to understand 'others' we have to accredit them with not only the beliefs and desires, but also the *values* that we all as human beings supposedly share.

Herder pushed the notion of incommensurability to the point where the very concept of a single human genus became, if not impossible to conceive, at least culturally meaningless. He seems even to have been sceptical of the Enlightenment's belief that peoples within a single but diversified culture, such as Europe, could usefully communicate with one another. The supposition that they could, he claimed, had been Joseph II's error. The Austrian Empire, which had no possessions outside Europe, was just as much a Trojan Horse as the scattered domains of Charles V had been.[162] If all peoples are, in effect, bound by the horizons of their own particular local understanding, if the only possible response to difference is not wonder but bewilderment, then the idea of 'human nature' itself becomes redundant. Herder's man might come to the aid of another from another culture because he could distinguish him from, say, a giraffe; but there was nothing in Herder's account to imply that he would have any *moral* obligation to do so. Nothing remains of what Shaftesbury – in a bid to escape what he saw as the necessarily dehumanizing consequences of Lockean sensationalism – claimed for all mankind; namely a common 'species-recognition'. It was this recognition which had driven Eskimos to rescue ship-wrecked French sailors, although to the Eskimo these neither looked nor behaved like anything which *they* could recognize as human. If we are to take Herder seriously (and, as Kant recognized, it is not always easy to do so) then one might as well argue that just as the 'Negro' can find happiness in his own way so, too, can he go to Hell in his own way.

This was just the conclusion which Diderot and all those (including Kant) who had argued for a universalism, a brotherhood of all mankind, had most feared. If anything could be saved from the European empires in the New World, it could only be a greater, rather than a lesser, awareness of the presence of others. This would not merely enable 'us' to help 'them', though that, too, was part of the project; it would also help to unravel some of the deleterious effects of our own murderous parochialism. On Diderot's account, the traveller and the colonist had effaced difference, and so had made Europeans insensitive to the suffering of others and increasingly incapable of responding to the creative demands of wonder. Colonies had made the 'other' all too familiar, a vehicle for European views like Orou, or a mere exotic, or even a potential laboratory for a new social science. But, in Diderot's view, this condition might still lead, now that the butchery was done and the older colonies were beginning to break away, to something altogether more subtle and more humane than Herder's 'nationalism'. It might lead into, not out of, contact with the 'other'.

For what Diderot hoped that we all, colonizer as well as colonized, might be able to salvage from centuries of enforced contact with 'other' peoples, is exactly what Herder would deny all possibility of: a reciprocity of understanding. For Diderot, this meant that we might learn from the Amerindian the limitations of our understanding of nature, and with that the absurdity of some of our moral codes. The Amerindian, in contrast, would be given access to our superior technology. Both societies would be improved, but both would remain firmly where they were and, except for the improvements which Enlightenment or technology would necessarily effect, they would remain the societies that they were. This could be the only possible embodiment of that midway station between the civil and the savage of which he had dreamed, that place 'where the happiness of the species resides'.

Afterword

Diderot's hope for a world poised midway between the savage and the civil is, though we may express it differently, recognizably one of ours. So, too, is Herder's insistence upon absolute incommensurablity, and consequent plurality of all cultures towards which we asked to extend, in Ernest Gellner's phrase, indiscriminate charity.[1] The modern European – and the modern 'American' – attitude towards the 'other', comes down to being one or other of these two: either we hope that we may be able to look forward to a more benevolent, less culturally divisive, future in which we may all understand what we most badly need to understand about each other, or we accept that all cultures can only mediate between one another on a number of very limited planes. In one sense, these limited options have always been with us. On the one hand, there was the response of Herodotus to what he had seen on his travels; a response which, like Herder's, while it expressed wonder at the strangeness of 'their' ways, never denied their right to act and believe as they wished. On the other, there was the far more murky claim of those, Aristotle among them, who, while they were prepared to take a long hard look at all that there was in the world, believed nevertheless that in the end, the optimum condition for all mankind was some kind of mean of which European culture was the obvious instantiation.

Like Diderot and Herder, we have enormously refined these two options. But since the late nineteenth century another interpretation has emerged. This claims that we – the cultures of the West – do not merely respond to the inescapable presence of the 'other': we actually construct him or her. On this account the two responses I have described are not responses at all: they are merely ways of capturing our own self-image in others. Both are essentially false if they are taken to be ways of understanding the world, and both are divisive. For all European cultures, the beneficiaries of a Greek ethnocentrism require the presence of something against which they can represent themselves, invariably to their own advantage. This, it could be said, is precisely why Europeans have always taken such an interest in other cultures, and in particular those which, in the terms by which they judge excellence, were notably inferior to their own. What, in the introduction to this book, I called the 'objectifying habit' could be ascribed simply to that need. The Huron or the Chichimeca has not the slightest concern for the practices or customs of his neighbours, except in so far as those practices touch upon or condition his own. Nor, it could be said, do the Ibo, the Javanese, or the Bengali. 'Anthropology' is a Western European science and its subject matter has, until very recently, been overwhelmingly the 'primitive'.

I do not wish to challenge this view. I wish, however, to suggest that the process by which this 'other' is constructed is not, as has so often been claimed, a rather simple act of political appropriation.

This book has attempted to describe a number of conceptual problems which Europeans have confronted – or constructed – in their dealings during a formative historical period with one highly significant 'other'. The writers with whom I began, Columbus, Las Casas and Oviedo, and those with whom I end, Diderot, Herder and Humboldt, were wholly unalike in the projects they pursued and in the composition of their mental worlds. Neither Columbus nor Oviedo, nor even Las Casas, for all his condemnation of the practices of the Spanish colonists, as prepared to challenge the culture to which they belonged to any significant degree. Diderot and Herder were. Indeed it is that critique which generated their concern with 'others' at all. But all of them – all of those who were compelled, in whatever way, to 'encounter' America – were driven by the need to make some sense of the beliefs and the ethical lives of others. This may have resulted in an attempt to *construct* 'others' better suited to the observer's own particular ethical life – it certainly did, as we have seen, in the case of Columbus. But the compulsion to construct brought with it conceptual challenges of its own. For however much we may, indeed, fabricate rather than find our counter-image, we do not fabricate it out of nothing. We cannot think counter-factually about less than whole worlds. Similarly we cannot imagine possible, if factual, worlds with no cultural specificity.[2] Even the 'states of nature' to which the great social and political theorists of the seventeenth century, from Locke to Grotius, made appeal, which were explicitly only *possible* states, 'other' worlds which could be used to explain the need for, and the subsequent development of society – even these were patiently constructed as if they had had some existence in historical time. To be at all effective, the 'other' has always had to be equipped with a dense and particular cultural identity. This is true even of those *bon sauvages*, Adario or Orou. Viewed from this distance, their cultural presence may seem thin enough, but for their contemporaries it was palpably there. And once this or that real 'savage' or 'barbarian' has been used in this way, his or her moral existence becomes a matter of real concern.

The discoveries by modern Europe of a huge range of 'other worlds', of which America was merely the first, if also the most striking, has made this the most deeply troubling, the most unsettling of modern cultural and ethical dilemmas. It is unsettling not only because so much – the whole tragic course of European colonialism – has been occasioned by it, but because it has always seemed, even to those with the best of intentions and the clearest of minds, inherently irresolvably. As Bernard Williams has written:

> When we ask what underlies the variety of human ethical practices, the truth is that we do not know and have no very clear idea of what an answer might look like. We do know one thing, or at least we have a very good reason to believe it: that if there is anything that could be an answer, it will come from actual interpretation of actual people.[3]

Diderot and Herder shared both these perplexities over what the answer to their question would look like, and they recognized the conviction that their attempts to find an answer had to be based upon the observation of 'actual people'. The trouble – and it is the problem that faces any attempt at cultural understanding – was how to identify actual persons. For the 'problem of the other' is clearly a problem about relationships. To see others, even to see them as reversed images of ourselves, we have to have some distance from them; and securing that distance while still preserving both their humanity and their actuality may well be impossible. This is, of course, one of the difficulties which 'attachment' presents. Columbus on Hispaniola was confronted by what were, indubitably, actual people. Yet he could only really identify them as such when he had translated whole areas of what it was that made them actual into a cultural language which to them would have been entirely without meaning. In the process, of course, although in his eyes they had become more like *people*, their actuality had very nearly vanished. Later generations, for whom the initial and unsettling encounter with America no longer seemed to be a problem – although it would surface again in exactly the same way in the South Pacific – were similarly convinced that they were confronting real cultural types.

The difficulty with grasping in any adequate way the lives or the beliefs of others – as distinct from understanding their methods of cooking or their kinship systems – lies in their very close proximity to our own lives and beliefs. There is, after all, relatively little at stake in dietary customs, or patterns of consanguinity. They can be very strange indeed without us feeling very different from the peoples who practise them. The process of acculturation which followed inexorably upon any process of European colonization sometimes demanded that these things be changed. The Castilians, for instance, tried to prevent their Arab, Christian subject from bathing. They did this, however, not because they believed that filthiness would make the Arab more familiar, less 'other'. They did it because they knew that for the Muslim washing was a significant part of ritual devotion and hence an integral part of an alien, and hostile, system of beliefs. Those, however, who live radically different lives or hold radically different beliefs from our own, those who worship unusual features of the landscape, offer food to agricultural implements or eat their neighbours, were alarming or frightening to those Europeans who first encountered these beliefs precisely because they touched directly upon recognizable areas of their ethical lives – on the nature of the sacred and on what it was to be 'human' – and yet remained terrifyingly other.

For most of the writers I have discussed in this book the problem, then, was precisely how to understand 'otherness' in terms which made sense both as an account of 'their' lives or beliefs, *and* as an account of the lives and beliefs of beings who were still sufficiently like 'us' to be clearly recognizable as part of what all contemporary Europeans understood to be the 'brotherhood of man'. In a sense all failed and, in a sense, those who continue to confront this problem continue to fail. We may formally have abandoned the notion of a common humanity in favour of something far closer to Herder's notion of pluralism. But if, unlike Herder, we wish to *understand* the beliefs of others, we simply cannot do without it. Modern ethnographical descriptions may seem, at first glance, more complex and more persuasive than their eighteenth-century predecessors. But that is generally an illusion which disappears on a second reading. We have a different set of concerns, a different 'grid' through which we read the evidence we have before us. But it need hardly be said that that grid is as powerfully present as it was two hundred years ago. Our 'Good Savages' are both good and savage to serve different cultural objectives, but they are frequently as far removed from whatever the lives of their originals may be like as Adario was from his. The plight of much contemporary anthropology, reduced to professional introspection, or historical self-criticism, is a reflection of the awareness of this. Similarly, the European moral concern with groups which European culture has exploited, oppressed or destroyed, seems often to be grounded in a corresponding sentimentalization of the 'other'. We all, it seems, need to salvage some notion of ourselves as potentially benevolent agents, to persuade ourselves that European civilization is not quite so rapacious and destructive of those who do not serve its ends as it so obviously appears to be.

To achieve that objective, the critics of colonialism have tended to construct 'others' quite as false as those invented by their opponents. *Every* image of the 'other' reflects intently upon itself. It has been one of the claims of this book that in the process, it might still be possible to capture something of the original, something of the true beliefs of those others. But we, the observers – who no longer have any faith in autopsy – are still in no position to say with any certainty what we have made and what we have only seen. There would indeed seem, as the students of colonial discourse claim, to be no way to escape from the circle, no way which will ever lead to an entirely *unconstructed* 'other'. But this constitutes a problem in *understanding*, a problem which has been hugely aggravated by the colonizing process but one which will not simply go away with the end of that process, or by the application of a good measure of anthropological *angst*. Rousseau, Diderot and Herder, for all their own loathing of colonization, knew this. Diderot and Herder's solutions were both, in the end, appeals to the ultimate inescapability of cultural incommensurability. For Herder, in particular, exceptionalism came very close to looking like a necessary condition of cultural identity. For both men, the legacy of the European empires in America – which might have been the fabrication of wholly new lives – had, in fact, been to demonstrate, finally and irrevocably, that conquest and annihilation was the only way in which cultures could deal with the differences between them. Diderot's 'half-way state' was, as he recognized, only a dream, and Herder's fully acculturated man, merely an evasion of the problem; for if the colonizer actually *becomes* the colonized, the problematic instantly vanishes.

If we could not accept the consequence of these melancholy facts – and clearly it was unacceptable to any enlightened person – then the only alternative was to leave 'them', physically and conceptually, alone. Communication could be maintained, or so it was hoped, through commerce, but commerce, if it were to achieve its 'gentilizing' mission, had to remain distinct from any form of colonization even, as Raynal recognized, from the minimum pattern of settlement practised by the Portuguese. And even then it was highly likely that if two trading partners were not equally matched militarily, colonization would inevitably follow: the British in India and the Dutch (all the more culpably because of their Republican origins)[4] in the Far East, had by the last decade of the eighteenth century demonstrated the truth of this. For Raynal, as for Diderot and for Herder, as even for Humboldt, the process of 'discovery' or 'encounter' with America seemed now to be over, a subject for regret, an historical lesson for all future European societies in those other 'New Worlds' in Asia, Africa, and the Pacific, which were soon to fall under the same 'civilizing', rapacious European gaze.

What Diderot believed that we might all learn from this lesson, was that all future forms of travel and commerce should be pursued only in those areas where contact or 'encounter' might prove mutually beneficial. But he also recognized, if only dimly, that what might follow for all 'savage' peoples from prolonged exposure to a world economy, from that 'time . . . when the sanctions of rulers will extend to the individual transactions between the subjects of different nations', might, in fact, turn out to be a deal less benign. If the discovery of America had taught enlightened Europe anything it was, in the end, a form of despair: the recognition that the 'savage', however defined, could ultimately have no place outside a world system whose character was already markedly European, yet could never survive *as* a 'savage' within it.

Notes

INTRODUCTION

1. Humboldt (1814), p. 57.
2. For Columbus's moment of hesitation, see pp. 22–3.
3. Quoted in Greenblatt (1991), p. 54.
4. Ulloa (1772), pp. 4–5.
5. I have used the male pronoun because that still seems unavoidable in the English language with its very limited range of inflections. Forms such as 'he/she' are too clumsy, and the simple replacement of 'he' by 'she' to designate the ungendered agent, although it may help to redress the balance, is merely a complimentary form of sexism. It is also the case that since so many of those I shall be discussing, the writers, colonists and explorers, *were* men, the general use of 'she' might cause unnecessary confusion. 'Human' and 'humankind' are, of course, no less gender-specific than 'man' and 'mankind', and since the term from which the latter derives, *Menschheit*, is a feminine noun, I take it that the English term 'man', when used to designate the whole race, may be feminine also.
6. Diderot (1955), p. 4. 'Le navigateur . . . traverse des espaces immenses, resserré et immobile dans une enceinte assez étroite'.
7. Diderot (1955), p. 6.
8. This incident is described and analysed in detail in Russell (1986).
9. See Pagden (1986).
10. Cf. the discussion in O'Gorman (1961), pp. 9–47.
11. Waldseemüller (1507), f. [c. iv^v], 'alia quarta pars per Americum Vesputium . . . inventa est'. He then goes on to describe Vespucci as the true 'inventor' of this New World, after whom it should therefore be named. O'Gorman convincingly translates 'invenio' in this context as 'conceive' rather than invent (O'Gorman, 1961, pp. 167–8, n. 117). The other term was the classical Latin, 'repertor', which the Milanese humanist, Peter Martyr, the first person to describe America as a 'New World', uses of Columbus. See p. 23.
12. Ferguson (1966), p. 6.
13. Raynal (1781), 3, pp. 210–11.
14. Mandrillon (1784), pp. 11–12. Mandrillon's *Recherches* were a submission for Raynal's prize essay. See pp. 169–70.

15. Las Casas (1951), I, p. 149.
16. Quoted in Pagden (1986), p. 53.
17. This is discussed in great detail by Gerbi (1973).
18. Humboldt (1810), pp. 1–3.
19. But the Europeans would be able to assist the Amerindians in this way only if they behaved other than the Spanish landowners whom Humboldt had met in America currently behaved. For the present brutality of the Indian, the fact that in three-hundred years of European rule, he seemed only, in fact, to have devolved, could, Humboldt believed, be attributed to the kind of government under which he had been compelled to live. See Pagden (1990), pp. 103–4.
20. Pliny (The Younger), Letters, VIII. 24. 2. Pliny is writing to one Valerius (?) Maximus prior to his departure for Achia, which, he says, is the 'true and genuine Greece, in which it is believed the first liberal arts, sciences and also agriculture are thought to have been invented' (in qua primum humanitas, litterae, etiam fruges inventae esse creduntur).
21. Quoted in Greenblatt (1991), pp. 36–7.
22. Ajofrín (1958–9), I, p. 84.
23. See p. 60.
24. On this dispute, see Pagden (1986), pp. 22–3.
25. Genty (1789), pp. 201–2. This, too, was a (rather belated) entry for Raynal's prize. See pp. 169–70.
26. See Farriss (1984).
27. Quoted in Michael Zuckerman, 'Identity in British America: Unease in Eden', in Canny and Pagden (1987), p. 144.
28. Quoted in Gilles Paquet and Jean-Pierre Wallot, 'Nouvelle France / Quebec / Canada: A World of Limited Identities', in

Canny and Pagden (1987), p. 99. And on Kalm, see pp. 134, 173.
29. See Boon (1982).
30. Montesquieu (1979), II, p. 527. For a more detailed discussion of the development of this distinction see Pagden, forthcoming.
31. Rousseau (1979–81), III, p. 560. And see his observations on the distinction in the second *Discours*, Rousseau (1979–81), II, pp. 171–3.

CHAPTER ONE

1. Oviedo (1959), I, pp. 120–21.
2. Pane's account of the customs of the Taino has not survived, but sections of it are quoted by the Milanese humanist Peter Martyr, see Martyr (1530), f.[CVIII]ʳ.
3. Colón (1982), p. 327.
4. Letter of February 1502, Colón (1982), p. 311.
5. Milhou (1983), p. 119.
6. Colón (1982), p. 257.
7. *Ibid.*, p. 250. On Columbus's indebtedness to the language of alchemy, see Milhou (1983), p. 131.
8. Las Casas (1951), p. 28.
9. Quoted in Carter (1987), p. xxv.
10. On this, see Trexler (1982).
11. Fernández-Armesto (1991), p. vi.
12. This, the process of an initial and direct relation which avoids the linguistic connection, is what Ernst Cassirer, in quite another context, called 'the pure category of relation'. Cassirer (1965), I, p. 312.
13. Colón (1982), p. 237. *Relación del tercer viaje*, August 13 1498.
14. Humboldt (1836–9), III, pp. 110–16; Humboldt (1850), p. 156.
15. Colón (1982), p. 218. For a more extended analysis of Columbus's quest for the Terrestrial Paradise,

see Pérez de Tudela y Bueso (1983), pp. 250–327. On Columbus's readings between text and experience, see Todorov (1982), pp. 23–5.

16. Acton (1960), p. 71.
17. Colón (1982), pp. 213–14.
18. 'Colonus ille orbis novus repertor', Letter to Ascanio Sforza, November 1 1493, Martyr (1530ª), f.xxxiiiv.
19. It might for classroom purposes, however, be merely set aside. See J. H. Elliott on the Nuremburg humanist, Cochaeus, who, in the preface to his edition of Pomponius Mela's *Cosmographia* of 1512, claimed that 'whether it [the discovery] is true or a lie has nothing to do with cosmography or history'. 'Renaissance Europe and America: A Blunted Impact?', in Chiapelli (1976), p. 10. And see pp. 94–5.
20. Bandini (1745), p. 68, and see Gerbi (1975), pp. 45–58.
21. See Pagden (1986), p. 25.
22. Humboldt's description of his instruments are in Humboldt (1814), I, pp. 56–60.
23. Quoted in Brading (1991), p. 516.
24. Humboldt (1814), p. 56.
25. Humboldt (1850), p. 354.
26. Humboldt (1846–58), I, pp. 8–9.
27. Humboldt (1850), p. 357.
28. Humboldt (1836–9), III, p. 20.
29. Humboldt (1836–9), II, p. 13.
30. Humboldt (1836–9), III, pp. 54–61.
31. This is most strikingly *not* true, of course, of places of residence, which is why so much of the discussion on the nature of civility, from antiquity to the present, hinges on the definition of the *domus*, the city and the family conceived of as a residential unit. It would be possible to write a natural history of civil society in terms of the tensions between the concepts of stability, permanence and motion and mobility.
32. Latour (1987), p. 227.
33. Cf. Latour's observation: 'You are ashamed of not grasping what it is to speak of millions of light years? Don't be ashamed, because the firm grasp the astronomer has over it comes from a small ruler he firmly applies to a map of the sky like you do to your road map when you go out camping. Astronomy is the local knowledge produced inside these centres that gather photographs, spectra, radio signals, infra-red pictures, everything that makes a trace that other people can easily dominate.' Latour (1987), pp. 229–30.
34. Latour (1987), p. 227.
35. Since the Cephalopod had originated in Asia this was, he claimed, evidence of monogenesis. Lafitau also claimed that they were merely men whose heads had been forced down into their shoulders. See Jean-Louis Fischer, 'Lafitau et l'acéphale: une preuve "Teratologique" du monogenisme', in Blanckaert (1985), pp. 90–105.
36. Humboldt (1807), pp. 34–5.
37. See Wolf Lepenies, 'Interesting Questions in the History of Philosophy and Elsewhere', in Richard Rorty *et al*, eds. (1984), pp. 146–7.
38. Cortés (1986), p. 28.
39. Latour (1987), p. 225.
40. This episode is brilliantly analysed in Greenblatt (1991), pp. 109–18.
41. Delisle de la Drévetière (1756), p. 36.
42. Bougainville (1771), p. 224, and see Moravia (1978), pp. 104–5.
43. Ulloa (1772), p. 7.
44. See Heikamp (1972), p. 107.
45. Thevet (1554), f.3ʳ and see Lestringant (1981), p. 207, 'La

vue n'est-elle pas en effet le sens générateur de la possession, la garantie de l'appropriation intellectuelle et politique?'
46. Diderot (1955), p. 13.
47. Todorov (1982), pp. 19–20. For the eschatalogical significance which the discovery had for Columbus, see Milhou (1983), pp. 136–42.
48. Las Casas (1951), I, p. 199.
49. Las Casas (1951), I, pp. 199–200.
50. *Carta a Santángel*, 15 February, 1493, Colón (1982), p. 140, and see the observations of Todorov (1982), pp. 33–5 on this passage.
51. See Fernández-Armesto (1991), p. 46.
52. *Carta a Santángel*, Colón (1982), p. 140.
53. Colón (1982), p. 15.
54. This was Martin Waldseemüller. See Waldseemüller (1507), f.ciiiˇ.
55. On this, see Stagl (1990).
56. Humboldt (1807), p. 27.
57. Humboldt (1814), p. 30.
58. Herder (1800), p. 187, and see p. 173.
59. Quiroga (1922), p. 40.
60. Quiroga (1922), pp. 42–3.
61. M*** (1785), pp. 9–10.
62. M*** (1785), p. 123.
63. Quiroga (1922), p. 49.
64. Quiroga (1922), p. 52.
65. Quiroga (1922), p. 54.
66. Sahagún (1975), p. 73. For the image of the ethnographer as doctor collecting and interpreting symptoms, see *ibid.* p. 17.
67. For an account of the composition of the *Histoire*, see Lestringant (1990a), pp. 47–52.
68. Léry (1585), pp. 260–61. On this point, see Lestringant (1990), pp. 202–3.
69. Léry (1585), pp. 105–7.
70. The classic source is *De Anima* III. 3. See Malcolm Schofield, 'Aristotle on the Imagination', Barnes (1979).

71. Léry (1585), p. 106.
72. Léry (1585), pp. 112–13.
73. Léry (1585), pp. 105–6, and quoted in J. H. Elliott (1970), 22, and see Steven Mulley, 'Strange Things, Gross Terms, Curious Customs: The Rehearsal of Cultures in the Late Renaissance', in Greenblatt (1988), p. 69.
74. Léry (1585), p. 307.
75. Léry (1585), p. 110.
76. Léry (1585), p. 227, and see Belorgey (1989), p. 26.
77. de Certeau (1975), p. 221.
78. See Pagden (1983), p. 45.
79. Humboldt (1814), p. 28.
80. Humboldt (1807), p. 14.
81. See Beck, (1959–61) II, p. 18.

CHAPTER TWO

1. Léry (1585), p. 96.
2. Léry (1585), p. 2.
3. de Certeau (1986), pp. 68, 72.
4. Léry (1585), Preface.
5. On the distinction between biblical exegesis which relies upon 'a theology which claims Yahweh as the agent of a history of deliverance', and what he calls 'philosophical hermeneutics', see Paul Ricoeur (1986), pp. 122–3.
6. See Pagden (1988).
7. The phrase is Stanley Fish's, 'meaning comes already calculated, not because of norms embedded in the language but because language is always perceived, from the very first, within a structure of norms'. That structure, however, is not, he claims, 'abstract and independent' but determined by an 'assumed background of practices, purposes [and] goods'. Fish (1980), p. 318.
8. See Pagden (1986), p. 200.
9. Hobbes (1985), p. 117.
10. Pagden (1986), p. 153.
11. Las Casas (1951), I, pp. 19–22.

12. For Acosta's project, see Pagden (1986), pp. 149–151.
13. See Stannard (1966).
14. Acosta (1962), p. 11.
15. Foucault (1976), p. 146. This is not to deny that the reasons for which a given text came to form part of the canon in the first place *did* have something to do with its inherent properties.
16. 'The problem with eyewitness accounts,' Stephen Greenblatt has written, 'is that they implicitly call attention to the reader's lack of that very assurance – direct sight – that is their own source of authority'. Greenblatt, (1991) p. 34.
17. Oviedo (1959), I, p. 10.
18. See Gerbi (1975), pp. 168–74.
19. Las Casas [1550], f.240ʳ.
20. Oviedo (1959), I, p. 111.
21. For this part of Las Casas's project, see Pagden (1986), pp. 119–145.
22. Oviedo (1959), IV, p. 267.
23. Léry (1585), Preface.
24. Las Casas (1951), III, p. 342.
25. Oviedo (1959), I, pp. 7, 9.
26. Oviedo (1959), I, p. 12.
27. Oviedo (1959), IV, p. 336.
28. Oviedo (1959), I, p. 12.
29. Oviedo (1959), V, p. 306. Yet echoing the long European tradition which saw all forms of travel as contrary to nature (and on which see pp. 157–8), he added, that for all this, 'no plant breeds more quickly, for we understand that it is done against nature, for flax burns the fields in which it grows and makes the land sterile'.
30. Oviedo (1959), I, p. 8.
31. Oviedo (1959), I, p. 7.
32. Oviedo (1959), IV, p. 267.
33. Gilii (1780–84), I, p. xviii.
34. Oviedo (1959), I, p. 7.
35. Pliny, *Natural History*, Preface, 14–15.
36. Oviedo (1959), I, p. 13.
37. Oviedo (1959), I, p. 141. 'While I have breath in me and the spirit of God in my nostrils,' Oviedo declared, 'my lips will speak no evil, nor my tongue any lie', an inescapable echo of Job's defiant cry, 'All the while my breath is in me and the spirit of God is in my nostrils; My lips shall not speak wickedness nor my tongue utter deceit'. Job Cap. XXVII, The Vulgate reads, 'non loquentur labia mea iniquitatem, nec lingua mea meditabitur mendacium'.
38. Las Casas (1951), II, p. 27 and cf. the similar observation by Oviedo (1959), I, p. 9.
39. Oviedo (1959), I, p. 141.
40. Oviedo (1959), II, pp. 182–3. Cf. Don Quixote, I, 6.
41. M*** (1785), pp. 14–15.
42. Díaz de Castillo (1904), I, pp. 270–71.
43. Amadís (1959), I, p. 9.
44. For Oviedo's movements at this time and the history of the composition and publication of *Claribalte* see the excellent *estudio preliminar* by Juan Pérez de Tudela Bueso in Oviedo (1959), I, pp. LXI–LXIX.
45. Oviedo (1519), ff.aijʳ–aiijᵛ.
46. 'Exil, satire, tyrannie: les *Lettres Persanes*' in Starobinski (1989), pp. 91–2.
47. Oviedo (1959), II, p. 182–3.
48. Oviedo (1880), p. 233.
49. Oviedo (1959), II, pp. 85–7.
50. Oviedo (1959), IV, pp. 308–417.
51. Oviedo (1959), I, p. 10: Pliny, *Natural History*, Preface, 15.
52. Oviedo (1959), II, p. 184.
53. Oviedo (1959), I, p. 245.
54. *Natural History*, Preface, 14–15.
55. Oviedo (1959), II, p. 304, Sahagún (1975), p. 75, similarly laments the 'muchos años y … muchos trabajos y desgracias' which his work has cost him and which are now offered as further proof of its truthfulness.

56. Montaigne (1933), p. 212 ('Des Cannibales').
57. de Certeau (1986), p. 73.
58. Oviedo (1959), II, p. 183.
59. *De ordine*, II. xix. 51.
60. Oviedo (1959), II, p. 182.
61. Oviedo (1959), II, p. 305.
62. Las Casas (1987), p. 69.
63. Brading (1991), p. 76.
64. Las Casas (1951), II, pp. 441–4.
65. Las Casas (1951), II, p. 92.
66. Las Casas (1951), II, p. 93.
67. Cf. Taylor (1989), p. 139.
68. Las Casas (1951), III, p. 84.
69. Las Casas [1950], f.242ʳ.
70. Las Casas (1951), I, pp. 92–3.
71. *Aquí se contiene una disputa o controversía*, in Las Casas (1958), p. 308.
72. 'Carta a los Dominicos de Chiapa y Guatemala' [1563], in Las Casas (1958), p. 470.
73. Las Casas (1951), I, p. 19.
74. See Kelley (1990), p. 89.
75. 'Carta a los Dominicos de Chiapa y Guatemala' [1563], in Las Casas (1958), p. 471. See *Treinta proposiciones muy iurídicas*, in Las Casas (1958), p. 257.
76. See e.g. his attack on the Scottish theologian John Major as one who, in American matters at least, 'knew neither the law nor the facts'. Las Casas [1550], f.228v.
77. See Prosdocimi (1954–5), p. 815, and Olivecrona (1939), p. 78.
78. See Schultz (1953).
79. Las Casas (1987), p. 69.
80. 'Carta a un personaje de la corte' [October, 15, 1535] in Las Casas (1958), p. 63.
81. Las Casas (1951), I, p. 20.
82. Las Casas (1951), I, p. 6. Las Casas's reference to Isidore is, as are most of his references, incorrect. It should read, *Etymologiarum*, Bk. I, cap. 41.
83. Las Casas denied that the crown had property rights in America (*dominium rerum*), but never challenged its claim to sovereignty (*dominium jurisdictionis*). In the political language in which Las Casas wrote, both constituted a form of possession. See Pagden (1990), pp. 13–36 *passim*.
84. Las Casas (1951), III, p. 342.
85. 'Carta al Consejo de Indias' [October, 15, 1535] in Las Casas (1958), p. 59.
86. Las Casas (1951), I, p. 22.
87. Las Casas [1550], f.243ᵛ. There is a strong linguistic similarity between this passage and the description in the *Historia de las Indias* (Las Casas, 1951, I, p. 3) of the 'Greek chroniclers'.
88. Las Casas (1951), I, p. 13.
89. Diodorus Siculus, *History*, Bk. 1, caps. 3–5.
90. Las Casas (1951), I, p. 3.
91. Greenblatt (1991), p. 129.
92. Las Casas (1951), I, p. 12.
93. Las Casas (1951), II, p. 316. He had, he said, copied out a passage, 'so that it may be seen how simply the Admiral lived and wrote, and also how, in those times, there was not the elevated, illustrious and magnificent mode of writing which is now used in the world, and that the words which are now used to puff up the titles used in letters were lacking'.
94. Some two hundred years later, Francisco Javier Clavigero, similarly engaged on writing a 'true' – and apologetic – history of the Indians, would make exactly the same claims for very much the same ends. See Pagden (1990), p. 100.
95. Oviedo (1959), II, p. 56.
96. See Schwartz (1978).
97. On this notion, see Greenblatt, pp. 10–11.
98. 'Memorial de los remedios', in Las Casas (1958), p. 121.
99. Las Casas (1987), p. 81.
100. Las Casas (1987), p. 159.
101. Las Casas (1987), p. 125.
102. Las Casas (1987), p. 169.
103. Las Casas [1550], f.241ᵛ.

104. 'Carta a los Dominicos de Chiapa y Guatemala', in Las Casas (1958), p. 472.
105. Las Casas (1987), pp. 160–3.
106. Geertz (1988), p. 17.
107. On which grounds, as he pointed out, 'Asia or Africa might well be described as a new world'. Léry (1585), f.cij^v. See p. 117.
108. See p. 77.
109. Las Casas (1987), p. 174.
110. This did not, however, prevent him from making prophetic utterances. See Milhou (1983), pp. 77–106.
111. Las Casas (1987), p. 69.
112. Vargas Machuca (1879), p. 216.
113. Geertz (1988), p. 79.
114. Acosta (1962), p. 10.
115. For the history of the development of this concept see the brilliant essay by Alonso Iacono, *L'Evento e l'osservatore* (Iacono, 1987).
116. Humboldt (1810), p. ii.
117. See his comments in Oviedo (1959), II, p. 305.
118. Ramusio (1978), I, pp. 3–4.
119. Purchas (1625), p. 2, *To the Reader*.
120. Prévost (1746), I, p. vj.
121. 'To this species of philosophical investigation, which has no appropriate name in our language, I shall take the liberty of giving the title *Theoretical or Conjectural History*, an expression which coincides pretty nearly in its meaning with that of *Natural History*, as employed by Mr. Hume, and which some French writers have called *Histoire Raisonnée*.' *Account of the the Life and Writings of Adam Smith LL.D*, in Smith (1980), p. 293.
122. Raynal (1781), I, p. 3.
123. Humboldt (1810), p. iii.
124. Blumenberg (1987), p. 94.

CHAPTER THREE

1. Gucciardini (1971), I, pp. 591–2. The Vulgate reads, 'In omnem terram excivit sonus eorum et finis orbis terrae verba eorum'. The meaning of the verse was much debated, and sometimes even used to suggest that the existence of America had been known in Antiquity. It could, of course, only have been prophetic and by most was merely taken to mean that Christ's word would one day be known to all the world. The discovery of America was one step on the way to that goal.
2. In a letter to the Duke of Saxony, Erasmus (1906–56), II, p. 584.
3. Temple (1909), p. 28.
4. Thevet (1975), p. 222.
5. Printed in Nardi (1965), pp. 41–2.
6. Galileo (1965), p. 17. Kepler also made the same comparison in a private letter to Galileo in 1610, Galileo (1929–39), X, 324; and see Jardine (1984), pp. 211–24.
7. Tassoni (1636), p. 532.
8. The best general accounts of the quarrel are still Rigault (1856), and Gillot (1914).
9. See Levine (1987), p. 155, who claims that, whereas in France the battle had begun as, and very largely remained, a literary affair, in England the 'inclination had been, ever since the days of Francis Bacon, to match the rivalry over the whole field of natural philosophy'. The same was true also of Italy and Germany.
10. Fontenelle (1825), III, p. 424.
11. Quoted in Elliott (1970), p. 10.
12. Voltaire (1963), II, p. 350.
13. Blumenberg (1983), pp. 339–40.
14. Campanella (1693), p. 6. Major (1519), f.1^v. Major, however, attributed the discovery to Vespucci.
15. Fontenelle (1825), III, p. 170.
16. 'Sur l'histoire', Fontenelle (1825), II, pp. 424–35.
17. Fontenelle (1825), III, p. 432.
18. 'Disgression sur les anciens et les

modernes', Fontenelle (1825), IV, p. 238.

19. Quoted in Shklar (1981), p. 644.
20. d'Alembert (1805), I, p. 239, 'Discours préliminaire de l'Encyclopédie' and on d'Alembert as a historian of science, see Gusdorf (1966), pp. 47–92.
21. Blumenberg (1983), p. 470.
22. Latour (1988), pp. 3–5.
23. Las Casas (1951), I, pp. 148–9.
24. Las Casas (1951), I, pp. 37–62.
25. Oviedo (1959), I, pp. 15–17. Oviedo's purpose, which won him few supporters, was to demonstrate that America was not only a re-discovered world, but that it was one which had once been part of the territory of Visigothic Spain. He also endorsed the myth of the 'unknown pilot' – the claim that Columbus had been told about the probable existence of America from a shipwrecked sailor he had met on an earlier voyage.
26. Oviedo (1959), I, p. 20.
27. Francis Bacon, as James Barry reflected from the other end of the eighteenth century, had 'like another Columbus [led] us to the discovery of new worlds in the regions of knowledge'. Barry (1775), p. 124.
28. Galileo (1929–39), XI, p. 66.
29. On Columbus's reading of signs, see Todorov (1982), pp. 22–39.
30. Galileo (1929–39), X, p. 296.
31. Galileo (1967), p. 339, and see Blumenberg (1987), p. 82.
32. Fernández-Armesto (1991), pp. 23–44, provides a useful, and usefully sceptical, account of the current understanding of Columbus's geographical theories.
33. Robertson (1777), I, p. 64.
34. Humboldt (1836–9), III, p. 10.
35. That this is so is clear from the reason which Robertson gave for omitting any mention of the discoveries from his celebrated *The Progress of Society in Europe*, which was first published as a preface to his *History of Charles V* (1769). 'I found,' he wrote, 'that the discovery of the new world . . . the genius of the European settlements in its various provinces, together with the influence of these upon systems of policy and commerce in Europe were subjects so splendid and important', that they required a work to themselves. Robertson (1972), p. 5.
36. Robertson (1777), I, p. 66.
37. Robertson (1777), I, p. 64. On Henry, see Russell (1984).
38. Robertson (1777), I, pp. 62–6.
39. Robinson (1774), pp. 36–7. Robinson also makes the, by then commonplace, connection between Columbus, Galileo and Copernicus.
40. Colón (1982), p. 217. See the observations in Fernández-Armesto (1991), pp. 30–31. Robertson (1777), I, pp. 65–6, had no doubt that this is what Columbus had done.
41. Las Casas (1951), I, pp. 148–9.
42. Raynal (1781), II, p. 7.
43. Burke (1757), I, p. 4.
44. Jardine (1984), p. 215.
45. Spratt (1667), p. 108.
46. de Pauw (1777), II, p. 160–61.
47. Galileo (1965), p. 37.
48. Michelet (1855), p. xciii.
49. Spratt (1667), p. 36.
50. d'Alembert (1805), I, p. 279, 'Discours préliminaire de l'Encyclopédie'.
51. Raynal (1781), III, p. 211.
52. Humboldt (1836–9), IV, p. 6.
53. Humboldt (1846–58), I, p. 232.
54. Humboldt (1836–9), III, p. 9.
55. Humboldt (1836–9), III, p. 12.
56. Humboldt (1836–9), III, p. 14.
57. Humboldt (1807), p. 29.
58. Humboldt (1807), p. 17.
59. Humboldt (1810), p. 3.
60. Quoted in Blumenberg (1987), p. 92.

61. Pratt (1991), pp. 119–20.
62. Humboldt (1973), p. 657. Letter to David Friedlander. Bacon, however, makes no such claim in the *Sylva Sylvarum*, which is an account of a series of physical and botanical experiments.
63. Humboldt (1860), pp. 17–18.
64. Humboldt (1846–58), I, p. 275.
65. Humboldt (1846–58), II, p. 53.
66. Humboldt (1846–58), II, p. 265.
67. Humboldt (1807), p. 54.
68. Goethe (1813), p. 7.
69. Humboldt (1846–58), II, p. 260.
70. Humboldt (1846–58), I, p. 230.
71. Humboldt (1836–9), III, p. 7.
72. Humboldt (1846–58), I, pp. 242–5.
73. Humboldt (1836–9), III, p. 153.
74. Humboldt (1846–58), I, p. 231.
75. Humboldt (1846–58), I, p. 297.
76. Humboldt (1836–9), I, p. x.
77. The link between the discovery of America and the discovery of printing was probably first made in 1539 by Pompanazzi's colleague at Padua, Lazzaro Buonamico. Elliott (1970), p. 9.
78. Hornius (1655), pp. 306–7.
79. Humboldt (1846–58), II, p. 299.
80. Michelet (1855), pp. ii–iii, and see Elliott (1972).
81. Humboldt (1836–9), I, p. ix.
82. Humboldt (1836–9), I, p. ix.
83. See Minguet (1969), p. 586.
84. Michelet (1855), p. iii.
85. Humboldt (1807), p. 43.
86. Condorcet (1970), p. 122.
87. Humboldt (1846–58), II, p. 299.
88. Humboldt (1807), p. 30.
89. In two works, *Plan einer vergleichenden Anthropologie* of 1795 and *Das achtzehnte Jahrhundert* of 1797. Previously the term had been used exclusively of the physical composition of man.
90. Humboldt (1807), p. 35.
91. Humboldt (1846–58), I, p. 54.
92. Humboldt (1846–58), II, pp. 354–5.
93. Humboldt (1846–58), II, pp. 298–9.
94. Humboldt (1836–9), III, p. 154.
95. Schiller (1982), p. 7.

CHAPTER FOUR

1. Léry (1580), f.cij^v.
2. Locke (1967), p. 319. All that Locke says in this famous phrase however is that 'no such thing as *Money* was any where known'.
3. The phrase is Peter Martyr's. See Pagden (1986), p. 24.
4. Described in Gerbi (1973).
5. Degerando (1978), pp. 131–2.
6. For the Spanish legislation, see Pagden (1986), p. 183, and for Brazil, Azevedo (1950), pp. 193–228.
7. *De partibus animalium*, 660 a 17–18. See Pagden (1986), p. 16.
8. Quiroga (1922), p. 52.
9. Lahontan (1931), pp. 160–61.
10. For the textual complexities of Lahontan's writings, see the excellent introduction by Gilbert Chinard to Lahontan (1931).
11. Quoted in Lahontan (1931), p. 53, n. 2.
12. Quoted in Lahontan (1931), pp. 55–6.
13. Voltaire (1954), p. 279.
14. Lahontan (1931), p. 183–4.
15. Lahontan (1931), p. 161–3.
16. Quoted in Aarsleff (1982), p. 290.
17. *Scienza nuova*, 428–430.
18. See p. 86 and n. Stewart's famous observation was made precisely of Adam Smith's *Essay on the First Formation of Languages*. And see Aarsleff (1974), p. 97, on the project of the language-theorists being to 'explore and perhaps explain the nature of the mind of man'.
19. Locke (1975), p. 408.
20. Lamy (1957), pp. 107, 270.
21. There is, however, very little sustained theoretical speculation

about the nature and place of Amerindian languages before 1700 and, as Hans Aarsleff has observed, the 'truly creative period' in the history of language-theory began with Condillac's *Essai* of 1746. Aarsleff (1974), p. 94.

22. See Hans Aarsleff, 'Leibnitz on Locke on Language' in Aarsleff (1982), pp. 42-83.

23. There were, however, still those, Vico among them, who claimed to be able to produce natural etymologies for all nouns. *Scienza nuova*, 433-434.

24. See Locke (1975), pp. 402-11 and Kretzmann (1976).

25. Locke (1975), p. 207. La Condamine claimed they could not count above three (La Condamine, 1745, p. 56), although as Rousseau observed in *Emile*, they could obviously see the five fingers on their hands. (Rousseau, 1979-91, IV, p. 572n.), and cf. Condillac (1947-51), I, pp. 432-83. 'Les hommes cessant de se faire de nouveaux besoins, cessant aussi de faire de nouvelles idées'.

26. Beattie (1783), p. 271.

27. Lahontan (1703), II, p. 199.

28. See p. 143.

29. Bougainville (1771), p. 224-5.

30. See Diderot (1955), p. 10. 'Il ne trouvera dans sa langue', observes 'B' of Aotoru, 'aucuns termes correspondans à celles dont il a quelques idées'.

31. Diderot (1955), p. 10.

32. Voltaire (1954), p. 243.

33. Voltaire (1954), p. 279.

34. Voltaire (1736), p. 15.

35. Rousseau (1968), pp. 127, 131.

36. Condillac (1947-51), II, p. 113.

37. Bougainville (1771), p. 226.

38. Mendelssohn (1764), pp. 43-4. He was speaking of the 'Greenlanders'. Cf. the observations of Charles de Brosses (1765,

pp. 32-3) who argues that all 'savages' speak the 'language of the imagination and the passions', a language which because it is not concerned with *explanation* (that is with science) depends not upon abstract ideas – for those are the modes for rational discourse – but on what he called 'material images'.

39. Quoted in Aarsleff (1982), p. 157.

40. This is what Galileo referred to as the *metodo risolutivo* and the *metodo compositivo*, which had already been developed at Padua during the sixteenth century by Jacobo Zabarella. See Schmitt (1969).

41. See Pagden (1986), pp. 184-5. 'J'ai entendú', as one of the characters in François Delise de la Drévetière's hugely popular play *L'Arlequin sauvage* (1756) puts it, 'que les sauvages parloient toujours par métaphore'. (Delisle de la Drévetière, 1756, p. 15.)

42. Lahontan (1703), pp. 48-52.

43. 'Dissertation sur les différents moyens dont les hommes sont servis pour exprimer leurs idées', in Maupertuis (1756), II, p. 44, and cf. Rousseau's observation that since language originated in a cry this 'gave to each word the sense of an entire proposition', 'Discours sur l'origine de l'inégalité' in Rousseau (1979-81), III, p. 149.

44. 'Les rêveries du promeneur solitaire', in Rousseau (1979-81), I, p. 995, and see Starobinski (1967), p. 284.

45. 'Cours d'études pour l'instruction du Prince du Parme', in Condillac (1947-51), I, p. 403.

46. Quoted in Aarsleff (1982), p. 99 n. 39.

47. Ulloa (1772), p. 386. He went on to claim that the languages of both 'Indians' and 'Jews' were similarly mendacious and deceptive since in both 'they can

affirm or deny a thing with equal facility', this not being a property of civil or 'Christian' languages.

48. Robertson (1777), I, pp. 311–2.
49. Rousseau (1979–81), III, p. 149. Cf. Baptiste du Tertre, whose account of the peoples of the French Caribbean provided Rousseau with many of the formal details from which he constructed his state of nature, and who claimed that such peoples, 'have no word with which to express those things which do not strike the coarseness of our corporeal senses. They do not know what understanding is, or will, or memory, because these things are hidden forces which produce no external effects'. Du Tertre (1654), p. 463.
50. Rousseau (1979–81), III, p. 151.
51. Quoted in Mannheim (1984).
52. Quoted in Pagden (1986), pp. 185–6. 'B' in the *Supplément au voyage de Bougainville*, makes much the same observation of the alphabet of the Tahitians. It lacks, he says, 'b, c, d, f, g, q, x, y, z'. Diderot (1955), p. 10.
53. See Pagden (1986), pp. 184–6.
54. Quoted by V. G. Kiernan, 'Noble and Ignoble Savages', in Rousseau and Porter (1990), p. 90.
55. Humboldt (1810), p. ix.
56. Court de Gébelin (1781), p. 492. Cf. Herder (*Über der Ursprung der Sprache* (1770) in Barnard, 1965, p. 57) for whom the diversity of the languages of America was merely the necessary outward expression of a plurality of human cultures which was itself the creation of nature.
57. Lahontan (1931), p. 236.
58. Lahontan (1931), p. 169.
59. Herder (1800), p. 194.
60. Herder (1800), p. 234.
61. Lahontan, pp. 159–60.
62. Herder (1800), p. 236.

63. *Scienza nuova*, 429.
64. Gouget (1758), I, p. 170. On the sameness of savage societies, see pp. 151–2.
65. Rousseau (1968), p. 57.
66. Rousseau (1968), p. 57.
67. 'Dissertation sur les differents moyens dont les hommes sont servis pour exprimer leurs idées', in Maupertuis (1756), III, p. 451, and see David (1965).
68. Lahontan (1931), p. 227.
69. Lamy (1757), p. 5.
70. Rousseau (1968), p. 81.
71. 'Lettre à M. de Beaumont' in Rousseau (1968), p. 217.
72. Rousseau (1968), pp. 197–8.
73. Diderot (1955), p. 27.
74. Lahontan (1931), p. 227.
75. Voltaire (1954), p. 108.
76. Derrida (1967).
77. Lahontan (1931), p. 83.

CHAPTER FIVE

1. Diderot (1955), p. 14. M. L. Perkins has noted how the *Supplément* reverses the traditional travel narrative. It begins with a farewell then takes up the story of Bougainville's arrival, while the ancient sage urges his countrymen to weep at the Frenchman's coming not his going. Perkins (1974).
2. Diderot (1955), p. 53.
3. Diderot (1955), p. 24.
4. Diderot (1955), p. 26.
5. On this point, and on Diderot's use of sensualism in general, see Taylor (1989), p. 329.
6. Diderot (1955), p. 64.
7. Montesquieu (1979), I, p. 150.
8. Diderot (1955), p. 19.
9. Rousseau (1825), II, p. 28.
10. I have followed the now definitive reconstruction of Diderot's contributions in Goggi (1976–7) and Duchet (1978). But because of the extreme rarity of Goggi's book

all the citations will be to Raynal (1781).

11. Bernard (1775), p. 39.
12. Tourneaux (1877), IX, pp. 487–8.
13. See Benot (1963).
14. 'Lettre apologétique de l'abbé Raynal à M. Grimm', in Diderot (1956), p. 640.
15. Raynal (1781), V, p. 16.
16. See, however, Duchet (1961), p. 187, who takes what amounts to the opposite view. For her *L'histoire* est pour lui [Diderot] un cadre de recherche aussi bien qu'un moyen d'expression'.
17. Paine (1782), p. 41.
18. Gadamer (1975), pp. 238–289, and Kelley, 'Civil Science in the Renaissance: The Problem of Interpretation', in Pagden (1987), pp. 75, 77.
19. Diderot (1955), pp. 59–60.
20. Raynal (1781), X, p. 285 and Diderot (1955), p. 52. And for the significance of the fact that these are *codes*, see Kelley (1990), p. 223.
21. Diderot (1955), p. 52.
22. Bougainville had been in Canada in 1756–7 and had been adopted by an Iroquois tribe. His 'Mémoires sur les coutumes et usages des cinq nations irqouoises du Canada', served Diderot as a basis for his fragmentary, 'Court essai sur le caractère de l'homme sauvage' (Diderot, 1875–7, VI, pp. 454–5) which, in turn, informed some of his claims in the *Histoire*. See Duchet (1963).
23. Raynal, V, pp. 1–2. 'On National Characters' in Hume (1882), p. 252.
24. Raynal (1781), I, p. 41.
25. Raynal (1781), I, p. 5.
26. Raynal (1781), I, p. 41.
27. de Pauw (1777), I, p. 130.
28. Torres (1781), I, p. 28.
29. 'On National Characters' in Hume (1882), pp. 248–9.
30. Raynal (1781), VIII, pp. 210–11.

31. See the observations in Kelley (1990), p. 90.
32. Buffon (1842), III, p. 221[b], and see Iacono (1989–1990).
33. Lafitau (1724), II, p. 484.
34. This point is also made by Duchet (1978), pp. 160–61.
35. *Voyage de Hollande*, in Diderot (1985–7), XVII, p. 368.
36. See pp. 170–72 and see Duchet (1978), p. 163.
37. Descartes (1970), I, p. 92.
38. Rousseau (1979–81), II, pp. 151–2.
39. Article on 'Société (Morale)' from the *Encyclopédie*, in Diderot (1875–7), XVII, p. 131.
40. 'Incomprehensible', in d'Alembert and Diderot (1765), VIII, p. 654.
41. Article on 'Société (Morale)' from the *Encyclopédie*, in Diderot (1875–7), XVII, p. 132.
42. See Hont and Ignatieff (1983), p. 7 and pp. 130–31.
43. Smith (1980), p. 40.
44. Grimaldi (1958), p. 562.
45. 'Lettre apologétique de l'abbé Raynal à M. Grimm', in Diderot (1956), p. 632.
46. Linguet (1767), I, p. 227.
47. Diderot to Sophie Volland, 30 October 1759, Diderot (1955–70), 2, p. 299.
48. Rousseau (1979–81), IV, p. 858, *Emile*, Bk. V.
49. Raynal (1781), V, pp. 13–14.
50. Raynal (1789), p. 11.
51. Rousseau (1979–81), II, p. 144.
52. Shaftesbury, *Philosophical Regimen*, quoted in Taylor (1989), p. 252, and see Taylor's comments on this passage.
53. Raynal (1781), V, p. 14.
54. For the political significance of these claims, see Pagden (1990), pp. 103–4.
55. Condorcet (1970), pp. 228–30.
56. 'Réfutation suivie de l'ouvrage de Helvétius intitulé L'Homme', in Diderot (1875–7), II, pp. 431–2. On this half-way state, see

Duchet (1971), pp. 459–63.
57. Diderot (1875–7), 8, p. 352, and see Imbruglia (1988–9), p. 343.
58. Beccaria (1832), p. 367.
59. Quoted in Imbruglia (1990), p. 509.
60. 'Réfutation suivie de l'ouvrage de Helvétius intitulé L'Homme', in Diderot (1875–7), II, p. 432.
61. Raynal (1781), V. pp. 15–16.
62. In Diderot (1968), pp. 105–6.
63. For d'Alembert's historical project, see Shklar (1981) and Hankins (1970), *passim*.
64. Raynal (1781), III, p. 256.
65. Bougainville's own account of this event is significantly different from Diderot's. He admits to giving orders to shoot at thieves, but only on the advice of the local chieftain, Ereti, who, Bougainville says, 'eut grand soin de montrer plusieurs fois ou étoit sa maison, en recommandant bien de tirer du côté opposé'. Bougainville (1771), p. 197.
66. Naigeon (1821), p. 291.
67. Quoted in Imbruglia (1990), pp. 508–9.
68. Raynal (1781), V, p. 2.
69. Montesquieu (1979), I, p. 367. *Lettre* CLV.
70. 'In interiore homine habita veritas', *De vera religione*, xxxix. 72.
71. Diderot (1955), p. 51.
72. Diderot (1955), p. 10.
73. Raynal (1781), V, p. 16.
74. Raynal (1781), X, p. 296.
75. Diderot (1955), p. 13.
76. Raynal (1781), V, p. 16.
77. Raynal (1781), X, p. 297.
78. 'Réfutation suivie de l'ouvrage de Helvétius intitulé L'Homme', in Diderot (1875–7), II, p. 431.
79. Raynal (1781), V, p. 138.
80. Chastellux (1787), pp. 60–61. This was originally written for a prize proposed by Raynal for the best essay on the subject of the relative benefits for Europe of the

discovery of America (see pp. 169–70) although, or so the author claims, it was never submitted.
81. Raynal (1781), X, p. 287.
82. Montesquieu (1979), I, p. 286, *Lettre* CV.
83. Raynal (1781), V, p. 3.
84. Raynal (1781), X, p. 297.
85. Raynal (1781), V, p. 2. Cf. Voltaire's description of pirates – another group who, because of their nomadism, travel down the chain of civility – as 'des tigres qui auraient un peu de raison'. Voltaire (1963), 2, p. 376. On the place of piracy in the *Histoire des deux Indes*, see Imbruglia (1990).
86. See Diderot, 'Sur les cruautés exercées par les espagnols en Amérique', in Diderot (1875–7), VI, pp. 451–2.
87. Raynal (1781), IX, pp. 107–9.
88. Chastellux (1772), II, p. 97.
89. Raynal, V, p. 2.
90. In the *Discours préliminaire* to his translation of Shaftesbury's *An Inquiry concerning Virtue or Merit* (1745). Diderot (1875–7), I, p. 9.
91. Raynal (1781), III, pp. 215–6.
92. See Pagden (1990), pp. 7–8.
93. See his commentary on Francis Hutchesons' *An Inquiry into the Original of our Ideas of Beauty and Virtue* (1725) in 'Sur l'origine et nature du beau', Diderot (1968), pp. 396–8.
94. Raynal (1781), V, pp. 44–5.
95. Diderot, *Essai sur la peinture* (1766) in Diderot (1968), p. 670, and quoted in Imbruglia (1988–9), p. 326.
96. Raynal (1781), V, p. 5.
97. Raynal (1781), III, p. 209.
98. Descartes (1970), I, pp. 362–5. Descartes goes on to say, however, that once we have acquired this disposition we must 'at the same time afterwards try to free ourselves from it [wonder] as much as possible. For it is easy to

supplement its defects by special reflection and attention which our will can always oblige our understanding to give on these occasions when we judge that the matter which presents itself is worth the trouble'. And see the comments in Greenblatt (1991), pp. 19–20.

99. Quoted in Imbruglia (1988–9), p. 341.
100. See Taylor (1989), p. 527 n. 10.
101. Quoted in Greenblatt (1991), p. 34.
102. Raynal (1781), X, pp. 10–11.
103. Diderot (1968), p. 213. For d'Alembert's use of the metaphor, see p. 103.
104. Raynal (1781), V, p. 140.
105. On the evolution of this term, see Starobinski (1989), pp. 11–59.
106. Humboldt (1846–58), I, pp. 20–21.
107. Humboldt (1846–58), I, pp. 271–2.
108. Humboldt (1974), p. 88.
109. Quoted in Alpers (1983), pp. 8–9.
110. Raynal (1781), V, p. 10.
111. Raynal (1781), I, p. 308.
112. Raynal (1781), X, p. 29. The empire he is discussing here is the Russia of Catherine the Great of which he had had first-hand experience. See Duchet (1971), pp. 463–8. But the same general rule, it is clear, applies to the Spanish and French empires in America.
113. Raynal (1781), V, p. 139.
114. Raynal (1781), VII, p. 3.
115. Turgot (1844), p. 551.
116. I would like to thank Antony Grafton for having suggested this possibility to me.
117. Raynal (1781), V, pp. 4–5.
118. Raynal (1781), V, pp. 69–70.
119. Raynal (1781), V, p. 3.
120. Raynal (1781), I, pp. 1–2.
121. The best account of this prize and of those who entered the com-

petition is Imbruglia (1983), pp. 378–88.
122. Mandrillon (1784), p. 57.
123. Mandrillon (1784), pp. 12–14.
124. Raynal (1781), III, pp. 204–5.
125. Paine (1782), p. 42.
126. Mandrillon (1784), p. 58.
127. Raynal (1781), X, pp. 152–7. On the eighteenth-century uses of the languages of 'trust' and of 'honour', see Pagden (1990), pp. 65–89.
128. M*** (1785), pp. 20–21. Commerce is, he says, 'la base et la conservateur de toute société', thus giving it more political prominence than even Diderot would have allowed. He also makes an interesting, but largely unexamined distinction between commerce and 'le commerçant'. His contemporaries, he claims, such as Diderot (or, as he believes him to be, Raynal) have frequently, in their enthusiasm, conflated the two, although they are no more the same thing than 'ceux qui allument les lampes, et les vierges d'un Temple, ne sont la religion qu'on y professe'.
129. Raynal (1781), I, p. 4.
130. Raynal (1781), IX, p. 152.
131. Raynal (1781), I, p. 2.
132. Raynal (1781), III, p. 205.
133. See Rouché (1940), p. 84.
134. Herder (1800), p. 185.
135. Herder (1800), p. 186.
136. Herder (1800), p. 189.
137. Herder (1800), p. 221.
138. Article on 'Société (Morale)' from the *Encyclopédie*, in Diderot (1875–7), XVII, p. 144.
139. Herder (1969), p. 199.
140. Herder (1800), p. 208.
141. Herder (1800), pp. 208–10.
142. Herder (1800), p. 218.
143. Herder (1800), pp. 246–8.
144. Herder (1800), p. 244.
145. Herder (1800), p. 218.
146. Herder (1827), pp. 12–15.
147. Herder (1800), pp. 202–6.

148. Herder (1827), p. 101.
149. Ferguson (1966), p. 3.
150. Herder (1800), pp. 200–202.
151. Herder (1800), p. 199.
152. A not dissimilar claim for the genetic transmittability of the instruments of material culture is to be found in Geertz, 'The Growth of Culture and the Evolution of Mind', in Geertz (1975), pp. 55–83.
153. Herder (1800), p. 224, and cf. p. 250 where the same image is used again.
154. Herder (1800), p. 249.
155. Constant (1815), p. 95.
156. Herder (1800), p. 228.
157. Herder (1969), p. 188.
158. Herder (1800), p. 219.
159. Berlin (1990), p. 84, n. 3. He quotes Herder's Journal for the year 1769: 'There is not a man, a country, a people, a national history, a state, which resembles each other: hence truth, goodness and beauty differ from one another'.
160. See 'Alleged Relativism in Eighteenth-Century Thought', in Berlin (1990), pp. 70–90.
161. Herder (1800), p. 241.
162. Barnard (1965), p. 59.

AFTERWORD

1. Gellner, 'Concepts and Society', in Wilson (1970), p. 36. Gellner, however, uses this notion in a wholly different context to Herder's.
2. Hawthorn (1991), pp. 6–7.
3. Williams (1991), p. 10.
4. See Raynal (1781), I, pp. 323–7.

Bibliography of Works Cited

Aarsleff, Hans, 'The Tradition of Condillac: The Problem of the Origin of Language in the Eighteenth Century and the Debate in the Berlin Academy Before Herder', in ed. Dell Hymes, *Studies in the History of Linguistics* (Bloomington, 1974), pp. 93–156.

—— *From Locke to Saussure. Essays on the Study of Language and Intellectual History* (Minnesota, 1982).

Acosta, José de, *Historia natural y moral de las Indias* [1590], ed. Edmundo O'Gorman (Mexico, 1962).

Acton, Lord, *Lectures on Modern History* (London–Glasgow, 1960).

Adams, D.J., 'A Diderot Triptych Re-examined', *Modern Language Review* (1981), 76, 47–59.

Ajofrín, Fray Francisco de, *Diario del viaje que . . . hizo a la América septentrional en el siglo XVIII*, ed. Vicente Castañeda y Alcover (Madrid, 1958–9).

d'Alembert, Jean and Diderot, Denis, *Encyclopédie, ou Dictionnaire raisonné des sciences des arts et des métiers* (Neufchatel, 1765).

d'Alembert, Jean, *Œuvres philosophiques, historiques et littéraires de d'Alembert*, ed. J.F. Bastien, 18 vols (Paris, 1805).

Alpers, Svetlana, *The Art of Describing: Dutch Art in the Seventeenth Century* (Chicago, 1983).

Amadís, *Amadís de Gaula*, ed. Edwin B. Place, 2 vols (Madrid, 1959).

Azevedo, Fernando de, *Brazilian Culture* (New York, 1950).

Bandini, Angelo Maria, *Vita e lettere di Amerigo Vespucci* (Florence, 1745).

Barnard, F.M., *Herder's Political Thought from Enlightenment to Nationalism* (Oxford, 1965).

Barnes, Jonathan, eds Jonathan Barnes, Malcolm Schofield and Richard Sorabji, *Articles on Aristotle*, vol. 4, *Psychology and Aesthetics* (London, 1979).

Barry, James, *An Inquiry into the Real and Imaginary Obstructions to the Acquisition of the Arts in England* (London, 1775).

Beattie, James, *Dissertations Moral and Critical* (London, 1783).

Beccaria, Cesare, 'I piaceri dell' immaginazione', in *Raccolta di operetti filosofiche e filologiche scritti nel secolo xviii* (Milan, 1832).

Beck, H., *Alexander von Humboldt*, 2 vols (Weisbaden, 1959–61).

Belorgey, Jean-Michel, *La vraie vie est d'ailleurs. Histoire de ruptures avec l'occident* (Mesnard-sur-l'Entrée, 1989).

Benot, Yves, 'Diderot, Pechmeja, Raynal et l'anticolonialisme', *Europe* (1963), 41, Janvier-Fevrier, 137–53.

Benrekassa, Georges, 'Dit et non-dit idéologique; à propos du *Supplément au voyage de Bougainville*', *Dix-huitième siècle* (1973), 5, 29–40.

Berlin, Isaiah, *The Crooked Timber of*

Humanity. Chapters in the History of Ideas, ed. Henry Hardy (London, 1990).

Bernard, F., *Analyse de L'Histoire Politique et Philosophique* (Leiden, 1775).

Blanckaert, Claude, *Naissance de l'ethnologie?* (Paris, 1985).

Blumenberg, Hans, *The Legitimacy of the Modern Age*, trans. Robert M. Wallace (Cambridge, Mass.–London, 1983).

—— *The Genesis of the Copernican World*, trans. Robert M. Wallace (Cambridge Mass.–London, 1987).

Boon, James, *Other Tribes, Other Scribes. Symbolic Anthropology in the Comparative Study of Cultures, Histories, Religions and Texts* (Cambridge, 1982).

Bougainville, Louis Antoine, Comte de, *Voyage autour du monde par la frégate du roi la Boudeuse, et la flûte l'Etoile en 1766, 1767, 1768 et 1769* (Paris, 1771).

Brading, David, *The First America. The Spanish Monarchy, Creole Patriots and the Liberal State, 1492–1867* (Cambridge, 1991).

de Brosses, Charles, Comte de, *Traité de la formation méchanique des langues et des principes physiques de étymologie*, 2 vols (Paris, 1765).

Buffon, Le Clerc, Georges, Comte de Buffon, *Œuvres complètes de Buffon*, 6 vols (Paris, 1842).

Burke, Edmund, *An Account of the European Settlements in America*, 2 vols (London, 1757).

Canny, eds Nicholas and Anthony Pagden, *Colonial Identity in the Atlantic World 1500–1800* (Princeton, 1987).

Campanella, Tomasso, *De Gentilismo non retiniendo quaestio unica* (Paris, 1693).

Carter, Paul, *The Road to Botany Bay. An Essay in Spatial History* (London, 1987).

Cassirer, Ernst, *The Philosophy of Symbolic Forms*, trans. Ralph Manheim, 3 vols (New Haven–London, 1965).

de Certeau, Michel, *L'écriture de l'histoire* (Paris, 1975).

—— *Heterologies: Discourse on the Other*, trans. Brian Massumi (Manchester, 1986).

Chastellux, François Jean, Marquis de, *De la félicité publique, ou Considérations*

sur le sort des hommes dans les différentes époques de l'histoire, 2 vols (Amsterdam, 1772).

—— *Discours sur les avantages ou les désavantages qui résultent, pour l'Europe, de la découverte de l'Amérique* (London, 1787).

Chiapelli, F., ed. *First Images of America: The Impact of the New World on the Old* (Berkeley–Los Angeles–London, 1976).

Colón, Cristóbal (Christopher Columbus), *Textos y documentos completos. Relaciones de viajes, cartas y memoriales*, ed. Consuelo Varela (Madrid, 1982).

Condillac, Étienne Bonnot, Abbé de, *Œuvres philosophiques de Condillac*, ed. Georges Le Roy, 33 vols (Paris, 1947–51).

Condorcet, Marie-Jean Antoine, Marquis de, *Esquisse d'un tableau historique des progrès de l'esprit humain*, eds O.H. Prior and Yvon Belaval (Paris, 1970).

Constant, Benjamin, *De l'esprit de conquête et de l'usurpation dans leurs rapports avec la civilisation européenne* (Paris, 1815).

Cortés, Hernán, *Hernán Cortés. Letters from Mexico*, trans. and ed. Anthony Pagden (New Haven–London, 1986).

Court de Gébelin, Antoine, 'Essai sur les rapports des mots, entre les langues du nouveau monde et celles de l'ancien', in vol. 8 of *Monde primitif, analysé et comparé avec le monde moderne*, 9 vols (Paris, 1781).

David, M., *Le débat sur les écritures et hiéroglyphes aux XVIIe et XVIIIe siècles* (Paris, 1965).

Degerando, Joseph-Marie, 'Considérations sur les divers méthodes à suivre dans l'observation des peuples sauvages', in eds Jean Copans and Jean Jamin, *Aux origines de l'anthropologie française. Les Mémoires de la Société des Observateurs de l'Homme* (Paris, 1978), pp. 129–69.

Delisle de la Drévetière, François, *L'Arlequin sauvage, comédie en trois actes* (Paris, 1756).

Derrida, Jacques, 'Le linguistique de

Rousseau', *Revue internationale de philosophie* (1967), 81, 443–62.

Descartes, René, *The Philosophical Works of Descartes*, trans. and ed. Elizabeth S. Haldane and G.R.T. Ross, 2 vols (Cambridge, 1970).

Diderot, Denis, *Œuvres complètes*, ed. Jules Assevat and Maurice Tourneaux, 20 vols (Paris, 1875–7).

—— *Supplément au Voyage de Bougainville* [1773], ed. Herbert Dieckmann, (Geneva–Lille, 1955).

—— *Correspondence de Denis Diderot*, 16 vols (Paris, 1955–70).

—— *Œuvres philosophiques*, ed. Paul Vernière (Paris, 1956).

—— *Salons*, ed. Jean Seznec and Jean Adhemar, III, 1767 (Oxford, 1963).

—— *Œuvres esthétiques*, ed. Paul Vernière (Paris, 1968).

Duchet, Michèle, 'Le "Supplément au voyage de Bougainville" et la collaboration de Diderot à "L'Histoire des deux Indes"', *Cahiers de l'Association Internationale des Etudes Françaises* (1961), 13, 173–87.

—— 'Bougainville, Raynal, Diderot et les sauvages du Canada. Une source ignorée de "l'Histoire des deux Indes"', *Revue d'Histoire Litteraire de la France* (1963), 63, Jan.–Mars, 228–36.

—— *Anthropologie et histoire au siècle des lumières. Buffon, Voltaire, Helvétius, Diderot* (Paris, 1971).

—— *Diderot et l'Histoire des deux Indes, ou l'écriture fragmentaire* (Paris, 1978).

Du Tertre, Jean Baptiste, *Histoire générale des Isles de Christophe, de la Guadaloupe, de la Martinique, et autres dans l'Amérique* (Paris, 1654).

Elliott, J.H., *The Old World and the New 1492–1650* (Cambridge, 1970).

—— 'The Discovery of America and the Discovery of Man', *Proceedings of the British Academy* (1972), LVIII.

Erasmus, Desiderius, *Opus epistolarum Des. Erasmi roterodami*, ed. P.S. Allen, 12 vols (Oxford, 1906–56).

Farriss, Nancy, *Maya Society under Colonial Rule: The Collective Enterprise of Survival* (Princeton, 1984).

Ferguson, Adam, *An Essay on the History of Civil Society* [1767], ed. Duncan Forbes (Edinburgh, 1966).

Fernández-Armesto, Felipe, *Columbus* (Oxford, 1991).

Fish, Stanley, *Is There a Text in This Class? The Authority of Interpretive Communities* (Cambridge, Mass., 1980).

Fontenelle, Bernard de, *Œuvres de Fontenelle*, 5 vols (Paris, 1825).

Foucault, Michel, 'What is an Author?', in ed. J. Hatarari, *Textual Strategies. Perspectives in Post-Structuralist Criticism* (Ithaca, 1979).

Gadamer, Hans-Georg, *Truth and Method* (*Wahrheit und Methode*) (London, 1975).

Galileo, Galilei, *Le opere de Galileo Galilei*, 20 vols (Florence, 1929–39).

—— *Kepler's Conversation with Galileo's Sidereal Messenger* [*Dissertatio cum nuncio sidereo*], trans. E. Rosen (New York, London, 1965).

—— *Dialogue of the World Systems* [*Dialoghi sui massimi sistemi*, 1632], trans. Stilman Drake (Berkeley and Los Angeles, 1967).

Geertz, Clifford, *The Interpretation of Cultures* (London, 1975).

—— *Works and Lives. The Anthropologist As Author* (Stanford, 1988).

Genty, Louis, *L'influence de la découverte de l'Amérique sur le bonheur du genre-humain* (Paris, 1789).

Gerbi, Antonello, *The Dispute of the New World* (Pittsburgh, 1973).

—— *La natura delle Indie nuove* (Milan–Naples, 1975).

Gilii, Filippo Salvatore, *Saggio di storia americana*, 4 vols (Rome, 1780–84).

Gillot, Hubert, *Le querelle des anciens et des modernes en France* (Paris, 1914).

Goethe, Johann Wolfgang von, 'Schreiben des Hrn. G.R. Göthe an den Herausgeber' in *Allegemeine geographischen Ephemeriden* (Weimar, 1813), vol. 41, pp. 5–8.

Goggi, Gianluigi, *Denis Diderot. Pensées détachées. Contributions à l'Histoire des deux Indes*, edizione a cura di Gianluigi Goggi, 2 vols (Siena, 1976–7).

Gouget, Antoine Yves, *De l'origine des*

loix, des arts et des sciences; et de leurs progrès chez les anciens peuples, 2 vols (Paris, 1758).

Greenblatt, Stephen, 'Murdering Peasants: Status, Genre and the Representation of Rebellion', in *Representing the English Renaissance*, ed. Stephen Greenblatt (Berkeley, 1988).

—— *Marvellous Possessions. The Wonder of the New World* (Oxford, 1991).

Grimaldi, Francesantonio, *Riflessioni sopra l'ineguaglianza tra gli uomini* [1779–80], in *Illuministi italiane*, ed. Franco Venturi (Milan–Naples, Vol V, 1958).

Guicciardini, Francesco, *Storia d'Italia*, ed. Silvana Seidel Menchi, 3 vols (Turin, 1971).

Gusdorf, Georges, *De l'histoire des sciences à l'histoire de la pensée* (Paris, 1966).

Hankins, Thomas L., *Jean d'Alembert: Science and the Enlightenment* (Oxford, 1970).

Hawthorn, Geoffrey, *Plausible Worlds. Possibility and Understanding in History and the Social Sciences* (Cambridge, 1991).

Heikamp, D., *Mexico and the Medici* (with contributions by F. Anders) (Florence, 1972).

Herder, Johann Gottfried, *Outlines of a Philosophy of the History of Man* [*Ideen zur Philosophie der Geschichte der Menschheit*], trans. T. Churchill (London, 1800).

—— *Treatise upon the Origin of Language* [*Abhandlung über den Ursprung der Sprache*] (London, 1827).

—— *Yet Another Philosophy of History* [*Auch eine Philosophie der Geschichte zur Bildung der Menschheit*], in trans. and ed. F.M. Barnard, *Herder on Social and Political Culture* (Cambridge, 1969).

Hobbes, Thomas, *Leviathan*, ed. C.B. Macpherson (Harmondsworth, 1985).

Hont, I. and Ignatieff, M. 'Needs and Justice in the *Wealth of Nations*: An Introductory Essay', in eds I. Hont and M. Ignatieff, *Wealth and Virtue, the Shaping of Political Economy in the*

Scottish Enlightenment (Cambridge, 1983).

Hornius, Georgius, *Historiae philosophicae libri septem* (Amsterdam, 1655).

Humboldt, Alexander von, *Essai sur la géographie des plantes accompagné d'un tableau physique des régions équinoxiales* (Paris, 1807).

—— *Vues des Cordillères et monumens des peuples indigènes de l'Amérique* (Paris, 1810).

—— *Essai politique sur le royaume de la Nouvelle Espagne*, 2 vols (Paris, 1811).

—— *Voyage de Humboldt et Bonpland. Première partie. Relation historique*, 3 vols (Paris, 1814).

—— *Atlas géographique et physique des régions équinoxiales du Nouveau Continent* (Paris, 1814–34).

—— *Examen critique de l'histoire de la géographie du nouveau continent et des progrès de l'astronomie nautique au quinzième et seizième siècles*, 5 vols (Paris, 1836–9).

—— *Cosmos: Sketch Of a Physical Description of the Universe* [*Kosmos. Entwurf einer physischen Weltbeschreibung*], translated under the superintendence of Lt.Col. Edward Sabine, 4 vols (London, 1846–58).

—— *Views of Nature: Or Contemplations of the Sublime Phenomena of Creation* [*Anshicten der Natur, mit wissenschaftlichen Erläuterungen*], trans. E.C. Otte and Henry G. Bohn (London, 1850).

—— *Letters of Alexander von Humboldt Written Between the Years 1827 and 1858 to Varnhagen von Ense* (London, 1860).

—— *Jugendbriefe Alexander von Humboldts* (Berlin, 1973).

—— *El libre progreso de la inteligencia* [an edition of thirty-five unpublished letters] (Caracas, 1974).

Hume, David, *Essays Moral, Political and Literary*, eds T.H. Green and T.H. Grose, 2 vols (London, 1882).

Iacono, Alfonso M., *L'evento e l'osservatore. Richerche sulla storicità della conoscenza* (Florence, 1987).

—— 'Tempi, congetture, storia. Aspetti del metodo comparativo nel XVIII secolo', *Il Pensiero. Rivista di Filosofia*,

Nuova serie (1989–90), vol. 30, 111–40.

Imbruglia, Girolamo, *L'Invenzione del Paraguay. Studio sull'idea di communità tra Seicento e Settecento* (Naples, 1983).

—— 'Dopo L'*Encyclopédie*. Diderot e la sagezza dell'immaginazione', *Studi settecenteschi* (1988–9), 11–12, pp. 305–58.

—— 'Diderot e le immagini della pirateria nel 700', *Belfagor* (1990), XLV, 493–511.

Jardine, Nicholas, *The Birth of History and the Philosophy of Science. Kepler's 'A Defence of Tycho Against Ursus' with Essays on its Provenance and Significance* (Cambridge, 1984).

Kelley, Donald, *The Human Measure. Social Thought in the Western Legal Tradition* (Cambridge, Mass. and London, 1990).

Kretzmann, Norman, 'The Main Thesis of Locke's Semantic Theory', in ed. Herman Parret, *History, Linguistic Thought and Contemporary Linguistics* (Berlin–New York, 1976) pp. 331–47.

La Condamine, Charles de, *Relation abrégée d'un voyage fait dans l'intérieur de l'Amérique méridionale* (Paris, 1745).

Lahontan, Louis-Armand de Lom d'Arce, Baron de, *Nouveaux voyages de M le Baron de Lahontan dans l'Amérique septentrionale*, 2 vols (The Hague, 1703).

—— *Dialogues curieux entre l'auteur et un sauvage de bon sens qui à voyagé, et curieux Mémoires de l'Amérique septentrionale*, ed. Gilbert Chinard (Baltimore–Paris–London, 1931).

Lamy, Bernard, *La Rhétorique, ou l'art de parler* (Paris [?] 1757)

Las Casas, Bartolomé de, *Argumentum apologiae adversus Genesium Sepulvedam theologum cordubensem* [1550], transcribed in Fray Bartolomé de las Casas, *Obras Completas*, Vol. 9, ed. Angel Losada (Madrid, 1990).

—— *Historia de las Indias* [1527–], ed. Augustín Millares Carlo, 3 vols (Mexico, 1951).

—— *Obras escogidas de Fray Bartolomé de las Casas*, ed. Juan Pérez de Tudela Bueso, *Biblioteca de autores españoles*, vol. CX (Madrid, 1958).

—— *Brevíssima relación de la destrucción de las Indias*, ed. André Saint-Lu (Madrid, 1987).

Latour, Bruno, *Science in Action. How to Follow Scientists and Engineers Through Society* (Milton Keynes, 1987).

—— *The Pasteurization of Paris*, trans. Alan Sheridan and John Law (Cambridge, Mass., 1988).

Léry, Jean de, *Histoire d'un voyage fait en la terre du Brésil autrement dite Amérique* (2nd ed., N.P., 1588).

Lestringant, Frank, 'Fictions de l'espace brésilien à la renaissance: l'example de Guanabara', in eds C. Jacob and F. Lestringant, *Arts et légendes d'espaces. Figures du voyage et rhetorique du monde* (Paris, 1981), pp. 207–56.

—— 'The Philosopher's Breviary: Jean de Léry in the Enlightenment', *Representations*, 33, pp. 220–11.

—— *Le Huguenot et le sauvage. L'Amérique et la controverse coloniale, en France au temps des Guerres de Religion (1555–1589)* (Paris, 1990a).

Levine, Joseph M., *Humanism and History. Origins of Modern English Historiography* (Ithaca–London, 1987).

Linguet, Simon, *Théorie des loix civil, ou principes fondamentaux de la société*, 2 vols (London, 1767).

Locke, John, *An Essay Concerning Human Understanding* [1689], ed. Peter H. Nidditch (Oxford, 1975).

—— *Two Treatises on Government*, ed. Peter Laslett (Cambridge, 1967).

M***, *Lettres critiques et politiques sur les colonies et le commerce des villes maritimes de France adressés à G.T. Raynal par M****** (Geneva, 1785).

Major, John (Johannes Maior), *In secundum librum sententiarum* (Paris, 1519).

Mandrillon, Joseph, *Le spectateur américain, ou remarques générales sur l'Amérique septentrionale et sur la république des treize états-unis. Suivi de, Recherches philosophiques sur le découverte du nouveau monde* (Amsterdam, 1784), 3 pts.

Mannheim, Bruce, '*Una nación acorralada*: Southern Peruvian Quechua language planning and politics in historical perspective'. *Language and Society*, 13, 291–309.

—— *The Language of the Inka Since the European Invasion* (Texas, forthcoming).

Martyr, Peter, *De orbe novo decades* (Alcala de Henares, 1530).

—— *Opus espistolarum petri martyris Angleria* (Alcala de Henares, 1530a).

Maupertuis, Pierre Louis Moreau de, 'Dissertation sur les différents moyen dont les hommes se sont servis pour exprimer leurs idées', in *Œuvres*, 3 vols (Lyons, 1756), vol. 3, pp. 437–68.

Mendelssohn, Moses, 'Drafel die Bestimmung des Menschen betreffend' in *Briefe di neueste Litteratur betreffend* (1764), 19.

Michelet, Jules, *Histoire de la France au seizième siècle* (Paris, 1855).

Milhou, Alain, *Colón y su mentalidad mesiánica en el ambiente franciscanista español* (Valladolid, 1983).

—— 'Las Casas à l'âge d'or du prophétisme apocalyptique et du messianissme', in *Autour de Las Casas. Actes du colloque du ve centenaire* (Paris, 1984).

Minguet, Charles, *Alexandre de Humboldt, historien et géographe de l'Amérique espagnole, 1799–1804* (Paris, 1969).

Montaigne, Michel Eyquem de, *Essais de Michel de Montaigne*, ed. Albert Thibaudet (Bibliothèque de la Pléiade) (Paris, 1933).

Montesquieu, Charles de Secondat, Baron de, *Œuvres complètes*, ed. Roger Caillois, 2 vols, (Bibliothèque de la Pléiade) (Paris, 1979).

Moravia, Sergio, *La scienza dell'uomo nel settecento* (Bari, 1978).

Naigeon, Jacques-André, *Mémoires historiques et philosophiques sur la vie et les œuvres de Denis Diderot* (Paris, 1821).

Nardi, Bruno, *Studi su Pietro Pompanazzi* (Florence, 1965).

Nobrega, Manuel da, *Cartas do Brasil e mais escritos*, ed. Serafim Leite (Coimbra, 1955).

Olivecrona, K., *Law and Fact* (Copenhagen–London, 1939).

O'Gorman, Edmundo, *The Invention of America. An Inquiry into the Historical Nature of the New World and the Meaning of History* (Bloomington, 1961).

Oviedo, Fernández de Oviedo y Valdes, Gonzalo, *Libro del muy esforçado y invencible Cavallero dela fortuna propriamente llamado don claribalte* (Valencia, 1519).

—— *Historia general y natural de las Indias*, ed. Juan Pérez de Tudela Bueso, *Biblioteca de autores españoles*, vols CXVII–CXXI (Madrid, 1959).

Pagden, Anthony, 'The Savage Critic: Some European Images of the Primitive', in *The Yearbook of English Studies* (1983) 13, 32–45.

—— *The Fall of Natural Man. The American Indian and the Origins of Comparative Ethnology*, 2nd ed. (Cambridge, 1986).

—— ed. *The Languages of Political Theory in Early-Modern Europe* (Cambridge, 1987).

—— 'The Reception of the "New Philosophy" in Eighteenth-Century Spain, *Journal of the Warburg and Courtauld Institutes* (1988), 51, 126–40.

—— *Spanish Imperialism and the Political Imagination* (New Haven–London, 1990).

—— *Indios e immaginazione europea: come l'indiano europeo divenne l'indiano americano* (Venice, forthcoming).

Paine, Tom, *A Letter Addressed to the Abbé Raynal on the Affairs of North America in which the Mistakes in the Abbé's Account of the Revolution of America are Corrected and Cleared Up* (London, 1782).

de Pauw, Joannes Cornelius, *Recherches philosophiques sur les Américains, ou Mémoires interéssants pour servir à l'histoire de l'espèce humaine*, 2 vols (Berlin, 1772).

Pérez de Tudela Bueso, Juan, *Mirabilis in altis. Estudio crítico sobre el orígen y significado del proyecto descrubridor de Cristóbal Cólon* (Madrid, 1983).

Perkins, M.L., 'Community Planning in Diderot's *Supplément au Voyage de Bougainville*', *Kentucky Romance Quarterly* (1974), 21, 399–417.

Pocock, J.G.A., 'The Mobility of Property and the Rise of Eighteenth-Century Sociology' in *Virtue, Commerce and History* (Cambridge, 1985).

Pratt, Mary Louise, *Imperial Eyes. Travel Writing and Transculturation* (London–New York, 1992).

Prévost, Antoine François, Abbé, *Histoire générale des voyages ou nouvelle collection de toutes les relations de voyages par mer et par terre qui on été publiées jusqu'à présent dans les différentes langues de toutes les nations connues*, 7 vols (Paris, 1746).

Prosdocimi, Luigi, ' "Ex facto oritur ius". Breve nota di diritti medievale', *Studi senesi* (1954–5), 66–67, 808–19.

Purchas, Samuel, *Hakluytus Posthumus or Purchas his pilgrimes* (London, 1625).

Quiroga, Pedro de, *Libro intitulado coloquios de la verdad*, ed. Julian Zarco Cuevas (Seville, 1922).

Ramusio, Giovanni Battista, *Navigazioni e viaggi* [1534], ed. Marica Milanesi, 4 vols (Turin, 1978).

Raynal, Guillaume-Thomas, Abbé, *Histoire philosophique et politique des établissemens et du commerce des Européens dans les deux Indes*, 10 vols (Geneva, 1781).

—— *Conversations entre messieurs Raynal et Linquet sur les natures et les advantages des divers governements* (Brussels, 1789).

Ricoeur, Paul, *Du texte à l'action. Essais d'hermeneutique, II*, (Paris, 1986).

Rigault, Hippolyte, *Histoire de la querelle des anciens et des modernes* (Paris, 1856).

Robertson, William, *The History of America*, 2 vols (London, 1777).

—— *The Progress of Society in Europe. A Historical Outline from the Subversion of the Roman Empire to the Beginning of the Sixteenth Century*, ed. Felix Gilbert (Chicago–London, 1972).

Robinson, Robert, *Arcana: Or the Principles of the Late Petitioners to Parliament*

for the Relief in the Subscriptions (Cambridge, 1774).

Rorty, Richard, eds Richard Rorty, J.B. Schneewind and Quentin Skinner, *Philosophy in History* (Cambridge, 1984).

Rouché, Marc, *La Philosophie de l'histoire de Herder*. (Publication de la Faculté des Lettres de l'Université de Strasbourg, 93) (Strasbourg, 1940).

Rousseau, G.S. and Roy Porter, eds, *Exoticism in the Enlightenment* (Manchester, 1990).

Rousseau, Jean Jacques, *Œuvres complètes de Jean Jacques Rousseau*, ed. P.R. Auguis, 27 vols (Paris, 1825).

—— *Essai sur l'origine des langues, où il est parlé de la mélodie et de l'imitation musicale*, ed. Charles Porset (Paris, 1968).

—— *Œuvres complètes*, (Edition publiée sous la direction de Bernard Gagnebin et Marcel Raymond. Bibliothèque de la Pléiade), 4 vols (Paris, 1979–81).

Russell, Peter, 1986, 'White Kings on Black Kings: Rui da Pina and the Problem of Black African Sovereignty', in *Medieval and Renaissance Studies in Honour of Robert Brian Tate* (Oxford, 1986), pp. 151–63.

—— *Prince Henry the Navigator: The Rise and Fall of a Culture Hero* (Oxford, 1984).

Sahagún, Bernardino de, *Historia general de las cosas de la Nueva España*, ed. Angel María Garibay (Mexico City, 1975).

Schiller, Friedrich, *On the Aesthetic Education of Man* [*Über die ästhetische Erziehung des Menschen*], ed. and trans. Elizabeth M. Wilkinson and L.A. Willoughby (Oxford, 1982).

Schmitt, Charles, 'Experience and Experiment: A Comparison of Zabarella's View with Galileo's *De Motu*', *Studies in the Renaissance* (1969), 16, 80–138.

Schulz, Fritz, *History of Roman Legal Science* (Oxford, 1953).

Schwartz, Stuart B., 'New-World Nobility: Social Aspirations and

Mobility in the Conquest and Colonization of Spanish America', in *Social Groups and Religious Ideas in the Sixteenth Century*, eds Miriam Usher Chrisma and Otto Grendler (Kalamazoo, 1978).

Shklar, Judith, 'Jean d'Alembert and the Rehabilitation of History', *The Journal of the History of Ideas* (1981), 42, 643–64.

Smith, Adam, 'The History of Astronomy', in *Essays on Philosophical Subjects*, eds W.P.D. Wightman, J.C. Bryce and I.S. Ross, Oxford (Vol. IV of the Glasgow Edition of the Works and Correspondence of Adam Smith, 1980).

—— *Lectures on Rhetoric and Belles Lettres*, ed. J.C. Bryce, Oxford (Vol. IV of the Glasgow Edition of the Works and Correspondence of Adam Smith, 1983).

Sprat, Thomas, *History of the Royal Society* (London, 1667).

Stannard, J., 'Dioscorides and Renaissance Materia-medica', in *Materia Medica in the Sixteenth Century, Analecta medico-historia*, 1, ed. M. Florkin (Oxford, 1966), 1–21.

Stagl, Justin, 'The Methodising of Travel in the 16th Century: A Tale of Three Cities', *History and Anthropology* (1990), 4, 303–38.

Starobinski, Jean, 'Rousseau et l'origine des langues', in *Europäische Aufklärung Herbert Dieckmann zum 60 Geburtstag*, eds H. Friedrich, F. Schalk (Munich, 1967), 281–300.

—— 'Diderot et la parole des autres', *Critique* (1972), 28, 3–22.

—— *Montaigne in Motion*, trans. Arthur Goldhammer (Chicago–London, 1985).

—— *Le remède dans le mal. Critique et legitimation de l'artifice à l'âge des Lumières* (Paris, 1989).

Tassoni, Alessandro, *Dieci libri di pensieri divers* (Venice, 1636).

Taylor, Charles, *Sources of the Self the Making of the Modern Identity* (Cambridge, Mass., 1989).

Temple, Sir William, *An Essay Upon the Ancient and Modern Learning (1690)*, ed. J.E. Spingarn (Oxford, 1909).

Thevet, André, *Cosmographie de Levant* (Lyons, 1554).

—— *Le grand Insulaire et pilotage d'André Thevet angoumoisin, cosmographe du Roi* [1588] in *André Thevet. North America, A Sixteenth-Century View*, ed. and trans. Roger Schelsinger and Arthur P. Stable (Montreal, 1975).

Todorov, Tzvetan, *La conquête de l'Amérique. La question de l'autre* (Paris, 1982).

Torres, Antonio de, *Saggio di riflessioni sulle arti e il commercio europeo dei nostri tempi e degli antichi*, 2 vols (Pesaro, 1781).

Tourneaux, M., *Correspondence litteraire, philosophique et critique par Grimm, Diderot, Raynal etc*, 16 vols (Paris, 1877).

Trexler, Richard C., 'Aztec Priests for Christian Altars: the Theory and Practice of Reverence in New Spain', in ed. Paola Zambelli, *Scienze credenze occulte livelli di cultura* (Florence, 1982), 175–96.

Turgot, Anne Robert Jacques, 'Mémoire sur le manière dont la France et l'Espagne devraient envisager les suites de la querelle entre la Grande-Bretagne et ses colonies, 6 Avril 1776', in *Œuvres de Turgot* (Paris, 1844), vol. 2.

Ulloa, Antonio de, *Noticias americanas: entretenimientos phisicos-históricos sobre la América Meridional y la Septentrianal [sic] Oriental* (Madrid, 1772).

Vargas Machuca, Bernardo de, *Apologías y discursos de las conquistas occidentales . . . en controversía del tratado Destruición de las Indias escrito por Don Fray Bartolomé de las Casas. In Colección de documentos inéditos para la historia de España*, vol. LXXI (Madrid, 1879).

Voltaire, François Marie Arouet de, *Alzire, ou les Américains. Tragédie* (Paris, 1736).

—— *Romans et contes*, ed. René Groos (Paris, 1954).

—— *Essai sur les mœurs et l'esprit des nations et sur les principaux faits de l'histoire depuis Charlemagne jusqu' à Louis XIII*, ed. René Pomeau, 2 vols (Paris, 1963).

Waldseemüller, Martin, *Cosmographie introductio quibusdam geometriae [ac] astronomiae principiis ad eam rem necessariis* (St. Die, 1507).

Williams, Bernard, 'Saint-Just's Illusion – Interpretation and the Limits of Philosophy', *London Review of Books* (1991), 13, no. 16, 29 August, 8–10.

Wilson, B.R., ed. *Rationality* (Oxford, 1970).

Index of Names

7 3 5 2 8 7 7 8   8

216